The status of woman in Islam is the same as that of man. Injunctions about honor and respect enjoined for one sex are enjoined equally for the other sex. So far as rights in this world and rewards in the Hereafter are concerned, there is no difference between the sexes. In the organization of daily living, both are equal participants and partners. Yet Islam sees man as man and woman as woman and, considering the natural differences, it advocates the principle of the division of labor between the two sexes rather than the equality of labor.

بسم الله الرحمن الرحيم

Some other books by the same author

Woman in Islamic Shari'ah
God Arises: The Evidence of God in Nature and in Science
God-Oriented Life
Muhammad: The Prophet of Revolution
Islam As It Is
Islam: The Voice of Human Nature
Islam: Creator of the Modern Age
Religion and Science
Indian Muslims: The Need For A Positive Outlook
Tabligh Movement
Tazkirul Qur'an
(Commentary of the Qur'an in 2 volumes)
Allahu Akbar
(God is Great, in Urdu)
Al-Islam Yatahadda
(Modern Challenges to Islam, in Arabic)

WOMAN

—— BETWEEN ——

ISLAM

—— AND ——

WESTERN
SOCIETY

•••

Maulana Wahiduddin Khan

The Islamic Centre, New Delhi

Translated by
Farida Khanam

Urdu version: *Khatoon-e-Islam* (New Delhi, 1993)
Arabic version: *Al-Mar'ah baina Shari'at al-Islam wa
al-Hadarah al-Gharbiyah* (Cairo, 1994)

© Goodword Press, 1999
First published 1995
Reprinted 1997, 1998, 1999

ISBN 81-85063-75-3

No prior permission is required from the publisher
for translation of this book and publication of its
translation into any language.

GOODWORD PRESS
AL-Risala, The Islamic Centre
1, Nizamuddin West Market, New Delhi 110 013
Tel. 4625454, 4611128 Fax 4697333, 4647980
e-mail: skhan@vsnl.com

Distributed in U.S.A. by

THE BESTSELLERS
61-38, 168 St. P.O. Box: 650654,
Fresh Meadows, NY 11365-00654
Tel. 718-3594861 Fax: 718-3594446
e-mail: akhan72252@aol.com

CRESCENT BOOKS
2221 Peachtree Road,
Suite D109, Atlanta, GA 30309
Tel. 770-662 6970
Fax 404-351 2832

Distributed in U.K. and Europe by

IPCI: ISLAMIC VISION
481, Coventry Road,
Birmingham B10 0JS
Tel. 0121-773 0137,
Fax: 0121-766 8577
e-mail: info@ipci-iv.co.uk

ALIF INTERNATIONAL
109 Kings Avenue, Watford,
Hertfordshire WDI 7SB
Tel. 01923-240844
Fax 01923-237722
e-mail: bandali@alif.co.uk

Printed by Nice Printing Press, Delhi

Contents

4. The Problems Facing Modern Civilization

5. Position of Woman in the Islamic *Shari'ah*

Foreword

An anthology of the Qur'an, prepared by English orientalist Edward William Lane (1801-1876), was published in 1843. It carried a foreword by way of introduction to Islamic teaching, which, inter alia, stated that "the fatal point in Islam is the degradation of woman."[1]

This ill-considered observation gained such currency that it was commonly repeated as if it were an established fact. Almost a century and a half has elapsed since then, and, with the passage of time, this conviction has, if anything, deepened. It has even been quoted as if it were gospel truth in a judgement passed in the Supreme Court of India by the Chief Justice of India, Mr. Y.V. Chandra Chud, in the now notorious Muhammad Ahmad-Shah Bano divorce case.

To interpret the Islamic concept of woman as "degradation" of woman is to distort the actual issue. Islam has never asserted that woman is inferior to man: it has only made the point that woman is differently constituted.

Let us suppose that a doctor tells his patient that his eye is a very delicate organ of the body, to be treated gently and with great care, unlike his fingernails, which can be cut and filed, if necessary. The doctor's instruction does not mean that he is degrading the eye vis à vis the nail. He is only pointing out the difference between the nail and the eye.

If all the laws relating to men and women in Islam are based on this fundamental reality that men and women are of two different sexes, it is because distinctive differences between man and woman are established biological facts.

This being so, male and female spheres of activity cannot be one and the same, whether in family or in social life. There must necessarily be differences in the kind of work that they do, and also in their places of work.

All the revealed scriptures have held the same concept of woman, and thousands of years have passed without its ever having been doubted. It is only in modern times that it has been challenged by the women's liberation movement, which holds that men and women are alike in every respect and that both should, therefore, be given equal opportunities.

This movement first reared its head in Britain in the 18th century, later spreading across the whole of Europe and America. In 1772, a certain impetus was given to the movement by the publication of a book by Mary Wollstonecraft, entitled *A Vindication of the Rights of Women.* The gist of this book was that women should receive the same treatment as men in education, work opportunities and politics, and the same moral standards should be applied to both sexes.[2] Such was the zeal and fervor with which this movement was launched that it spread far and wide. Both men and women participated in it, and even talking about the differences between man and woman was brushed aside as being a sign of backwardness. By the beginning of the 20th century, this trend of thought had established its hold all over the world, and laws came to be made or modified accordingly. All doors were to be thrown open to men and women alike.

In practice, however, this experiment has met with utter failure. Even after a struggle of almost 200 years, women have failed to achieve a status equal to that of men. They are almost as backward today as they were before the launching of the "women's lib" movement. The only practical result has been that women have come out of the home, and are to be seen everywhere in the company of men. By degrees they have lost their femininity without having achieved the goal of equal status with men in every domain for which they paid this very high price.

The failure of women's liberation has led to wide-ranging research being carried out on this topic, employing strictly scientific methods. Finally, the patent biological differences between men and women have been scientifically proved. These differences have all along been a reason for women's failure to find an equal place in every department of life. Where philosophers had cast doubts upon the religious concept of women — quite erroneously as it turned out — scientific findings have now re-established this concept's veracity.

Now the question arises as to why it is that once science has supported the religious concept of man and woman as being the right one, the allegation continues to be made that Islam has "degraded" woman. For instance, the Indian freedom fighter, S.M. Joshi, who was interviewed in connection with a government-sponsored scheme to record the voices of freedom fighters for posterity, stated that "the Shariat of the Muslims and the Manusmruti of the Hindus — followed by both communities for centuries — were equally socially reactionary."[3]

Such remarks are made so indiscriminately and so frequently that it is high time we concerned ourselves less with our own sense of injury and more with the possible root causes. The main reason is that the results of research on the differences between man and woman have remained only an academic finding and have not yet formed the basis of a popular intellectual revolution. The social penetration of these ideas will have to take place in the same way as monotheism replaced polytheism, that is, through the kind of intellectual revolution set in motion by the Prophet Muhammad and his Companions with the special succor of God.

Such an intellectual revolution in our own times is certainly not far-fetched, since modern science has provided all the arguments in its favor. It is only a question now of sufficient number of believers engaging themselves wholeheartedly in the dissemination of those findings for a popular, intellectual revolution to take place. It is my earnest desire that the following chapters should provide the inspiration for this history-making task.

Wahiduddin Khan
May 19, 1994

The Islamic Centre
C-29, Nizamuddin West
New Delhi

Notes

1. Edward William Lane, *Selections from Kuran* (London 1982), p. XC.
2. *Encyclopaedia Britannica* (1984), vol. 10, p. 733.
3. *The Times of India,* April 6, 1986.

CHAPTER 1

A Survey

Human intelligence having its limits, the universe seems difficult to interpret. Man can only guess at facts: he is in no position to comprehend them. The history of man's struggle to come to grips with the baffling factors in his terrestrial and celestial environment has been recorded throughout the ages in the writings of sages, philosophers and men of religion, one more recent, and very commendable effort being a book by Sir James Jeans (1877-1946) which gives us prior warning in its very apt title — *The Mysterious Universe* — of just how impenetrable the secrets of the cosmos can be.

It was this mystery surrounding the universe which gave rise in ancient times to many stories, now called myths. On the basis of pure conjecture, man developed many suppositions which, in the course of time, became widespread beliefs, rooted in the human imagination.

We find that in every age man has had a set of beliefs which molded his thoughts and deeds. In ancient times this set of beliefs was entirely based on myths. It was not until the 7th century A.D. that there was any change in this pattern of thinking. Now importance was attached to facts instead of superstitions. A revolution indeed, and it was brought about by the advent of Islam.

Myths were developed to account for the cosmos. How did the gods bring heavens, earth, plants, beasts and men into existence? What is the divine origin of human institutions and of the *ecumene*? What divine process is responsible for prosperity or failure? To explain such basic questions etiological (origin or causal) myths were developed. For example, the attraction between man and woman (and the consequent institution of marriage) is explained by the myth that primeval man was one creature, subsequently divided into two parts, male and female, which are attracted to one another to regain their pristine unity. Aristophanes expresses this theory of sexual attraction in *Plato's Symposium.* Genesis has the same theory in the familiar myth that a rib, taken out of Adam, was fashioned into Eve; and precisely because woman was taken out of man, man forsakes his father and mother to "cleave unto his wife" so that they become "one flesh" (Gen. 2:23-24).[1]

Here are two examples which illustrate, on the one hand, the difference between science (knowledge) and superstition, and on the other, how Islam was originally responsible for putting an end to the age of myth and superstition and heralding the new era of enlightenment.

One of the phenomena of nature in our world is the eclipse, sometimes the sun going into eclipse and at other times the moon. Today we have discovered the astronomical laws governing these phenomena but, in ancient times, man was ignorant of what these phenomena and their causes actually were. Strange and wonderful stories on the basis of conjecture were, therefore, concocted to bring them within the realm of human understanding. The Chinese account of the eclipse and its "remedy" is one of the more fanciful:

> When an eclipse occurred, the Chinese thought that the sun was being swallowed by a huge dragon. The whole population joined in making as much noise as possible to scare it away. They always succeeded![2]

Considering their "success," it is little wonder that the Chinese used the same tactics with happy conviction on subsequent occasions. It is now common knowledge that the dates and durations of such eclipses are entirely calculable, just as the course of Halley's comet was entirely predictable.

It was during this age of superstition that Islam appeared on the horizon to herald a new era of enlightenment. Its account of the solar eclipse was just one of the ideas which were totally at variance with the beliefs of the day, and which have subsequently been deemed quite in accordance with the findings of modern research. The Prophet Muhammad's own explanation of the solar eclipse is worthy of note. It so happened that the death of his only son, Ibrahim, at the age of one and a half, coincided with a solar eclipse in the tenth year of the Hijra (January, 632 A.D.). The ancient belief still being prevalent that eclipses were caused by the death of an important person, some of the inhabitants of Medina began spreading the story that the eclipse was due to the death of the Prophet's son. The Prophet, therefore, felt it necessary to gather his people together and explain the truth to them. This account of his is set forth in the Hadith of two writers of peerless authenticity, Muslim and Bukhari:

> After praising and glorifying God, he said: "Eclipses of the sun and moon are not due to the death of any human being; they are just two signs given by God. When you observe an eclipse, you should pray to God, praise Him, ask for His mercy and blessings, and give something in charity."[3]

He again stressed the fact that they were signs from God, had no connection with the life or death of any particular individual, and that, through them, God wished to convey to man His warnings. Therefore, when you see any such thing, remember God, fear Him, pray to Him and ask His forgiveness.[4]

Thus Islam put an end to myths and superstitions of this kind for the first time in human history. Another incident of this nature which took place during the time of the second Caliph, 'Umar ibn al-Khattab, has been recorded in history as follows: "Ibn Luhai'a relates that, according to Qais ibn Hajjaj, when Egypt was conquered, its inhabitants went to 'Amr ibn al-'As, the Amir (governor) of Egypt at that time, and told him that when, according to the local calendar, the month of Bauna came round, the river Nile had to be offered the customary sacrifice, without which it would not flow. It seemed that after the twelfth night of that month, they had to find a young girl who was a virgin and the only child of her parents, then they had to persuade her parents to give her in sacrifice, whereupon they dressed her in the finest clothes and jewels and cast her into the river Nile."

'Amr ibn al-'As told them that such practices were prohibited by Islam, which indeed had put an end to all idolatrous practices which had been prevalent prior to its advent.

The people of Egypt, therefore, refrained from making the sacrifice, and waited for the water to flow into the bed of the Nile, but the entire month of Bauna passed without the water making its appearance. They then decided to migrate.

At this point, 'Amr ibn al-'As wrote to explain the entire situation to the Caliph, 'Umar ibn al-Khattab. The latter replied that the action he had taken was correct, and, in his letter, he enclosed a note which he said should be thrown into the River Nile.

On receiving this letter, 'Amr ibn al-'As opened the note and found these words written therein: "To the Nile, river of the Egyptians, from 'Umar ibn al-Khattab, Chief of the Faithful and humble servant of God. If the flow of your waters is under your control then let your waters not flow. But if it was Almighty God who made your waters flow, then we pray to Him to make your water flow again."

'Amr ibn al-'As duly complied with the Caliph's injunction and cast the note into the river. The very next morning, the people saw with their own eyes that the waters had started to flow — by the will of God. In the course of a single night its level rose by 12 feet. Thus God put an end to this inhuman custom of the Egyptians, and never again to this day has there been a repetition of it.[5]

A PRACTICAL NECESSITY

The myths and superstitions of ancient times had affected people's thinking to the point where their approach to most things had become unrealistic. This was especially true of society's determination to regard woman as inferior to man. But there was an additional reason for this flawed concept having evolved, and that was the failure to recognize the importance of the home as the basic unit which collectively constitutes society, the training ground for future generations, in short, the cohesive force without which society would cease to exist. Just as the strength of a building lies in the quality of its individual bricks, so does the strength of society depend upon the quality of its constituent families.

The work done within the home is, therefore, of prime importance. It may take greater gentleness and delicacy than responsibilities outside the home, which require greater vigor, superior physical strength and stronger nerves, but, for the survival and progress of human civilization, feminine qualities are just as essential as masculine qualities — which is why nature has cast man and woman in very different molds. Women are endowed by nature with more of the passive qualities in order to make them better suited to domesticity, while men are endowed with more of the active qualities

which make them better qualified to shoulder responsibilities outside
the home. This ensures a natural and effective complementarity in
family life.

SUPERSTITIONS CONCERNING WOMEN

This down-grading of women, because they came to be identified with
"inferior" tasks, resulted in their debasement in society. In the eyes
of the law, women could not enjoy the same rights as men and,
therefore, were not considered deserving of a share in family property.
In practice, there was little distinction made between women and
slaves. The opprobrium attaching to womanhood became so great that
in certain tribes it lead to female infanticide: it was considered
humiliating to be the father of a female child.

Ancient legends which perpetuated these erroneous ideas grew
out of the all-too-common human tendency to exalt the supposedly
great and to deprecate the supposedly inferior. Woman then became
not only inferior, but truly despicable in the eyes of society. These
ideas, which spread with the legends, were quite false, but took root
so firmly in the cultures of many nations, that they came to be
universally accepted as the truth. We shall mention here two such
stories.

The first is an ancient Greek tale which later gained currency
in Europe. It concerns the very first woman, who was created out
of earth by Hephaestus at the instance of Zeus, the king of the gods,
and sent down into the world with a box containing all kinds of misery
and evil. It was the intention of Zeus in so doing to set at naught
the blessing of fire which Prometheus had bestowed upon mortals
by stealing it from heaven. The story goes that from the moment the
box was opened, the world has been plagued with wickedness and
sorrow. This woman was given the name Pandora, a Greek word
which originally meant "all-giving," but which came to be
synonymous with "giver of all evils."

The second story has certain points of similarity. It too concerns
the first woman, Eve, and having already become famous among Jews,
was even incorporated into the Bible, which meant, of course, that

it was later accepted by Christians too. The Bible version as told in the second chapter of the book of Genesis is as follows:

7.   And the Lord God formed man of the dust of ground, and breathed into his nostrils the breath of life; and man became a living soul.

8.   And the Lord God planted a garden eastward in Eden; and there he put the man he had formed.

9.   And out of the ground made the Lord grow every tree that is pleasant to the sight and good for food; the tree of life also in the midst of the garden, and the tree of knowledge of good and evil.

15.   And the Lord God took the man, and put him in the garden of Eden to dress it and to keep it.

16.   And the Lord God commanded the man, saying, Of every tree of the garden thou mayest freely eat:

17.   But of the tree of knowledge of good and evil, thou shalt not eat of it: for in the day that thou eatest thereof thou shalt surely die.

18.   And the Lord God said, It is not good that the man should be alone; I will make him an help meet for him.

21.   And the Lord God caused a deep sleep to fall upon Adam, and he slept: and he took one of his ribs, and closed up the flesh instead thereof;

22.   And the rib, which the Lord God had taken from the man, made he a woman and brought her unto the man.[6]

Chapter 3 tells the story of the fall of man.

1.   Now the serpent was more subtil than any beast of the field which the Lord God had made. And he said unto the woman, yea, hath God said, Ye shall not eat of every tree of the garden?

2.   And the woman said unto the serpent, We may eat of the fruit of the trees of the garden:

3.   But of the fruit of the tree which is in the midst of the garden, God hath said, Ye shall not eat of it, neither shall ye touch it, lest ye die.

4.   And the serpent said unto the woman, Ye shall not surely die:

5.   For God doth know that in the day ye eat thereof, then your eyes shall be opened, and ye shall be as gods, knowing good and evil.

6.   And when the woman saw that the tree was good for food, and that it was pleasant to the eyes, and a tree to be desired to make one wise, she took of the fruit thereof, and did eat, and gave also unto her husband with her; and he did eat.

7.   And the eyes of both of them were opened, and they knew that they were naked; and they sewed fig leaves together, and made themselves aprons.

8.   And they heard the voice of the Lord God walking in the garden in

the cool of the day: and Adam and his wife hid themselves from the presence of the Lord God amongst the trees of the garden.

9. And the Lord God called unto Adam, and said unto him, Where art thou?

10. And he said, I heard thy voice in the garden, and I was afraid, because I was naked; and I hid myself.

11. And he said, Who told thee that thou wast naked? Hast thou eaten of the tree, whereof I commanded thee that thou shouldest not eat?

12. And the man said, The woman whom thou gavest to be with me, she gave me of the tree, and I did eat.

13. And the Lord God said unto the woman, What is this that thou hast done? And the woman said, The serpent beguiled me, and I did eat.

14. And the Lord God said unto the serpent, Because thou hast done this, thou art cursed above all cattle, and above every beast of the field; upon thy belly shalt thou go, and dust shalt thou eat all the days of thy life:

15. And I will put enmity between thee and the woman and between thy seed and her seed; it shall bruise thy head, and thou shalt bruise his heel.

16. Unto the woman he said, I will greatly multiply thy sorrow and thy conception; in sorrow thou shalt bring forth children; and thy desire shall be to thy husband, and he shall rule over thee.

17. And unto Adam he said, Because thou hast hearkened unto the voice of thy wife, and hast eaten of the tree, of which I commanded thee, saying, Thou shalt not eat of it: cursed is the ground for thy sake; in sorrow shalt thou eat of it all the days of thy life;

18. Thorns also and thistles shall it bring forth to thee; and thou shalt eat the herb of the field;

19. In the sweat of thy face shalt thou eat bread, till thou return unto the ground; for out of it wast thou taken: for dust thou art, and unto dust shalt thou return.

20. And Adam called his wife's name Eve; because she was the mother of all living.

21. Unto Adam also and to his wife did the Lord God make coats of skins, and clothes them.

22. And the Lord God said, Behold, the man is become as one of us, to know good and evil: and now, lest he put forth his hand, and take also of the tree of life, and eat, and live for ever:

23. Therefore the Lord God sent him forth from the garden of Eden, to till the ground from whence he was taken.

24. So he drove out the man; and he placed at the east of the garden of Eden Cherubims, and a flaming sword which turned every way, to keep the way of the tree of life.[7]

This story, enshrined as it is in the pages of the Bible, would have us believe that the cause of Adam's expulsion from a life of comfort and happiness and his subsequent trials and tribulations was Eve's having yielded to temptation, and that this was how the first man came to bear the burden of Original Sin which according to Christianity was to be shared by the entire human race.

This story has no basis whatsoever in fact, but it had such a strong hold over the popular imagination that it spread not only amongst the Jews and Christians, but amongst almost all the nations of the world. In becoming a part of language and literature, it managed to reach every class of people.

Just as the Qur'an has rectified many distortions of the accounts of the Bible, so has it also refuted this distorted account of Adam and Eve. The following passage from the Qur'an puts the incident in its true perspective:

> To Adam He said: "Oh Adam! Dwell with your wife in Paradise, and eat from whatever you please; but never approach this tree or you shall both become transgressors."
>
> But the devil tempted them, so that he might reveal to them that which had been hidden from them of their shame. He said: "Your Lord has forbidden you to approach this tree only to prevent you from becoming angels or immortals." Then he swore to them that he would give them friendly counsel.
>
> Thus he cunningly seduced them. And when they had eaten of the tree, their shame became visible to them, and they both covered themselves with leaves of the garden.
>
> Their Lord called out to them, saying: "Did I not forbid you to approach that tree, and did I not warn you that the devil was your sworn enemy?"
>
> They replied: "Lord, we have wronged ourselves. Pardon us and have mercy on us, or we shall surely be among the lost."
>
> He said: "Go hence, and may your descendants be enemies to each other. The earth will for a while provide your sustenance and dwelling-place. There you shall live and there you shall die, and thence you shall be raised to life."[8]

In the above-quoted passage the dual form of the verb in Arabic has been used throughout, so that it is made abundantly clear that for every transgression both Adam and Eve have been held equally responsible. Thus it becomes quite evident that Satan tempted them together, both fell into his trap, both ate the forbidden fruit and both were equally held responsible and both suffered equally in consequence. This surely demonstrates that they were on an equal footing in the eyes of God.

CELIBACY

Celibacy has existed in some form or another throughout man's religious history and has appeared in virtually all the major religious traditions of the world.[9]

It is true that prior to Islam, in almost every religion, celibacy was considered to be the highest criterion of piety, the fundamental reason for this being the inferior status of women. There were periods in the history of certain countries when women were considered almost sub-human and a source of sin. Those who associated with them were, therefore, regarded as being inferior. By contrast, those who lived a life of celibacy had an aura of sanctity about them and basked in the esteem of society.

The basic function of celibacy was to establish the internal wholeness and spiritual self-sufficiency of the truly religious person, so that he might become a living symbol of sacredness and purity. It was meant to prove to him that the ultimate reality was beyond his physical needs, so that he in turn might demonstrate to others that fulfillment may be achieved by total dependence upon what is sacred. Throughout the history of primitive religions, priests have been forbidden sexual activity, and abstinence therefrom has been regarded as ritual purification. Religious literature has perpetuated such notions about celibacy with the objective of enhancing the moral and spiritual advancement of the religiously inclined. The exemplary perfection attained in this way was supposed to make it possible to induce certain altered states of mystical consciousness which gave one direct experience of the spiritual absolute. Those who wished to attain this state or perform certain special religious services were required to make a vow of celibacy in the presence of another.

Celibacy probably derives originally from taboos of sexual power as being a rival to religious power, and of sexuality as being a polluting factor, especially in situations where sanctity was all-important. The Romans, for example, adhered to the dictum of ascetic philosophers and priests that the ideal teacher should be unmarried. For women too, virginity and celibacy have been considered to be assets in the attainment of spiritual goals. The ideal held up before them was that they should remain unmarried throughout their lives, and pass into the next world in the same virgin state.

Take, for example, what must be the fate of women living in Jain communities. The monastic groups of Jainism being marked by the greatest austerity, all Jain monks are to avoid even looking at women, for, according to a Jain source, "they are to monks what a cat is to a chicken."[10] Buddhism and allied religions take a very similar view.[11]

The Prophet Muhammad, upon whom be peace, was the first of the historical personalities to refute these fallacies in word and deed: celibacy was shown to be no genuine symbol of spirituality. He showed that true spirituality meant remaining in the midst of the family, and adhering to the limits prescribed by God. Woman was then clearly seen to be a good in life and not an evil.

Not only did the Prophet break the tradition of celibacy, but he repeatedly encouraged his Companions to do so as well. In order to show that celibacy and sanctity did not go hand in hand, he went so far as to say "woman and perfume has been endeared to me,"[12] thus breaking with an age-old tradition. In ancient times, the notion of a man of religion having relations with a woman was so abhorred that, if the Prophet had not spoken out forcefully on this issue, people would have continued to revere the tradition of celibacy under the influence of the past.

Research carried out in modern times has proved that the concept of celibacy is wholly unnatural and unrealistic. In comparison, Islamic ideology is perfectly natural and in accordance with reality. On this subject the Noble Laureate, Dr. Alexis Carrel, has this to say:

> The sexual glands have other functions than that of impelling man to the gesture which, in primitive life, perpetuated the race. They also intensify all physiological, mental, and spiritual activities. No eunuch has ever become a great philosopher, a great scientist, or even a great criminal. Testicles and ovaries possess functions of overwhelming importance.[13]

Far from considering marriage with a woman to be a shameful act, Islam, which is basically a realistic religion, considers it praiseworthy for a man to marry a woman. This is a clear indication that the teachings of Islam are wholesomely consistent with modern scientific findings and in complete consonance with nature.

ORDER OF NATURE

Sculpture is an ancient form of art. There is, no doubt, an obvious resemblance between living beings and statues, but if someone were to presume that the concerns of human beings were the same as those of statues and began to study man under the heading of sculpture, what would be the outcome? This method of study would certainly lead to strange conclusions. A carved image has no need of food and drink; therefore, the student of sculpture would naturally assume that arrangements to this effect were not necessary for man either. He would proceed to the assumption that if a statue can be locked inside a room for any length of time, so could a man be put inside a locked room for years without anyone having to worry about him.

During the time of the former President of Egypt, Jamal Abdun Nasir, an ancient statue of Abu Simbel, 20 meters high and firmly fixed in the rocks, had to be removed from its place to make way for the construction of a huge dam. This work, undertaken between 1964 and 1966, necessitated the use of special machines which could cut the statue into several pieces so that they could be shifted to a safer place, and then reassembled. Now, on this parallel, the student who views man as a statue, can also, as part of some scheme, start chopping up the human body.

Of course, there is no sculptor in this world who would do such a thing. But in another department, that of education, such experts have come into being in modern times as are experimenting with man as if he were a statue, and doing everything to him that could be done to a statue. This branch of knowledge is called "anthropology." This field of study began at the turn of the 19th century. In the light of data collected on external information regarding the conditions of ancient man, his beliefs, customs, traditions, certain conclusions about human beings in general were arrived at.

Religion naturally came within this field of study, necessitating the collection of information on the religions practised by different tribes and communities. Thus a list of the customs which went under the name of religion was produced.

A natural outcome of this method of study was that religion came to be regarded as a social phenomenon. That is to say, religion was presented as something which had evolved out of the influences of human myths, customs and social conditions. Religion is essentially a divine truth (a commandment of God), but thanks to the anthropologists' particular method of study, it has been reduced to a mere artifact of historical accretion.

The greatest harm done to religion by this method of study is that in modern times it has been shorn of its credibility, and reduced to insignificance, whereas, as the commandment of God's religion it had an unassailable authenticity, because it possessed divine credibility in its own right. Every religious statement was accepted as the ultimate statement of a superior being and, as such, worthy of being adhered to. Conversely, when religion is regarded merely as a social phenomenon, all its credibility is dissipated. This can be compared to relegating the science of chemistry to the position of alchemy, or to equating astronomy with astrology.

The fact is that this method of study, when applied to religion, is totally wrong. It turns a reality into a non-reality. It is to accord human status to something which is essentially divine. To understand the reality of religion let us peruse this verse of the Qur'an: "Are they seeking a religion other than God's when every soul in heaven and earth has submitted to Him, willingly or by compulsion? To Him they shall all return."[14]

According to this verse, the religion which God desires man to adopt in his daily living is the same divine law which God has imposed upon the entire universe. Religion is the name of this same universal law.

THE LAW OF BALANCE

Now let us examine this divine law. In the words of the Qur'an it is the law of balance: "He raised the heaven on high and set the balance, that you might not transgress the balance. Give just weight and full measure."[15]

The universe is not composed of just one item. It is rather a collection of highly disparate elements. Besides this, each and every one of its components is in motion. Not a single constituent, from the minutest atom to the most gigantic galaxy, can ever for a second remain static. For the precise functioning of this infinitely complex assemblage of moving components, limits in space and time had to be applied so that the different parts did not come into conflict with each other. God, therefore — besides creating all these things — established a systematic balance between them. This principle is known as the "Law of Nature."

Similarly, in the human world — also a vast assemblage of disparate individuals — everyone is in motion. And in order that each should continue on his life's journey without colliding with his fellow men, it was likewise necessary to establish boundaries, both moral and physical, for all human beings without exception: a balance had to be struck so that there should be no clash between individuals or societies. It is, indeed, this law of nature which has been revealed to humanity through the medium of the prophets. God's will on this subject is recorded in the Qur'an: "We have sent our Messengers with clear signs and brought down with them scriptures and the scales of justice so that men might deal with fairness."[16]

That is to say that God sent a balance of justice in the form of a book through His prophets. This book was supported by arguments and evidence so that people could believe in its authenticity and would not hesitate to order their lives according to this balance, that is, the just law. While the law of balance is inherent in the rest of creation, for man, it has been provided externally through the revelations of this divine book.

THE BANEFUL EFFECTS OF DEVIATION

Any deviation from the divine balance established by God leads to chaos and confusion. It is, therefore, laid down in the Qur'an that no changes should be made in the balance God has created by means of His laws of reform.[17]

One example of universal balance is the fixity of the distance between the sun and earth (about 90 million miles). This distance is extremely balanced, ensuring a whole range of temperatures on earth which is favorable to the continuance of the human species. If this balance were upset in any way, it would result in all kinds of disasters. For instance, if the distance between the sun and the earth were reduced by half, temperatures would rise to such extremes, that everything and everyone on the surface of the earth would be reduced to ashes. There would be no possibility of life existing in any form whatsoever.

The same applies to the girth of our planet. Its present circumference is about 25,000 miles, but if this were reduced by half, the pull of its gravity would be so weakened that we should all go flying off into space. If, on the contrary, the circumference were doubled, the effect of gravity would be so overwhelming that all growth would cease. Man would be reduced to the size of a mouse and a mouse would be little bigger than an ant.

The unparalleled balance that exists on earth is aptly illustrated by the strange example of the insects which, unlike human beings, do not possess lungs, but breathe through tubes. When insects grow large the tubes cannot grow in ratio to the increasing size of the body of the insect. Hence there never has been an insect more than a few inches long with a slightly longer wing spread. Because of the mechanism of their structure and their method of breathing, there never could be an insect of great size. This limit in their growth held all insects in check and prevented them from dominating the world. If this physical check had not been provided, man could not exist. Imagine a man meeting a hornet as big as a lion or a spider equally large.[18]

Of course, the notion of order in the world has periodically been called into question. A certain western writer has suggested that the gravitational pull of the earth is far greater than is absolutely essential, hence the difficulty one experiences in carrying even a weight of ten kilos. Had it been less, he points out, we should have been able to walk about, carrying a weight with ease. But this objection is ill-founded. It is entirely due to gravity having the pull that it does, that our homes remain firmly fixed to the ground. Had it been less, they would have flown about like kites, and civilization as we know it would hardly have been possible.

It is fortunate that the order of the universe is not in the hands of men. If it were, we should experience intermittent tampering with the immutable laws of nature. Gravity would wax and wane, the earth would move nearer to or further from the sun and, on the pretext that nature had been cruel to insects in fixing the size of their breathing tubes, the said creatures would be encouraged to grow to elephantine proportions, thus filling the whole earth with them. None of these developments would, however, be encouraging to the human species!

Luckily, man cannot effect such changes in the universe, since he has no power over its ordering. But he is free to act as he wills in his own world, and the result has been chaos on a grand scale. The extremes to which he has gone are thus referred to in the Qur'an: "Evil appears on land and sea as a result of the (evil) which men's hands have done."[19]

WOMAN VERSUS MAN

In view of the divine law of balance, let us consider the relationship between man and woman. According to divine law, this relationship was set up on the principle of the division of labor, i.e. it is the responsibility of the man to carry out tasks outside the home, while the woman takes charge of tasks within the home. The Qur'an states that "men are the protectors and maintainers of women."[20]

This does not make a man a woman's superior, or her master. This only means that in running a home and bringing up a family, it is for the man, with his more active capabilities, to earn a living, deal with all official matters, and, when called upon, defend his country. A man is by nature more suited to such tasks, and that is why it is in the nature of things that they should be his responsibilities and not woman's. The word qawwam in the above verse, is an intensive form of qa'im meaning, "one who is responsible for or takes care of a thing or a person." Thus the use of this word is indicative of the wisdom of the division of labor rather than the superiority of man over woman. It should be conceded that if the woman finds herself in a position of responsibility in running the home, it is because her more passive nature, her talent for household tasks, her gentleness and affection all fit her admirably for domesticity, to which she is certainly better adapted than her male counterpart.

Since time immemorial life had been equably systemized by this division of labor. Earning a living had most often meant hunting, farming, fishing, working in orchards, transporting merchandise for barter or trading, all tasks physically difficult to perform, and, therefore, better and more easily done by men. While men were thus engaged, it was simply more practical for women to stay at home and manage the household. But with the advent of the industrial revolution, conditions were created which tended to break up this natural order, for now jobs came into existence which, to some extent, were suitable for women, and, since tradition in western countries did not require women to segregate themselves from men and live in seclusion, they came out of their homes and began working in offices and factories. Gradually, the traditional pattern of living began to change. Men were no longer the sole breadwinners: women had begun to share that responsibility. With economic independence came the realization in women that they should "break out of the shackles forged for them by men" to make new and independent lives for themselves. This trend in thinking eventually paved the way for the women's liberation movement. Since feminism was given its first impetus by the industrial revolution, "women's lib" began in those countries where industrialization had first made its appearance. The first noteworthy book to demand equal rights for women was published in London in 1792. Authored by Mary Wollstonecraft, it was entitled, *A Vindication of the Rights of Woman*. The industrial revolution came later to America and that is why the women's liberation movement did not begin there until the nineteenth century. With the progress of the industrial revolution, women's liberation gained momentum, reaching its zenith in the 20th century.

The upholders of this movement maintained that the cause of the difference existing between men and women in societies with ancient traditions lay not in nature but in a man-made social framework. Their contention was that a woman could do anything that a man could do, but that outdated social customs prevented her from coming into her own. They held that, once given the opportunity to demonstrate her capabilities, a woman would be able to work shoulder to shoulder with men in every walk of life. In no respect would she lag behind.

This movement is now over two hundred years old and, in modern developed countries, it has been so successful that neither the law nor tradition now places the slightest obstacle in the path of women who wish to step into the shoes of men. Yet women still lag far behind men, there being very few instances of their having actually placed themselves on an equal footing with them.

Encyclopaedia Britannica has this to say on the subject of women in modern society:

> In the economic sphere women who work outside the home are heavily concentrated in the lowest paying work and that having the lowest status. Women also earn less than men in the same kinds of jobs. The median pay of women workers in the U.S. was 60 percent that of men in 1982. In Japan the percentage of average pay was 55. Politically, women are greatly underrepresented in national and local government and in political parties.[21]

Today the social boundaries set by time-honored conventions have broken down, and all countries now have laws favoring equality of the sexes. Yet modern woman still finds herself on a lower rung than man, not having been able to achieve equal status in any of the economically or professionally important areas of modern living. This state of affairs would appear to indicate that, contrary to the women's libbers' way of thinking, social conditioning cannot be blamed for the centuries-old difference in the status of men and women. If this had been so, surely by the end of the 20th century women would have been enjoying an equal status with men. Obviously, we must search for the reasons elsewhere.

THE DIFFERENCE BETWEEN MEN AND WOMEN

In every period of history — even today in western developed countries — women have remained subordinate to men. The western upholders of the so-called women's lib movement are still saying that this is not a natural division and that the difference should be attributed to artificial social conditioning. Recent research, however, has discredited this supposition.

We reproduce below a report on this issue published in *Daily Express*:

"It is a rough old world for women, as the feminists never cease to remind us. They blame centuries of social conditioning — a kind of conspiracy whereby men all over the world somehow contrive to keep women in a subordinate role. A much simpler, and more probable explanation is that universal male dominance stems not from social oppression but fundamental differences between the sexes." This is the view put forward by Professor Steven Goldberg of New York in his book, *The Inevitability of Patriarchy*, which has earned him some shrill abuse from feminists in America ("Fascist Pig" and "Male Sadist" are two of the milder epithets), and has upset a few here, too, since he arrived to launch the British publication. "The feminists hate me," Goldberg told me cheerfully, "I like to think their intense wrath stems from my inherent rightness. Putting it simply, I believe that the universality of male dominance in all societies cannot be explained by social conditioning."

But it can be explained by the male hormone testosterone which "programmes" the infant male for a life of greater aggression and dominance while he is still in the womb. That's why little boys are clearly more aggressive than little girls even before they've had a chance to be socially conditioned. And in later life, same dominance means that men are far more ready to sacrifice holidays, health and family for the sake of their career. In truth the feminist case is none too strong. If it really were true that male dominance was due to social conditioning rather than innate male qualities, then surely somewhere in the world at some time a society would have evolved in which women were dominant. None has. And even in societies like those behind the Iron Curtain which boast of sexual equality, one sex is obviously "more equal" than the other. You can see it in Russia's 62-strong council of ministers. Not one is a woman.

After a lifetime spent researching the diverse societies of the world that expert woman anthropologist, Margaret Mead, who is commonly thought to be on the feminist side, has declared: "All the claims so glibly made about societies ruled by women are nonsense. We have no reason to believe that they ever existed... Men have always been the leaders in public affairs and the final authorities at home."

Does that mean that men are better than women? Professor Goldberg wags a warning finger. "Not better, but different." The male brain works differently from the female brain. In I.Q. tests with men and women of similar intelligence levels, the men tend to score higher on logical and deductive problems, though the women will generally do better in verbal skills.

Unquestionably women have greater emotional awareness even before they have children. Little girls are commonly more thoughtful and sensitive to parental moods than little boys.

Professor Goldberg's proposition is quite simply, that they are much less likely to get to the top — and all because of testosterone. The masculinization of the brain by this hormone has been demonstrated conclusively by experiments on female rats and other mammals. "And we have now found the same thing with human beings," says Goldberg. The professor concludes: "The central fact is that men and women are different from each other from the gene to the thought to the act. These differences flow from the biological natures of man and woman."

Women who deny their natures and covet a state of second rate manhood are forever condemned to argue against their own juices. The experience of men is that there are few women who can out-fight them and few who can out-argue them, but when a woman uses feminine means she can deal with any man as an equal. In this and every other society men look to women for gentleness, kindness and love. The basic male motivation is protection of women and children. The feminist cannot have it both ways: If she wishes to sacrifice all this, all that she will get in return is the right to meet men on male terms. She will lose.[22]

FUNDAMENTAL DIFFERENCE

Nobel Laureate Dr. Alexis Carrel (1873-1944) has discussed this issue with great perception. After enumerating the biological facts which are crucial to the issue, he sums up the profundity of the difference between men and women:

The differences existing between man and woman do not come from the particular form of the sexual organs, the presence of the uterus, from gestation, or from the mode of education. They are of a more fundamental nature. They are caused by the very structure of the tissues and by the impregnation of the entire organism with specific chemical substances secreted by the ovary. Ignorance of these fundamental facts has led promoters of feminism to believe that both sexes should have the same education, the same powers and the same responsibilities. In reality woman differs profoundly from man. Every one of the cells of her body bears the mark of her sex. The same is true of her organs and, above all, of her nervous system. Physiological laws are as inexorable as those of the sidereal world. They cannot be replaced by human wishes. We are obliged to accept them just as they are. Women should develop their aptitudes in accordance with their own nature, without trying to imitate the males. Their part in the progress of civilization is higher than that of men. They should not abandon their specific functions.[23]

Another article, "Why Women Are Second Rate," which appeared in the *Illustrated Weekly of India* on April 2, 1978, stresses the findings of professor H.J. Eysenck, the inventor of Intelligence Quotient (I.Q.) tests: "As an ardent supporter of equal opportunities for women, I am constantly nagged by doubts about their creative ability. How is it that women have produced so few writers, poets, composers, artists of top calibre? How is it that even in professions which are traditionally regarded as theirs, e.g. cooking and dress-designing, men beat them to the second place. All the famous chefs and dressmakers (even women's wear) are men. Hitherto I had accepted the sociologist's point of view that it was tradition and environment that militated against them. Somehow the sociological answer did not carry total conviction and I felt there was more than environment and lack of opportunity behind women's second-ratedness."

Professor H.J. Eysenck who pronounced that the black and brown races had a lower I.Q. than the white, has now proclaimed the same about women. Their genes make them what they are: from the time of conception their feminineness is programmed as in a computer. It is not, as sociologists maintain, tradition or environment which makes a female child play with dolls while her brother plays with toy soldiers, but her biological constitution. Even within the womb, the female develops a broader pelvis than the male. The broader the pelvis, the more feminine will its possessor be, says Eysenck. Males with broad pelvises tend to be feminine, passive, even homosexual. Females with narrow pelvises tend to be masculine, aggressive, even lesbian. Random sampling amongst your own acquaintances will confirm some of Eysenck's postulates. "Eysenck had earlier brought the wrath of the champions of racial equality on his head. Now women's libbers are out for his scalp with their rolling pins."[24]

THE HELPLESSNESS OF WOMAN

In an attempt to provide women with an equal status, modern civilization has, in fact, only managed to provide her a permanently unequal status. In whatever sector of the western economy a woman may be working, she is considered second rate as compared to a man. Even to achieve this second-rate position, a woman has to pay a certain price. She must willy-nilly become the plaything of men, allowing herself to be subjected to masculine cruelty and lasciviousness. The following is an extract about a report on American working women:

> They sound like experiences in a Delhi bus. Lewd gestures, offensive language, attacks on your person — the American workplace is for its women workers what public transport is for women in Delhi. A bank teller, Michelle Vinson, suffered physical abuse and alleged rape by the bank's vice-president Sidney Taylor for four years until finally, assisted by a women's organisation, she went to court. The district court rejected her appeal, largely because she had remained silent for four years and had not used the bank's complaint procedure to ask for help. It held that any relationship between the two was voluntary. The higher court of appeal rejected every finding of the district court and the matter finally found its way to the Supreme Court.

> The Supreme Court of the United States ruled that sexual harassment is a direct infringement of a woman's right to employment. It creates a hostile and abusive work environment in which she may be forced to leave her job or in which she cannot function to her full potential, even if such unwelcome sexual demands are not directly linked to concrete employment benefits. In other words, the court ruled that it violates U.S. civil laws against sex discrimination in the workplace.

> Sexual harassment of working women is endemic, said the friends-of-the-court brief filed by numerous women's organisations for this case. In the last five years, about half the American female working force has suffered this type of harassment at work. This does not just happen to women in factories or at blue collar workplaces. Within the fibreglass, multi-storied skyscrapers, the American office is not as pleasant for its women secretaries, lawyers, and other professionals as its air-conditioned, carpeted and muted decor makes it appear.

> About 42 percent of federally employed women were harassed in their jobs, stated a recent two-year survey done by the Official Merits Protection Board. Another 60 percent of the members of the American Federation of State, Country and Municipal Employees said that sexual harassment was a frequent problem for them. And between 1981 and 1985, the number of such complaints to the Equal Employment Opportunities Commission, established to monitor employment practices, shot up by 70 percent. The complaints vary from the physical violence of rape and assault to the insidious harassment of unwanted pushing and touching, persistent sexual demands, offensive sexual

comments, constant conversations containing sexual innuendoes and coarse language.

The offender usually makes his moves swiftly and silently, when there are not witnesses around. He is usually confident that fear, embarrassment, and often the hopelessness of the situation will keep the victim from making public complaints. And when complaints are made, he can use every defence that this grey area of social attitudes and innuendoes provides. When it is so hard for a rape victim to prove she has been violated, one can imagine how much harder it is for a victim of the less dramatic forms of violence to prove her case.

In such instances, if the offenders are their supervisors, women who resist or complain find themselves burdened with an increased workload, scathing work evaluation, unwarranted reprimands and sheer hostility. So many quit their jobs rather than go to court. When neither alternative seems feasible, they give in, quietly.[25]

This is the condition of the American female worker, in spite of laws having been passed assigning equal status to both sexes. There are even laws prohibiting harassment of women workers by men, but this has not prevented women being victimized by unprincipled male colleagues and superiors. Their helplessness stems from the fact that they have already left their parents and husbands and need to work for a living. If they left their offices as well, there would be nowhere left for them to go. If the factory or office were not last in the line of social and economic refuges for women, many workplaces would find their female task force becoming rapidly depleted.

The state of women workers in western offices is no mere accident, so that legislation can do little to improve the situation. It is such a serious and complex matter that no rule or regulation can effectively deal with it. If we hold that a bird and a bull are equal and bring them into a field to fight a duel on an equal footing, as a result of which the bird gets crushed, can we then stop this cruelty by imposing laws to this effect? Can there be a law to prevent a bird from being trampled on when it encounters a bull?

It has to be conceded that nature has cast men in the stronger and women in the weaker and more delicate mold. This accounts for nature making different demands upon men and women, resulting in a convenient division of labor. Any alteration in the division of labor is a deviation from nature: the solution to the ensuing problems lies only in a reversion to nature. They can never be solved while continuing on the path of rebellion from nature.

A flower, for instance, finds a prestigious position for itself as part of a bouquet, but if the same flower is placed under a rock, it will get crushed beyond all recognition. The same is true of a woman. In her own natural setting — the home — she is in a position of honour and prestige, and all her qualities shine forth as a result. But the moment she steps out of it to enter a crassly competitive world, she descends from the pedestal on which her family has placed her, and sinks deep into the mire of masculine oppression. Instead of her feminine talents coming into play quite naturally within the domestic framework, and bringing joy to herself and to her nearest and dearest ones, they become the object of the lustful exploitation of total strangers, and sources of frustration and stultification to the woman herself. The humiliations of the office, the shop and the factory are no fair exchange for the honor of family life. Outside the home, a woman feels constantly under siege.

There is no doubt that nature has cast men in the stronger, and women in the weaker mold. This accounts for nature making different demands upon men and women, resulting in a convenient division of labor. Any divergence from this pattern only creates problems in the home, especially for children. Many solutions have been sought to these problems, but the only effective way of setting matters right is to return to the order established by nature.

THE CURSE OF AIDS

AIDS, the most terrible scourge of modern times, has proved how fatal it is to deviate from nature. The high-risk groups are promiscuous homosexuals, bisexual men, intravenous drug-abusers and those having multiple sexual partners. Its highest incidence is among male homosexuals. For such people, AIDS (Acquired Immune Deficiency Syndrome) is the ultimate in divine retribution. With the defence mechanisms of the body rendered completely useless, the AIDS victim has as little hope of recovery as malaria victims used to have before the advent of modern therapeutics. AIDS renders medication ineffective, fevers do not respond even to injections and the body's acceptance of food is almost nil. The victim becomes weak, his joints ache and he is in a constant state of depression. What is worse is that AIDS victims have become social outcasts. Even their gifts are not acceptable for fear of contagion from them. They find themselves deserted by friends of both sexes and when they travel, hotel servants and call girls are afraid to approach them. Now a stage has come when the department of health in America has had to issue strict orders to doctors to carrry out tests on blood taken from blood banks for transfusion, as this has been found to be a source of infection. During the year 1985-86, there were in America nearly 50,000 AIDS patients who were not direct victims of AIDS but who had contracted the disease due to contacts with such patients. Here is a report based on 1986 statistics:

> AIDS IN AMERICA: The dreaded AIDS disease and related diseases are far more prevalent in the U.S. than is generally realised, according to a report in the *Wall Street Journal*. The paper said the number of Americans who suffer from AIDS is 21,000 and nearly half of them are expected to die. About 100,000 to 200,000 have AIDS-related diseases including lymphadenopathy, thrombocytopemia, condidiasis, diarrhoea, fever, hairy leukoplakia, dementia, neuropathy and Hodgkins.[26]

Here is another report, this time of a conference held in the first week of July 1986 in Paris:

> According to experts participating in a conference on AIDS held in Paris last week, there will be 300,000 new cases of AIDS in 1991 alone if the virus spreads in the rest of the world as it has in the U.S. In the U.S., 74,000 new AIDS cases are forecast for the same year. It was estimated that by then more than a quarter of a million Americans would have caught the disease and 179,000 would have died. The U.S. hospital bill for AIDS for 1991 is forecast to be $ 8 billion. At present, France is the worst affected European country and had recorded about 700 cases by the first quarter of this year. West Germany is next with 457, Britain third with 340 and Italy fourth with 219.[27]

In a society where homosexuality had come out into the open, AIDS had to be meted out as a kind of punishment to stem this massive upsurge of gross unnaturalness. Having now discovered that AIDS is contracted through sexual promiscuity in general and homosexual practices in particular, would-be sexual partners are beginning to flee from one another.

Research in zoology has brought to light the "green monkey," a native of the jungles of Africa. Of all the known species of monkey, this is the only one which indulges in homosexual practices and suffers from a disease similar to AIDS. Perhaps God created it with its perversions and afflictions in order to provide a salutary lesson for mankind. But all such lessons have been swept away by the wave of permissiveness which is carrying all before it in the western world of today. A glaring example is provided by San Francisco:

> AIDS is sweeping San Francisco, the city known as the 'gay capital of the world,' according to medical statistics published on Wednesday. Of the 520 new cases of AIDS recorded in the first six months of the year, more than two out of three — 67 per cent — proved to be fatal. This compared with the previous record of 58 per cent fatalities last year.[28]

Now AIDS victims are being fled from as plague victims used to be in the old days. Localities which used to be the happy hunting grounds of "gays" now wear a deserted look. According to the *Encyclopaedia Britannica,* homosexuality had been practised in western countries long before the recent spate of publicity given to it, but it had not been studied scientifically until early in the 20th century. It was only after World War II that there was any proper collection of data on the subject. A.C. Kinsey, who conducted a large-scale, systematic appraisal of the incidence and social correlates of homosexuality (1948,1953), found that 37 percent of all U.S. males and 13 percent of all U.S. females had at least one overt homosexual experience with orgasm. In other western countries, the facts largely corresponded with these figures.

In most countries, there are no laws against homosexuality per se, almost all of them having repealed the laws against homosexual activities between "consenting adults in private," and, whereas homosexuals used to be denoted by a term loaded with opprobrium — sodomites — they are now referred to by the newly coined expression, "gay," which would appear to lend a harmless aspect of lively cheerfulness to their activities. Society now only draws the line at an adult having homosexual relations with a minor or with an unwilling partner by force. It appears to have forgotten that it was exactly this practice which led to the destruction of the Prophet Lot's compatriots. In Britain, in addition to having been legalized in 1967, it has 'progressed' to the point of attaining a legal status similar to that of marriage. Denmark has also followed suit:

> Denmark has granted homosexual and lesbian couples the same rights of inheritance as married couples, reports Reuter. The Danish parliament on Friday voted by 78 votes to 62 in favour of a law granting inheritance rights to couples who can prove they are living together. The new inheritance rights will also apply to brothers and sisters who share a home.[29]

In modern times, it is the concept of unlimited freedom which has led to the acceptance of homosexuality and the breakdown of the traditional institution of marriage. A clever phrase has even been coined to denote the sexual relations established between man and man and woman and woman: sexual preference. But the consequences of this deviation from the natural order have been nothing short of evil. In truth, there is only one right path for man to follow and that is the natural order shown to us by the prophets of God. No one who deviates from this path can hope to be spared from its evil consequences.

The West has had to pay a doubly high price for its transgressions. By exposing the delicate female sex to the strong male world, it has permanently lowered their status. What Dr. Louise F. Montgomery has said about the status of women in the publishing world is true also of American women in all spheres of life: Women in the United States remain in the lower ranks in the newspaper hierarchy. Even in TV news programmes, the leaders who influence Americans are males.[30] An even greater harm done by deviation from nature has been the fatal degeneration arising from the innumerable evils of widespread sexual promiscuity in the developed world.

Notes

1. *Encyclopaedia Britannica*, vol. 12 pp. 919-920.
2. Ian Nicolson, *Astronomy*, 1978.
3. Al-Bukhari, *Sahih, Abwab al-Kusuf*, (*Fath al-Bari*, 2/424).
4. Ibid., 2/437.
5. Ibn Kathir, *Al-Bidayah wa an-Nihayah* (Beirut, 1932), 7/111.
6. Bible, Genesis, 2:7-22.

7. Bible, Genesis, 3:1-24.
8. Qur'an, 7:19-25.
9. *Encyclopaedia Britannica* (1984), vol. 3, p. 1040.
10. Ibid., vol. 3, pp. 1040-42.
11. Ibid., vol. 16, p. 599.
12. An-Nasa'i, *Sunan, Kitab 'Ishrah an-Nisa'*, 7/61.
13. Alexis Carrel, *Man, The Unknown* (London,1984), p. 91.
14. Qur'an, 3:83.
15. Qur'an, 55:7-9.
16. Qur'an, 57:25.
17. Qur'an, 7:85.
18. Alexis Carrel, *Man, The Unknown*, pp. 79-80.
19. Qur'an, 30:41.
20. Qur'an, 4:34.
21. *Encyclopaedia Britannica* (1984), vol. X, p. 732.
22. *Daily Express* (London), July 4, 1977.
23. Alexis Carrel, *Man, The Unknown* (New York, 1949), p. 91.
24. *Illustrated Weekly of India* (Bombay), April 2, 1978.
25. *Indian Express* (New Delhi), August 3, 1986.
26. *The Times of India* (New Delhi), June 1, 1986.
27. Ibid., July 5, 1986.
28. Ibid., July 4, 1986.
29. Ibid., June 1, 1986.
30. *The Hindustan Times* (New Delhi), August 23, 1986.

CHAPTER 2

Woman in Society

WOMEN IN ANCIENT SOCIETY

In almost every inhabited corner of the globe, the societies of ancient times regarded the status of women as being inferior to that of man. "In Athens," says the *Encyclopaedia Britannica,* "woman's status had degenerated to that of slaves. Wives were secluded in their homes, had no education and few rights, and were considered by their husbands no better than chattels... In ancient Rome, a woman's legal position was one of complete subordination, first to the power of her father or brother and later to that of her husband, who held paternal power over his wife. In the eyes of the law, women were regarded as imbeciles."[1]

The reason for the ill-treatment of women in ancient times was the prevalence of superstition. There were, in fact, very few matters upon which irrational beliefs of one sort or another had not been adopted. Such perverted thinking became elevated to the status of religion and, as such, had a pervasively baneful influence upon all human relations.

Speculation was another mode of thought which produced strange, and often pernicious results. Ridiculing the thought processes of the ancient Greeks, Bertrand Russell writes: "Aristotle maintained that women have fewer teeth than men; although he was twice married, it never occurred to him to verify this statement by examining his wive's mouths."[2]

Christianity did little to improve this situation, having attached great importance to the erroneous belief given in the very first book of the Bible, that it had been Eve's wrongdoing which had caused Adam's ejection from the garden of Eden. Referring to women in general in this context, the *Encyclopaedia Britannica* says: "[According to Christianity] they were regarded as temptresses, responsible for the fall of Adam, and as second class human beings."[3] With such a myth ever-present in the collective consciousness of society, it is little wonder that women were allotted an inferior positon in both religious and secular matters. In the first letter addressed to the Corinthians, St. Paul says: "For the man is not of the woman; but the woman for the man."[4] In this, St. Paul is simply reaffirming what is laid down as gospel truth in the Old Testament Book of Genesis.

WOMEN'S STATUS IN ISLAM

In ancient times, thanks to the unreasoning and unreasonable approach fostered by superstition, speculation and other forms of irrational thinking, woman came to be considered inferior, one distressing result of which was that she was deprived, among many other things, of the right to inherit property. She was not even entitled to a share of family property. How great an incapacitating factor this was may be judged from the neglect and degrading treatment which women had to suffer for centuries. It was not until the advent of Islam, that, for the first time in the history of mankind, women were given their due legal rights over property. The famous historian J.M. Roberts writes:

> Its coming was in many ways revolutionary. It kept women, for example, in an inferior position, but gave them legal rights over property not available to women in many European countries until the nineteenth century. Even the slave had rights and inside the community of the believers there were no castes nor inherited status. This revolution was rooted in a religion which — like that of the Jews — was not distinct from other sides of life, but embraced them all.[5]

The same point has been made about ancient India by a retired Chief Justice of the Delhi Court, Mr. Rajindar Sachar:

> ... Historically, Islam had been very liberal and progressive in granting property rights to women. It is a fact that there were no property rights given to Hindu women untill 1956, when the Hindu Code Bill was passed, whereas Islam had granted these rights to Muslim women over 1400 years ago.[6]

This is not, however, just a matter of anteriority. What is significant is that, in granting women equal status and their proper rights, Islam set up an important precedent which had as far-reaching an effect on the civilization of the times as western civilization has had on the world of today. If Islam was able to accomplish such a revolution in human affairs, it was because it did not remain just a philosophical creed, but went on to conquer most parts of the inhabited world of the times.

In the world of today, even those commentators who generously acknowledge the virtues of Islam, often repeat the dictum that Islam has relegated women to an inferior status. But to say that Islam gives women a share in property and then to say at the same time that Islam has degraded women is contradictory. From ancient times till today, the question of inheritance has been the most important social issue, and might well be considered the sole criterion of status in society. Entitling women to have a share in property, contrary to the custom of the time, is a clear proof that Islam had no desire to degrade them. Had this been so, the first demonstration of this desire would have been to deprive them of their share in property, a correct and justifiable practice according to the traditions of the times.

It is interesting to see the reverse side of the coin as presented by a recent convert to Islam, namely, the English pop singer, Cat Stevens, now known as Yusuf Islam. Asked by a Jewish woman how he intended to deal with the problem of Islam's "degradation" of women, he said that he had not actually made a study of women's status in Islam, but that for his own part, he had, since his conversion, asked his mother to come and stay with him and that he loved looking after her. His relations with his wife had also considerably improved.

In its assessment of the status of women, the western mind has made the same error as was made by ancient man: it has formed opinions based on irrational beliefs. This accounts for latter-day distortions of thought regarding women in the advanced western countries and for the resultant grave distortion in the concept of women.

WOMEN IN MODERN CIVILIZATION

Where modern western man fell deeply into error, was in his blind acceptance of the concept of the equality of the sexes without giving due consideration of what equality — in its best sense — ought to mean, or what in practice it entails. According to modern thinking, giving equal status to women meant bringing them out of their homes and standing them face to face with men in all facets of life without any regard for the practical and moral problems which might ensue. Islam, on the other hand, defines separate roles, and, therefore, separate spheres of work for men and women, since it is natural and realistic to do so. The other great error made by modern western thinkers was to assume that a role which was separate and different, and played out in other than traditionally masculine strongholds, was necessarily of trifling importance — in short, inferior. As such, the West concluded that in giving a separate role to woman Islam gives them an inferior position. Conversely, since it is held in the West (in theory) that women must be given a place in all masculine spheres it is also concluded that the West gives her a superior position.

So modern man imagines that his feminine counterpart has, in actuality, been accorded a superior position. But let us examine what, in fact, is the state of women's affairs. In the societies of the West, which have attained a high level of material development, theory has yet to be put into practice, and men and women still live and work in their own very separate domains. The status of women is, in practice, almost the same as it was in ancient times, there still being mutually exclusive divisions into male and female spheres, with the corresponding attitudes still very much in evidence. If this were not so, what need would there be for "women's lib?"

Fourteen hundred years ago, Islam launched a much-needed "women's lib" movement, whose purpose was to free women from artificial curbs, and to give them the position which any normal human being should have in society. (One instance, for example is to give them a share in family property). This movement raised their status without any sacrifice of femininity or traditional values, and without creating any perversion in society.

Having launched its movement under the guidance of revelation, its Islamic exponents were in no doubt as to what limits should be set to societal change. The West, however, in its preoccupation with modernity, plunged headlong into experimentation with the old order of values, sweeping away traditional moral precepts and "restrictive" conventions. All of this was done under the banners of "reason," "empiricism," "logic," "liberalism," and so on, but, in actual fact, the whole "liberation" movement has been swamped in a welter of emotion, creating a number of social problems.

UNNATURAL EQUALITY

Selected readings from the Qur'an were prepared in English by the English orientalist, Edward William Lane, and were first published in London in book form in 1843. In his foreword, Lane wrote that "the fatal point in Islam was the degradation of woman." Since then this remark has been regularly taken up as a stick with which to beat Islam. In fact, whenever Islamic affairs were mentioned; it became such a common observation, that not only the enemies of Islam, but also relatively fair-minded writers such as the historian, J.M. Roberts, who did justice to Islam in pointing out its virtues, mentioned it as if it were an established fact.

We have shown in detail, at another point in this book, that this allegation is entirely baseless. The facts are quite the reverse. Islam has, in actual fact, raised the status of woman. If the truth were told, woman's degradation has come about at the hands of two major civilizations, one ancient and polytheistic, the other modern and atheistic. The former has been culpable both in theory and in practice, while the latter has been so in practice, despite its theorizing to the contrary.

We must never lose sight of the fact that what governed the ethics and lifestyles of ancient polytheistic civilizations were myths. Certain highly fanciful, but obviously baseless suppositions were believed in as truths, and all aspects of human existence were subordinated to them. For instance, ancient man regarded certain natural phenomena, such as the sun and the moon, with the awe of ignorance, and venerated them as deities. Conversely, he supposed certain other phenomena to be inferior, therefore, undeserving of respect. It was into the latter category that women fell, possibly because menstruation and their inability to fight alongside their menfolk were interpreted in an adversely superstitious manner. Woman was regarded as the inferior sex and, therefore, deserving of degrading treatment by men.

Modern western civilization has hardly produced a better result in ostensibly exalting the status of women. It may have pronounced men and women equal in every respect and decreed that all work that can be done by a man can be done by a woman too: it may have encouraged women to come out of their homes and try to find a position equal to a man's in every department of life (hence the slogan, "Don't make coffee, make policy"); but, in practice, this concept of equality has done more to degrade women than any traditional view could have done. The next chapter deals with this topic in detail.

What is the reason then for this state of affairs? The reason, to put it briefly, is the erroneous concept of absolute equality in western countries. For example, equality between men is held to be an indisputable fact. But if this equality between men is taken to mean that in every field every man can compete with every other man, the upholder of such an unnatural concept should be able to take an Einstein to a boxing ring and expect him to put up a good fight against the heavyweight champion. Conversely he would also expect the boxer to be able to hold his own while presiding over international, scientific conferences. This may seem laughable, but that is what absolute equality would mean. The Einstein who was at the top of the list in university or science conferences would be seen as a sadly inferior person in a bout with a boxer and the boxer would be completely out of his depth at the conference table. It is clear that applying this rule of equality would result in disaster.

True equality means equality not in the workplace but in status. Human equality does not mean that every man should be engaged in the same work as everyone else. It means rather that every man should be looked upon with the same respect, and should be able to expect the same treatment, legally and morally.

The error into which the West has fallen is its attempt to establish an unnatural equality in the workplace for men and women. The result is as might have been expected: the greatest inequality in human history has developed between men and women. If men and women are of two different sexes, it is because they were created to serve separate purposes. Place them in their respective fields and they will be equally successful, although in different ways. Place both men and women in the same field, and the women will fail to excel: the men will do better due to their natural abilities. As a result, the women will suffer a fall in status vis-à-vis the men.

Inspired by false notions of equality, a certain country girl once fled her home to seek an independent life in a city intending to make money as men do. She failed, however, to find a place in the world of men. What remained at her disposal now was her femininity. This she traded for an independent life. This independent life was not, however, gained by securing "equality" in social life, it was gained rather by having condescended to become the plaything of men.

Somewhat similar, but on a larger scale, has been the case of western women. The West encouraged women to come out of their homes to earn like men. They did so only to find that it was impossible to have an independent life by working like men in the outside world. The only alternative available to them to making money was their femininity. Like the country girl who fled her home, they had to sell their femininity in the market place. Such unnatural and immoral acts failed to give women an equal status. This resulted rather in the creation of innumerable new problems. One of them is pornography, which is not a separate problem in itself, but the inevitable result of unrestricted freedom having given way to licence.

PORNOGRAPHY

Pornography is the representation of erotic behavior, as in books, pictures, or films, intended to cause sexual excitement. Pornographic matter has fallen under legislative prohibition in most countries in the world on at least one of the following assumptions: (1) pornography will tend to deprave or corrupt the morals of youth, or of adults and youth; and, (2) consumption of such matter is a cause of sexual crimes.[7]

The demand for pornography has become so great that, in western countries, it has developed into a regular industry. In America itself this industry has an annual turnover of $ 8 billion. The problems created by it are of such magnitude that a U.S. government commission has issued a report linking sex crimes with hard-core pornography. The commission, headed by then U.S. Attorney General Mr Edwin Meese, called for a law enforcement effort of unprecedented scope against the $ 8 billion-a-year pornography industry.[8] Another commission set up by the U.S. Justice Department has come to a similar conclusion. This report, entitled *Degrading Women,* was published in the national press.

In an introduction to its final report, the Attorney General's commission on pornography urged action against the pornography industry, including more severe penalties for violation of obscenity laws. The report found that exposure to most pornography bears some causal relationship to the level of sexual violence, sexual coercion or unwanted sexual aggression. The commission's conclusions conflict with those of a 1970 presidential commission that found no link between pornography and violence or other anti-social behavior. The 11-member commission formed by Attorney General Edwin Meese said most pornography in the United States would be classified as "degrading," particularly to women. "We have reached the conclusion, unanimously and confidently, that the available evidence strongly supports the hypothesis that substantial exposure to sexually violent materials as described here bears a causal relationship to anti-social acts of sexual violence and, for some subgroups, possibly to unlawful acts of sexual violence," the report said. The commission also concluded that there were ties between the pornography industry and organized crime. "There seems strong evidence that significant portions of the pornography magazine industry are either directly operated or closely controlled by La Cosa Nostra members or very close associates," the commission said.[9]

THE CONSEQUENCES OF UNRESTRICTED FREEDOM

Women's emergence from their homes, the free mixing of the sexes and the pervasiveness of pornography add up to a situation in which sexual excitement is inevitable. The institution of marriage having proved inadequate for the satisfaction of such artificially stimulated and now unbounded sexual urges, free sexual relations have gradually become the order of the day, and in the modern West, there seems to be no limit to the occasions on which sexual liberties may be indulged in. By representing free relations between men and women as being as harmless as shaking hands with one's friend, books, films, plays, etc., have played a major role in encouraging the acceptance of such behaviour as the norm.

The marriage bond, as a result, has come to be viewed as burdensome, superfluous and outdated. So many young men and women have started to live together without being married that the term "unmarried couple" has now come to be considered just as lawful a term as "married couple."

Where the divine *shari'ah* has established a balance between men and women such as renders them complements to each other, "women's lib" claims that they are duplicates of each other — almost like clones. This ill-judged concept has become tremendously popular in recent years, upsetting the balance which had existed for hundreds of years between men and women. The results, however, have been no gain to humanity, while the harm done is too much even to quantify.

The first and most obvious result of women's new-found economic independence has been the higher incidence of divorce. Scientific research has proved that women are more emotional than men, and, as such, can take hasty, ill-considered decisions. Before the industrial revolution, having no permanent, independent, economic footing acted as a check to their emotionalism. When, for example, they felt aggrieved at what they considered the negative aspects of married life, the question of how and where they would live if they opted for divorce inevitably acted as a deterrent. But such fears have been swept away in modern times. On this point the *Encyclopaedia Britannica* says:

> Industrialization has made it easier for women to support themselves, whether they are single, married, divorcees, or widowed. In this connection it is interesting to note that the Great Depression the 1930s stopped the rise in the number of divorces in the United States for a time.[10]

In some western countries the divorce rates have increased to an alarming degree. In France half the number of marriages end in divorce, while in Canada the divorce rate is about 40 percent. In the U.S. the divorce rate is as high as the marriage rate. Ten percent of American women have gone through the experience of divorce.[11]

JUVENILE DELINQUENCY

Modern times have seen women coming out of their homes to enter every department of life. But they have not benefitted by being accorded equal status with men in life outside the home. What this new departure has done is leave insoluble problems in its wake, one of them being illegal sexual relationships. For the free mixing of men and women can seldom culminate in any other way.

A sexual relationship which is formed outside the fold of marriage seems initially to be a simple matter, but when a child is born in such a situation, it becomes evident — generally too late — that it is not such a simple matter, and that normally welcome event — the birth of a child — can have the gravest of consequences both for the child and the parents. It is a sad fact that a large number of illegitimate children are born in the West, despite contraceptive devices being in general use. An official report in 1985 revealed that nearly one in five children born in Britain was illegitimate and that nearly one in three had been conceived by unmarried parents. Such illegitimate children frequently begin their lives in ignorance of who their fathers and mothers are. They are looked after in official institutions and then enter society more in the manner of animals than human beings.

The subject of juvenile delinquency has been studied exhaustively. The *Encyclopaedia Britannica* says that it is among the most baffling social maladies of the 20th century. A world-wide phenomenon, it varies in quality and frequency from country to country.[12] The child delinquent is depicted as a nervous, negative creature suffering from psychological abnormalities, which can be traced to their having been deprived of their parents and which sooner or later manifest themselves in criminal activity.[13]

In a report of *Time* magazine it is revealed that in America each year about 300 children kill either their father or mother.[14]

It is a known fact that the weakest of all newborn creatures is the human child. He needs, more than any living thing, the love, care and guidance of his parents. But the encouragement given by western civilization to women to do something so unnatural as to leave home and enter into illicit relationships has resulted in children having been deprived of blessings which God had intended to provide for them through their parents. Sometimes they are denied the attention they need because their parents are out at work for the whole day in some office. Sometimes it is because their parents have separated that they are left alone; and sometimes it is because they were born out of wedlock, that the parents do not consider it their responsibility to look after them.

In western countries, where the marriage bond has weakened to a very great extent, and even quite trifling differences can result in separation, divorce has become common, and the resultant broken homes have had the same disastrous effects on children as illegitimacy. It is little wonder that children, who are deprived of the normal tender, loving care of a united family, degenerate into animal-like creatures and frequently develop criminal tendencies. One glaring example is Charles Sobhraj, the internationally notorious criminal. Sobhraj's Indian father and European mother did marry, but separated soon after his birth, so that he never knew what it was to live in a united home. He was brought up independently without receiving any proper education, and it is not, therefore, surprising that he gradually developed criminal tendencies. After a life of the most horrifying crime, he is now serving out a lengthy sentence in an Indian jail.

Should not this give pause to the headlong rush into women's emancipation and all the social instability which ensues?

Notes

1. *Encyclopaedia Britannica* (1984), vol. 19, p. 909.
2. Bertrand Russell, *The Impact of Science on Society* (1976), p. 17.
3. *Encyclopaedia Britannica* (1984), vol. 19, p. 909.
4. Bible, I Corinthians, 11:8.
5. J.M. Roberts, *The Pelican History of the World* (New York, 1984), p. 334.
6. *Statesman* (New Delhi), April 26, 1986.
7. *Encyclopaedia Britannica* (1984), vol. VIII, p. 127.
8. *The Times of India* (New Delhi), July 11, 1986.
9. Ibid., May 23, 1986.
10. *Encyclopaedia Britannica* (1984), vol. III, p. 586.
11. *Plain Truth,* May 1987.
12. *Encyclopaedia Britannica* (1984), vol. II, p. 913
13. Ibid., vol. 5, p. 273.
14. *Time,* October 19, 1987, p. 60.

CHAPTER 3

Western Woman

The "New Woman" has been proclaimed with a certain regularity for a century or more, *Time* magazine reminded its readers in a 1972 special edition devoted to an exploration of the status of women in America.[1] In 1989 the Scots traveller James F. Muirhead observed that it was man who was subservient in American life because he was "the hewer of wood, the drawer of water and beast of burden for the superior sex" (i.e. females). The feminists disagreed, insisting it was they who were dominated.

In 1920 American women won the right to vote, and in the 1920s and 1930s began to go to college in considerable numbers, with the expectation of entering the professions. Women believed that "the battle had been won." But, after the vicissitudes of the Great Depression of post-World War II economic boom, the feminist movement was reborn. It was a time of turmoil in American society: President John F. Kennedy had been assassinated in 1963, and the U.S. engagement in the Vietnam War prompted radical protests and widespread questioning of traditional values and institutions, especially among the youth.

The "new feminism" movement was a phenomenon of the restlessness found in the American woman of the 1960s and 1970s. "By all rights, the American woman today should be the happiest in history," Bonnie Angelo observed in *Time's* 1972 cover story. "She is healthier that U.S. women have ever been, better educated, more affluent, better dressed, more comfortable, pampered by gadgets. But there is a worm in the apple. She is restless in her familiar familial role, no longer quite content with the homemaker-wife-mother part in which her society has cast her...Many are in search of a new role that is more independent, less restricted to the traditional triangle of — children, kitchen and church."

According to Angelo, all but the staunchest advocates of "women's liberation" agree that woman's place is different than man's — but the restless American woman of the 1970s was not so sure just *what* that place was. The "new feminism" increasingly influenced young women to stay single, and transformed marriages by ending once automatic assumptions about woman's place, stated Angelo. Widespread commercial dissemination of oral contraceptives — the Pill — together with the overturning of state laws prohibiting abortion on demand — a process which began in the mid-1960s, but remains *enmired* in controversy today — had the effect of separating sexual relations from the solemn institution of marriage.

In 1972, women already made up one third of the U.S. work force, but their pay was much lower than men and they were generally confined to the lower ranking and lower skilled jobs. A soaring divorce rate, however, meant that in 1972 some 20 million Americans lived in households dependent on women as the sole or principal bread winners. A *Psychology Today* survey at the time found that even among male respondents, 51 percent agreed that "U.S. society exploits women as much as blacks."[2] In the more colorful phraseology of the American politician, diplomat and author, Booth Luce: "Power, money and sex are the three great American values today, and women have almost no access to power except through their husbands. They can get money mostly through sex — either legitimate sex, in the form of marriage, or non-married sex."[3]

Indeed, the changes in sexual morality in Europe and the United Status during the 1960s and 1970s were drastic and pervasive. Unlike their parents, many members of the young generation view premarital sex as good instead of bad. A Gallup poll in 1970 in the United States found that three out of four students were indifferent to virginity, or the lack of it, in the person they marry.[4] Said British gynecologist John Slome: "The kiss of the 1940s and 1950s has become the sexual intercourse of the '60s and '70s."[5]

The effect on women has been dramatic. For those feminists who decried the fact that woman's reproductive role made her a "prisoner of sex," the Pill appeared as the key to freedom. "Without the full capacity to limit your own reproduction," wrote Lucinda Cisler in *Sisterhood Is Powerful*, "a woman's other freedoms are tantalizing mockeries that cannot be exercized."[6] But in the view of University of Michigan psychologist Judith Bardwick, instead of liberating women to enjoy sex, the Pill has replaced fear of pregnancy with fear of being used. "Far from giving young women the sexual license that men have so long enjoyed, the Pill has caused some women to resent male freedom even more," Bardwick stated. "Far from alleviating anxiety over sexual use of the body, the Pill has exacerbated it."[7]

The pill notwithstanding, unwanted pregnancies still occur by the tens of thousands, and the fight over legalization of abortion-on-demand remains on center stage. And, the effects of long-term use of the Pill, which acts to prevent ovulation, are now a matter of public record. The changed hormonal balance caused by the Pill is blamed for headaches and weight gain in some women. British and other medical studies have found a connection between the Pill and the formation of blood clots that can cause strokes as well as an increased susceptibility to various forms of uterine cancer. Successive generations of female contraceptives — oral, sub-dermal and all the rest — have become even more potent and questionable in their long-term effect.

It should not be surprising to find that as of the 1970s female suicide was on the rise in the United States. Though it has always been the case that more men than women kill themselves, trends had begun to change in certain large cities. In Los Angeles, for example, whereas in 1960 of those who committed suicide 35 percent were women, by 1970 the percentage of women among suicides had jumped to 45 percent.[8] Another indication that women had begun to experience more conflict came from a University of Wisconsin study during the same period, which found that women psychiatric patients complained of more anxiety, depression, alienation and inability to cope with stress than did their counterparts of ten years earlier.[9]

THE "WOMEN'S LIB" MOVEMENT

"Women's liberation" began formally with the founding in 1966 of the National Organization for Women (NOW), the largest and most influential movement group. In 1985 NOW had a nationwide membership in the United States of some 185,000 women and men. NOW was conceived as a civil rights lobby for women, active in organizing support for enactment and enforcement of law prohibiting discrimination against women in employment, education and so forth. NOW has also led numerous campaigns in the Congress and in the courts on issues ranging from child care to abortion reform.

The National Women's Political Caucus is another mass-based organization, with a membership of 77,000 in 1985, and a commitment to get women involved full time in politics. "Women! Make policy, not coffee!" is the organization's motto.[10] The Congressional Caucus for Women's Issues, formed in 1977 and opened to male congressmen and senators in 1981, supports federal policy initiatives to improve the status of women and families. There are in addition a myriad old and new women's groups and organizations concerned with specific issues such as education, abortion or pension rights.

This current of the "new feminism," led predominantly by professional women and women in the labor movement, was joined by another current of younger women who were active in the civil rights and student protest movements, including the anti-Vietnam War and youth "counter-culture" movements, of the 1960s and 1970s. The latter group's focus was less on legal or policy changes affecting women than on a frontal challenge to cultural definitions of maleness and femaleness.[11]

As a result of its varied composition, the women's liberation movement's goals range from the modest, sensible amelioration of the female condition to extreme and revolutionary visions.[12] The first camp emphasizes a more egalitarian society: equal pay for equal work, a nation in which women are not blocked from access to education, political influence and economic power. The more radical wing of the movement, however, is disdainful of such mundane concerns and wants nothing less than a drastic revision of society in general. In their view, the sexual roles must be redefined to free both sexes from the stereotypes and responsibilities that have existed for ages. The concept of man as hunter and woman as keeper of the hearth, these feminists declare, is obsolete and destructive for both sexes.

Language itself became an issue for the "new feminists:" namely, do males use language to help perpetuate their roles as masters?[13] Yes! shout the feminists, language is "living proof" of women's oppression. Thus titles such as "chairperson" — instead of "chairman" — and "congressone" — instead of "congressman" — have begun to be heard in the West. Likewise, "sportsoneship" instead of "sportsmanship," "herstory" instead of "history," and "spokesone" instead of "spokesman." More well known is the feminists rejection of "Mrs." and "Miss" as a form of address — because it allegedly stigmatizes women by revealing their marital status. Instead, "Ms." — pronounced *miz* — has been widely adopted.

At the extreme radical fringe, the "new feminists" are waging an assault not just on society, but on the limitations of biology. Some argue that through the science of eugenics the genetic code could be altered to produce a different kind of man or woman. *Sputnik* magazine of October 1987 gave substance to this view with an article titled, "Should Daddies Be Mummies?" The article dealt with the theory of sex change forwarded by a German doctor, in which the uterus of a woman is taken out by surgery and placed into a man's stomach so that the man, too, can perform the child-bearing task, thus putting an end to the inequality created by nature itself between the sexes. Short of that, extremist feminists demand a complete withdrawal from dependence on men, including sexual ties, and advocate embrace of lesbianism.[14]

The views and aims of the women's liberation movement are wide-ranging, and sometimes contradictory. Likewise, the broad response to the "new feminism" has been as varied as the circumstances in which ordinary American women have found themselves. A series of Vignettes of women interviewed by *Time* magazine in 1972, and excerpted below, makes this variety clear.[15]

• *Betty Jackson* dreamed of being a singer or a nurse and, someday, a wife. Instead, at 15 she had an illegitimate child. "I live in dope city and on one of the worst streets," said Betty. "We have no heat. We get hot water once in a while. The wall is coming apart from the leaks. Roaches are everywhere. The rats minuet and waltz around the floor." The Welfare Department paid Betty's rent, but the two additional checks they provided monthly barely covered the purchases of necessities, much less "luxuries" such as a telephone, radio, TV or vacuum cleaner. "I am a slave to my financial problems," Betty said, "and my life is meaningless as far as having things that people are supposed to have." Whatever hopes she had of returning to work were dashed, Betty reported, when her 19-year-old daughter gave birth to an illegitimate child.

Survival, Betty explained, was her primary concern. Women's lib? "I'm not interested." Religion? "I don't go to church. They're robbers. I can prey at home, and He'll hear me just the same. I don't have to pay for it."

• *Luaretta Galligan* married in 1944. She found herself alone most of the time when her husband's company assigned him a job that kept him away from home six days a week. To make friends and keep busy, Lauretta opted for a job and attended night school. As her household expanded to include five sons, she dropped her outside interests to spend more time at home, "making sure everyone is going in the right direction," as she put it. At age 52 she still rises at 6:30 to prepare her husband's breakfast and get the two sons off to school. She smiles happily when her husband, Thomas, calls her his "greatest asset."

Said Lauretta: "My first priority is my family and my husband's work, and then I work on other things." She never plays bridge and only occasionally goes to fashion shows or luncheons. Most of her social life revolves around her husband's business. "Being a homemaker and mother is very stimulating. I realize there are many things about homemaking that are a little bit monotonous, but a lot of things about a woman's career or a man's career can be monotonous too."

• "Why should I have children?" asked *Suzanne Sape,* 23, and a happily married woman who is upward bound in a management planning career. "I'm glad I'm married," Suzanne said, "and I enjoy being feminine. I like to sew, and I was once really interested in fashion." But Suzanne's bent toward homemaking and shared joys did not extend to having children. "If I were to conceive," she stated frankly, "I would have an abortion. I like children very much. I consider it an enormous challenge to raise them the way they should be raised. It takes an awful lot of time and energy and intellect to raise them to cope with the problems of a pretty crummy world." Suzanne had talked with doctors, she said, about sterilization, but concluded that she did not want to risk the possible physical and psychological side effect.

"If you are a career woman, how can you bring the child up?" Suzanne asked. "If a woman has a child, it should be a full time occupation for at least the first year, perhaps two or three. Three years is an awful big bite out of a career, and I've spent a long time preparing for my career."

• *Noraine O'Callaghan* is against abortion — "It's murder she told *Time* — and she worried that some mothers use day care centers as a substitute for child rearing. But she sympathizes with most of the aims of women's liberation, she said. Her one reservation: "In order to get into the system, a woman has to become like a man, and is therefore, probably no better."

• *Marcia Heuber's* world is one of seasons and crops, dawn-to-dusk farm chores, the kitchen and children in a rambling farmhouse. When she was in high school, Marcia told *Time,* "My biggest goal was to get married." Though she works just as hard as her husband, Roger, she has no doubts about where she stands in relation to him: "I still feel the male sex should be dominant. I want my husband to feel he is the head of the household. We decide things together, but I think the final word should mostly be his."

Marcia also found time for social service activity like teaching Sunday School, playing the church organ, and so on. She is deeply proud of the life she has carved out for herself: 'Being married and having a family were the most important things for me. I'm very happy with my profession."

• *Lynn Young* is 33, attractive, unmarried and likes it that way. "I wanted to be a surgeon," she admitted, "but a friend at Stanford medical school discouraged me. He showed me how tough medicine is for a woman." Lynn never feels the least pressure to marry. "There simply aren't that many marriages I envy," she said. "A lot of women are just hanging in there for the security, but that's a dumb reason to get married."

• I used to call my husband, "A.B — arrogant bastard," started *Eleanor Driver.* "And he was, but he was strong and dominant, and I liked that. When the university offered me a job, he said, 'Go ahead — but I want my socks washed.'"

A revealing portrait of the average American housewife and her response to "women's lib" was drawn by author, wife and mother, Sue Kaufman:[16]

> She is anywhere from 24 to 45 — a wife, a mother, a housewife. She is usually far from mad (crazy or angry), far from being wildly bitter — but also far from being satisfied with what or where she is. Though she isn't too clear on where she would rather be, she knows it isn't up there on the big, steam rolling bandwagon of Women's Lib, or in the front ranks of the marching phalanx, waving banners. Much as she admires them.

> And she does admire them...

> She is overwhelmed by a terrible sense of wrongness, of jarring *inconsistency*. There was that surging, powerful feeling in the hall (when she went to hear a prominent feminist speak), and now, stranded on the linoleum under the battery of fluorescent kitchen lights, there is this terrible sense of isolation, of walls closing in, of being trapped...

> She has begun to think about the necessity of financial independence... about a job, part-time now, full-time later. If she has money of her own, she has begun to ask questions about separate bank accounts...

> But most likely she will not divorce. At least not casually, and certainly not for any principle or idea. Moreover, she like, or loves, her children, and though they are often a terrible drain on her emotions and strength, she is simply not prepared to delegate most of their care to someone else. She also likes, or loves, her husband, and though she is no longer willing to put up with anything she considers an infringement on her rights or dignity, she is not about to blow up the whole works by refusing to do what was contracted at the onset of her marriage — namely Women's Work — which covers everything from enduring labor pains to counting laundry...

The siren song of "women's liberation" is complicated and contradictory. Indeed, as soon as the vote was won, American suffragists split over a proposed Equal Rights Amendment (ERA) to the U.S. Constitution. Many women with a background in the social reform movement believed strongly in female differences, and feared that the ERA would preclude legislation protective of women.[17] More than 50 years later, in 1972, the ERA was passed in the U.S. Congress, but then failed to receive sufficient backing from state legislatures to be adopted.

"If the feminist revolution simply wanted to exchange one ruling class for another, if it aimed at outright female domination, the goal would be easier to visualize," concluded Bonnie Angelo in her overview of American women's status in 1972.[18] "The demand for equality, not domination, is immensely complicated. True equality between autonomous partners is hard to achieve even if both partners are of the same sex. The careful balancing of roles and obligations and privileges, without the traditional patterns to fall back on, sometimes seems like an almost utopian vision.

While nearly everyone favors some of the basic goals of the New Feminism — equal pay for equal work, equal job opportunity, equal treatment by the law — satisfying even those minimum demands could require more wrenching change than many casual sympathizers with the women's cause have seriously considered. Should women be drafted? Ought protective legislation about women's hours and working conditions be repealed?

WOMEN INTO THE MARKETPLACE

Complex currents of social change converged to produce the "new feminism" of the 1970s, but British historian and writer Arnold Toynbee identified an essential dilemma years earlier. Middle-class woman acquired education and a chance at a career, wrote Toynbee, at the very time she lost her domestic servants and the unpaid household help of relatives living in the old, large family; she had to become either a "household drudge" or "carry the intolerably heavy load of two simultaneous full-time jobs."[19]

In 1972, though American women already made up more than one third of the national workforce, they were concentrated in lower-skilled and lower-paying positions. An average woman employed in a full-time job earned only two thirds of the salary paid to a man with a similar job. Child care facilities were few and far between, and often too expensive. The same number of women as men graduated from high school that year, but only 41 percent of the women compared to 59 percent of the men went on to college. There had never been a woman justice on the U.S. Supreme Court, and less than 3 percent of the nation's lawyers were women. The first five female agents for the U.S. Secret Service were only then beginning training. And politically, women were barely visible: in 1975, only one in ten statewide elected officials and state legislators were women; and, at the national level, only 4 percent of the members of congress were women.

During the next two decades, from 1970 through 1990, all of these indicators of women's status changed, most rather dramatically, and women are now visible if not prominent in virtually every walk of life in the United States.[20]

• Justice Sandra Day O'Connor was appointed to the U.S. Supreme Court in 1982, and as of 1990 12.5 percent of all U.S. federal judges, and more than 8 percent of the judges on state benches, were women.

• In 1984, Representative Geraldine Ferraro, a wife and mother, was the Democratic Party's Vice Presidential candidate and the first woman in American history to run on a presidential ticket.

• In 1991, 17 percent of all elected mayors were women, up from just 1 percent in 1971. During the same period the number of statewide elected officials and legislators doubled, from 10 percent to just under 20 percent. At the national level progress has been slower: the proportion of female members of congress went up from 4 percent in 1975 to 10 percent in 1994.

• In 1991, 20 percent of then-President Bush's Senate confirmed appointments — that is, the higher-ranking appointments — were women, up from18 percent in 1977 under then-President Jimmy Carter. President William Clinton's cabinet is peppered with women — as of September 1993, Attorney General Janet Reno, Energy Secretary Hazel O'Leary, and Health and Human Services Secretary Donna Shalala were in the Cabinet proper. Laura D'Andrea Tyson was Chairman of the prestigious Council of Economic Advisers, Sheila Widnall was Secretary of the Air Force, Dr. Joycelyn Elders was U.S. Surgeon General, and the heads of the Peace Corps, the Environmental Protection Agency and Commodity Futures Trading Commission were women. One out of the five governors on the Federal Reserve Board and one out of the four commissioners on the U.S. International Trade Commission are women. There are about ten women in top posts within the Executive Office of the President, and there are more than 25 women under-secretaries in the various government departments or ministries.

• Women have also broken into the front ranks of the media, with Connie Chung holding a prized anchor position on the evening news for one of the three major commercial television networks and scores more women in the position of network reporters, and even more women anchoring and reporting for local news stations, not to mention hosting some of the most popular talk and variety shows.

• In 1989, a survey of 'Fortune 500' companies found that women made up 12.7 percent of corporate board membership, up from a single digit figure in 1970. And, businesses owned by women soared in the decade 1977-1978, from 7.1 to 30 percent of all business.

• In education, where women have historically lagged behind men, especially in post-secondary education, over the decade from 1970 to 1990 women's achievements converged with and in some cases surpassed men. From 1966 to 1987, the percentage of female high school graduates who completed four years of college increased from 16 to 25 percent, to equal that of men.

In 1989, the majority of degrees at all levels except doctorate were earned by women: whereas in 1970, 43 percent of the Bachelor's degrees and 39 percent of the Master's degrees were awarded to women, in 1989 it was 53 and 52 percent respectively. Though only 36 percent of the doctorates were awarded to women, that was a substantial jump from 13 percent in 1970.

Significantly, too, the proportion of degree in science and engineering earned by women showed a dramatic increase from 1960 to 1990. In 1989, 50 percent of all biological science degrees were earned by women, up from 28 percent in 1970. The proportion of degrees awarded to women in computer science and the physical sciences doubled from 14 percent in 1970 to 31 and 30 percent respectively in 1989. Mathematics, also a traditional preserve of men, saw an increase in degrees awarded to women during the same period of from 37 to 49 percent. And in business, 47 percent of the degrees went to women, compared to 9 percent in 1970. Though in 1989 women earned only 15 percent of all Bachelor's degrees in engineering, this was up from just 1 percent in 1970.

In the medical and other professional areas too, women have become increasingly qualified. In 1989, 26 percent of the dentistry degrees, 33 percent of the medical degrees, 50 percent of the veterinary medicine degrees and 40 percent of the law degrees were awarded to women.

From 1975 to 1989 the number of colleges and universities headed by women doubled, but women continued to be under-represented in the upper management of higher education. In 1989 only 10 percent of the chief executive officers of colleges and universities were female. Women's position in college faculties is likewise still insecure. In 1910 women made up 20 percent of college faculties: in 1985, a full seventy-five years later, just 28 percent of college faculties were female, and most women educators were clustered in the lower ranks, below the level of full professor, with lower pay and less job security.

A CLOSER LOOK

Western women have come out of the house and into the marketplace in full force, but a closer look raises the question as to how much of this is "liberation," and, even more important, what is its cost in human and social terms for women and for society.

In 1990, 53.5 million women, or 58 percent of all American women, were in the labor force — three fourths of them working full time. From 1975 to 1990, 20 million women had been added to the work force. Labor force participation of all women between 16 and 65 years of age rose dramatically, but the steepest increase was among married women with a husband present in the home. In 1990, nearly 60 percent of all married mothers with children under six years of age were working outside the home. In 1980 less than 20 percent of married mothers with toddlers under three years of age were full-time workers; by 1990 more than 33 percent of these mothers were in the work force.

Though women have made substantial advances in professional, technical and administrative-management occupational areas, they are still overwhelmingly employed in the administrative support occupa-tions, including clerical and secretarial jobs, and services (such as sales-girls, waitresses, hairdressers, etc.). In 1975, only 5.2 percent of employed females were in executive, administrative or management occupations, whereas by 1990 this had grown to 11.1 percent.

Similarly, in 1975, 13.2 percent of employed women worked in the traditional professions (i.e., as physicians, lawyers, registered nurses), and 2.7 percent worked in technical and related professions but, by 1990 this had increased to 15.1 percent and 3.5 percent respectively. In 1975, 63.7 percent of female employees were confined to four areas — namely, sales, administrative support, private household and other service occupations. In 1990 58.6 percent of employed women still worked in these fields.

So, although women in America are now 13.9 percent of all police and detectives, 19.3 percent of all physicians, 36 percent of all computer programmers, 43.5 percent of all manufacturing assemblers, 44.3 percent of all financial managers and 51.5 percent of all bus drivers, they are also 99 percent of all secretaries, 89.2 percent of all textile sewing machine operators, 84.8 percent of all health aides and 80.8 percent of all waitresses.

Among government employees, though women are a minority at the highest grade levels, their representation there has been increasing sharply. For instance, in 1982, 22.4 percent of the employees in Grades 11-12 and only 9.7 percent in Grades 13-15, were women. By 1988 31.9 percent of Grades 11-12 employees and 15.9 percent of Grades 13-15 employees were women. Still, the bulk of women in government employment are concentrated at the six lowest grades. In 1982, and still in 1988, fully 75 percent of the employees in the lowest six levels were women.

Though the pay gap between men and women has closed somewhat, and more so in some occupations than in others, discrimination in earnings and benefits remains pervasive. In 1980 women earned, on average, 64 cent for every dollar earned by men in the United States; by 1990 it was 72 cents. In certain areas, such as technical, sales, administrative support and service jobs, the male-female wage gap narrowed in recent years as much because of declines in men's salaries (due to recession condition) as of increases in women's wages. As of 1989, women were still more likely than men to be working at minimum wage jobs. Female workers were less likely than males to have employer or union-sponsored pension plans in 1987 (but between 1980 and 1987 the proportion of male workers with pension plans dropped by 6 percentage points).

In spite of the fact that nearly half the American work force consists of women, neither maternity/paternity leave nor child care support was by any means the norm in American firms, even in 1989. At that time, no more than 3 percent of medium and large size firms, on average, provided paid maternity leave, and this went down to 2 percent for small firms (with less than 100 employees). In 1988, more than 60 percent of American children under age 18 had working mothers, but as far as child care assistance is concerned, no more than 10 percent of firms of all sizes provided any real benefits or support for child care. However, 35-45 percent of all firms did provide flexible schedules and flexible leave times for parents with young children.

"Flexitime" notwithstanding, in 1987 6.2 million working mothers in America paid for child care. Of these 750,000 had incomes at or below the poverty line, and for them child care expenses ate up 20 percent of their income. Though mothers with children under age 21 and no father present are entitled to government child support, often they do not get it at all or do not get the full amount.

Closely related to the issue of women's earnings and benefits in the fact that between 1970 and 1989 the number of women workers of age 16 and above holding multiple jobs increased by almost 400 percent — from 636,000 to more than 3 million. Women who worked more than one job in 1989 were more likely than men to be doing so because the additional earnings were necessary to meet regular household expenses.

THE TRADITIONAL FAMILY UNDER SIEGE

Sweeping as the change may be, the phenomenon of working mothers is the least of the shock to the traditional American family over the past several decades. Though married couple families still heavily predominate, that predominance has dropped from 87 to 80 percent in just two decades as "other family types" became more common. The "male householder with no spouse present" from 11 to 16.5 percent. This varies by race: among black Americans, for instance, only the barest majority of families were married couples in 1989. The overall result: in 1990, fully one quarter of all American children resided with just one parent.

Already climbing in the 1960s, the divorce rate in America literally soared from 1970 to 1990. In 1990, the divorce ratio (i.e., the number of currently divorced persons per 1000 currently married persons) was at an all-time high of 166 for women and 118 for men. In that year 56 percent of American women over age 18 were married, with husband present; 3.7 percent were married with husband absent; 12.1 percent were widowed; 9.3 percent were divorced; and 18.9 percent were single (i.e., never married).

Though most women continued to marry, the average age at first marriage increased from 21 to 24 years between 1970 and 1988, and marriage tended to become a kind of way-station for many, only one of several different, and now acceptable, "family types." After entering adulthood, many women will live with a man prior to marriage. Such "co-habitation" outside of marriage, as it is called, was uncommon prior to 1970. In that year the U.S. Bureau of the Census counted 523,000 households with two unrelated adults of the opposite sex; by 1984 the number had grown to nearly two million. For most women such co-habitation is a temporary stage before marriage. But statistics do show that while at least five out of six young women in 1985 will marry, lifelong singleness (possibly in combination with one or more co-habiting relationships) is becoming more acceptable and common.[21]

Not only has the divorce rate soared, but the birth rate (i.e., the number of live births for each 1000 women of childbearing age) plunged — down from 118 in 1960 to 67.2 in 1988, a nearly 50 percent drop. By the early 1980s voluntary childlessness had become so acceptable and common — among married couples as well as among never-married women — that one researcher estimated that perhaps as many as 25 percent of the young women of the 1970s would in fact *never* have children.[22] In 1990, four out of every ten American families contained children, though the presence of children was more common in families maintained by women than either those maintained by men or in married couple families.

Simultaneously, the number of legal abortions has more than doubled. In 1987 in the United States, 1,354,000 pregnancies were terminated by abortion, up from 588,000 in 1972. Approximately 70 percent of the legal abortion are obtained by unmarried women, and these women are concentrated in the lower end of the income scales. Women with an annual household income at the poverty line or below account for only 15 percent of all American women, but they account for 33 percent of the women obtaining abortions.

NATURE'S VERDICT

The equality of man and woman is one of the main concepts of western civilization. It has been in vogue in the western world for the last one hundred years, but that has been quite long enough to show that, as an experiment in living, it has been a failure. In spite of women having been legally accorded equal status with men in many countries, and in spite of advances in the educational level of women and their entry into most arenas of economic and political life, in practice they have yet to achieve an equal professional status or secure an equal footing in society. And, meanwhile, the shift in women's role and identity in society has led directly to the breakdown of the family and a serious breakdown of public morality generally in the West.

Initially, supporters of the concept of equality of the sexes claimed that the differences between men and women resulted from environmental influences, but modern investigation shows that the cause must be sought elsewhere. Research carried out on a wide cross-section of society and over a broad range of different fields has established that this difference, far from having been externally imposed, by the environment, or through historical processes, is innate. That is to say, that it is biological in nature, something that women are simply born with and not something which is eradicable by legislation or the whipping up of popular sentiment. It is nature and not nurture which is to be blamed.

In 1981, *Newsweek* magazine reported in detail on the conclusions drawn from in-depth research carried out in America by both male and female investigators on the differences in the physical and mental make-up of men and women, namely, that women are emotional in their thinking and that men are superior to them in mathematics, problem solving, leadership and fighting.[23] Women's differences are traced not to their conditioned responses to a traditionally male dominated society, but to their own biology which fits them for an altogether different sphere of living.

It has now been established that hormones play an important role in creating this difference between the two sexes. When the male hormone testosterone was experimentally injected into females, they began to develop masculine characteristics. Girls who had been injected with male hormones while still at the foetal stage showed less fondness for playing with dolls, and even developed aggressive temperaments like boys. Researchers found that hormones can change the structure of the brain itself, so that if the male and female brain structures differ, the cause may be traced to the difference in hormones.

Although this research has clearly established that a difference does exist, physically and mentally, between men and women — obviously indicating separate spheres of activity for them — old adherents of the male-female equality concept are still reluctant to accept the reversal of a favorite theory. As a western scholars says: "Whether these physiological differences destine men and women for separate role in society is another and far more delicate question."[24]

Almost a decade prior to the *Newsweek* report, *Time* magazine, in its special issue on the status of American women, asked the question: "Are women immutably different from men?" Their review of the research findings at that time, summarized in the following pages, is instructive.[25] Women's liberationists believe that any differences other than anatomical are a result of conditioning by society. The opposing view is that all of the differences are fixed in genes. The idea that genetic predispositions exist is based on three kinds of evidence. First, there are the 'cultural universals' cited by anthropologist Margaret Mead: Almost everywhere, the mother is the principal caretaker of the child, and male dominance and aggression are the rule. Some anthropologists believe there has been an occasional female dominated society: others insist that none has ever existed.

Then there is the fact that among most ground dwelling primates, males are dominant and have as a major function the protection of females and offspring. Some research suggests that it is true even when the young are raised apart from adults, which seems to mean that they do not learn their roles from their society.

Finally, behavioral sex differences show up long before any body could possibly perceive subtle differences between his parents or know which parent he is expected to imitate. "A useful strategy," says Harvard psychologist Jerome Kagan, "is to assume that the earlier a particular difference appears, the more likely it is to be influenced by biological factors." Physical differences appear even before birth. The heart of the female fetus often beats faster, and girls develop more rapidly. "Physiologically," says sociologist Barbette Blackington, "women are better-made animals." Males do have more strength and endurance — though that hardly matters in a technological society.

Recent research hints that there may even be sex differences in the brain. According to some experimenters, the presence of the male hormone testosterone in the fetus may "masculinize" the brain, organizing the fetal nerve centers in characteristic ways. This possible "sex typing" of the central nervous system before birth may make men and women respond differently to incoming stimuli.

In fact, newborn girls do show different responses in some situations. They react more strongly to the removal of a blanket and more quickly to touch and pain. Moreover, experiments demonstrate that twelve-week-old girls gaze longer at photographs of faces than at geometric figures. Boys show no preference then, though eventually they pay more attention to figures.

Even after infancy, the sexes show differential interests that do not seem to grow solely out of experience. Psychoanalyst Erik Erikson found that boys and girls aged ten to twelve used space differently, when asked to construct a scene with toys. Girls often build a low wall, sometimes with an elaborate doorway, surrounding a quiet interior scene. Boys are likely to construct towers, facades, with canons and lively exterior scenes. "The difference," Erikson says, "seems to parallel the morphology (shape and form) of genital differentiation itself: in the male, an external organ, erectible and intrusive; and, internal organs in the female, with vestibular access, leading to statically expectant ova."

In aptitude as well as in interest, sex differences become apparent early in life. Though girls are generally less adept than boys at mathematical and spatial reasoning, they learn to count sooner and to talk earlier and better. Some scientists think this female verbal superiority may be caused by sex-linked differences in the brain. While girls outdo boys verbally, they often lag behind in solving analytical problems, those that require attention to detail.

It is a paradox that even though the number of educated women is at an all-time high, the representation of women in traditionally male professions is still extremely low. Harvard psychologist Matina Horner guessed that one reason for this may be that women actively fear success, and began seriously looking into this when she discovered that the few studies that had been made of women's motivation for achievement showed they had high anxiety. Reasonably certain that this meant women were afraid of competition, Horner decided nonetheless to test that assumption. Putting men and women into competitive and noncompetitive situations, she found that males showed a spurt of motivation in competition. Females did not. It was anxiety about competition that apparently held the women back.

There are personality differences between the sexes too. Some distinctions turn up remarkably early. At New York University, for example, researchers found that a female infant stops sucking a bottle and looks up when someone comes into the room; a male pays no attention to the visitor. Another experiment showed that girls of twelve months who become frightened in a strange room drift toward their mothers, while boys look for something interesting to do. At four months, twice as many girls as boys cry when frightened in a strange laboratory. And, according to Jerome Kagan, since similar differences can be seen in monkeys and baboons we are forced to consider the possibility that some of the psychological differences between men and women may not be the product of experience alone but of subtle biological differences.

Many researchers have found greater dependence and docility in very young girls, greater autonomy and activity in boys. When a barrier is set up to separate youngsters from their mothers, boys try to knock it down; girls cry helplessly.

Animal studies suggest that there may be a biological factor in maternal behavior; mothers of rhesus monkeys punish their male babies earlier and more often than their female offspring; and, they also touch their female babies more often and act more protective toward them.

The definitive research on hormones is still to be done, but one trait thought to be affected by hormones is aggressiveness. In all cultures, investigators report, male infants tend to play more aggressively than females. Some suggest that female may be as aggressive as men — but with words instead of deeds. However, it has been established that the female hormone estrogen inhibits aggression in both animal and human males. It has also been proved that the male hormone androgen influences aggression in animals. For example, castration produces tractable steers rather than fierce bulls.

The influence of androgen begins even before birth. Administered to pregnant primates, the hormones make newborn females play more aggressively than ordinary females. Moreover, such masculinized animals are unusually aggressive as long as they live, even if they are never again exposed to androgen. According to some experts, this long-lasting effect of hormones administered or secreted before birth may help to explain why boys are more aggressive than girls even during their early years when both sexes appear to produce equal amounts of male and female hormones.

Will there some day be a "unisex" society, with no differences between men and women except anatomical ones? *Time* magazine asked. It seems unlikely. According to psychoanalyst Therese Benedek: "Biology precedes personality."

"Nature has been the oppressor," observed psychologist Michael Lewis. Women's role as caretaker was the evolutionary result of their biological role in birth and feeding. The baby bottle may have freed women from some of the tasks of that role, but, says University of Michigan psychologist Judith Bardwick, "the major responsibility for child rearing is the woman's, even in the Soviet Union, the Israeli Kibbutz, Scandinavia and mainland China." Furthermore, though mothering skills are mostly learned, it is a fact that if animals are raised in isolation and then put in a room with the young of the species, it is the females who go to the infants and take care of them.

"Perhaps the known biological differences can be totally overcome, and society can approach a state in which a person's sex is of no consequence for any significant activity except child bearing," admits Jerome Kagan. "But we must ask if such a society will be satisfying its members." As Kagan sees it, "complementarity" is what makes relationships stable and pleasurable.

Psychoanalyst Martin Symonds agreed. "The basic reason why unisex must fail is that in the sexual act itself, the man has to be assertive, if tenderly, and the woman has to be receptive. What gives trouble is when men see assertiveness as aggression and women see receptiveness as submission." Unisex, he sums up, would be "a disaster" because children need roles to identify with and rebel against. 'You can't identify with a blur. A Unisex world would be frictionless environment in which nobody would be able to grow up."

The crucial point, however, is that a difference is nota deficiency. As one biologist put it: "We are all human beings and in this sense equal. We are not, however, the same."

AT WAR WITH NATURE

In practice, men still have the upper hand. The cause is not social conditioning, as feminists would have us believe. It is wholly biological and psychological. It is the biological factor which — we are forced to conclude after 100 years of feminist struggle — is the stumbling block in according women an *equal position* (that is, in the outside world) with men. It is the cruelty of nature rather than the cruelty of society which is to blame. Now that this has been established, the more militant among the feminists have started demanding that, in the womb itself, the science of eugenics should be applied to changing the genetic code in order to create a new biological system which will in turn produce a new breed of women. They maintain that, in this way, the male-dominated society could be replaced by one in which the sexes are equal in ability and performance. This suggestion is rather like saying that fish, like goats, should be able to produce milk, and then, when, in spite of every encouragement the fish fails to produce milk, proclaiming that one will create, with the help of medical science, a new strain of milk-producing fish. Exactly like goats.

If, one fine day, it occurred to a doctor that the mouth should be situated not on the face but on the stomach, and he thereupon set about removing the mouth from the face, the world would ridicule his foolishness, for the places which nature has allotted to the various physical features are unalterable. Our successful control of them depends upon our dealing with them as they are, and not in attempting to reshuffle them to suit man-made concepts.

This fanciful repositioning of women in society is rather like trying to juggle with the unalterable features of the human physiognomy. Similarly, when modern civilization began to draw up a new map of life, one of its features was to bring about complete equality between man and woman The whole family and social structure had to be turned topsy turvy in order to turn the fanciful supposition into a reality. In the end, women have come out of their homes, but they have been unable to become the equals of men in practical life. The reason is simple — nature did not obligingly go along with the human imagination.

The Russian scientist, Anton Nemilov, who himself desires to see total equality of the sexes become a reality, admits that this desire of ours has no basis in biology and agrees that this is the reason for this idea never having materialized. Citing scientific experiments and observations, he writes:

> Very few people will agree if it is said today that women should be given limited rights in the social set up. We, too, are wholly against such a suggestion. However, we should not deceive ourselves in thinking that establishing equality between men and women in practical .fe is a simple matter. Nowhere have more attempts been made than in the USSR to establish this equality. Nowhere in the world have such unbiased and generous laws been made than in the USSR, yet it is a fact that the position of woman in the family has hardly changed for the better.[26]

He goes on to say:

> Up till now the concept of inequality between men and women has been so deeply rooted not only in the lesser educated people but also in the highly educated Soviet people as well as in women themselves, that if, on occasion, women are treated as having full equality with men, this is attributed to men's weakness and impotency. If we pursue the thoughts of any scientist, writer, student, businessman, or hundred percent communist, we shall soon realize that he does not in his heart of hearts regard woman as his equal. If we read any recent novel, however free a thinker the writer might be, we shall certainly find

something or the other in it which will expose as superficial his concept of woman as equal to man.[27]

The reason is that this revolutionary concept clashes with an extremely important fact, i.e. that in respect of biology, both sexes are not equal, both are not meant to shoulder an equal amount of burden.[28]

Deviation from nature not only fails to achieve any positive gain, but also entails the loss of desirable features of human existence. The correct place for a thing is that assigned to it by nature. Any bid on our part to displace or reorient it inevitably leads to a variety of evils.

This is exactly what has happened in the case of women who have been taken out of their homes in order to make them men's equal. The result has not for them been the achievement of equal position. The result has been their becoming the objects of a flood of licentiousness and pornography.

Of this situation, Anton Nemilov writes:

> The truth is that all signs of sexual anarchy have become apparent in the workers. This is a situation fraught with grave dangers threatening to destabilize the whole socialist system. It should be countered in all possible ways. Great difficulties will be faced to fight on this point. I can cite thousands of instances of sexual licentiousness, which goes to show that this has spread not only in the lower echelons but on the top rungs of the ladder as well as among the intellectuals.[29]

Nemilov's view, published as long as fifty years ago, has been substantiated by recent experience. In fact, his words may be applied with even greater force and accuracy to the state of affairs prevailing today.

Modern man, regarding the old concept of man and woman as outdated, attempted to create equality between the two sexes. But this amounted to waging war with nature itself, to clashing with reality and his efforts proved counterproductive. Far from achieving equality between the two sexes, efforts made to reach this artificial goal paved the way to the spread of various evils in society.

SOME EXAMPLES

Here are some examples of the grave results of deviation in the matter of women under the influence of western civilization.

NOT GETTING MARRIED — A MISTAKE

It is thanks to erroneous western concepts that marriage has come to be equated with bondage. This, in turn, has resulted in the emergence of a permissive society with all the attendant social and familial evils. One such problem is typified by Greta Garbo, a Swedish film actress who was one of the most famous Hollywood personalities of her time. In her heyday she had been greatly sought after, but when she grew old, her charms faded and her friends, one by one, deserted her. On the 18th of September, 1980, at the age of 75, she celebrated her birthday all by herself. Her biographer, who was present at that time, asked whether she regretted having opted for a single and, consequently, lonely life. Greta Garbo replied sadly: "Not getting married was a mistake."[30]

In their prime, such women attract people by their youthful charm. But as they advance in years, they lose their attraction for the opposite sex, and their friends forsake them like rats leaving a sinking ship. It becomes less and less possible for them to continue to enjoy all the different kinds of entertainment which had formerly engaged them day in and day out. Too late, it dawns on them that all their past activities have been of no value. They had been living in a dream world from which they have now been rudely awakened. It is only at this point that they realize the futility of regarding permanent loyalty as an obstacle to the enjoyment of life. The delights of youth are replaced by the emptiness and boredom of old age. Pets become their only solace, as there is no life partner with whom to share their joys and sorrows, and no children to give them tender, loving care. There is no one of their own who will keep their name alive when they leave this world. There isn't even anyone to whom they can bequeath their life's savings with any degree of satisfaction. There is no one to love and no one to return their love. They find themselves left alone and bewildered in a world which abounds in life. For them there can be no greater punishment than this.

BE A GOOD WIFE

Frank Borman, an American astronaut went into space with a woman astronaut in the same spacecraft. After his return from the voyage he said: "Having women on the spacecraft was okay except that it would be upsetting to put a male and a female too close together for a long time." Borman's comment certainly upset the feminists. One American lady remarked in the course of a fiery speech: "Mr. Frank Borman would never have existed had his parents not come together."

Scientific research together with the realities of practical life have shocked the cherished concepts of feminists leading some of them to rethink their ideals. An American lady, Mrs. Marabel Morgan, a mother of two, recently published a book entitled *Total Woman*. Here is the simple magic formula she divulged to her American sisters so that they may lead successful married lives. "Be nice to your husband, stop nagging him and understand his needs." In less than a year this book sold three million copies. To the writer the perfection of womanhood lies in her ability to become a good companion of her husband rather than seek an independent life.[31]

The truth is that the total woman is one who can be a total companion to her husband.

ADMITTING DEFEAT

Another example of the baneful consequences of western civilization's deviation from nature's course is that of Jean Seberg, an American actress who also achieved extraordinary fame and popularity because of her charming personality. Not only in the U.S., but also in Europe, she was the cynosure of all eyes. At an early stage in her career, she opted to become an object of entertainment to millions in preference to making a home for herself on the traditional pattern. But when her diary was gone through after her death, the last line turned out to be: "I wish I had stayed home."[32] How ironic that such a "successful" career should have ended in helpless failure.

God has endowed everything pertaining to the world of matter with particular characteristics. The objects of His creation are, therefore, able to perform satisfactorily only if they function strictly in accordance with their own particular properties. In the same way, God has created man and woman with their particular traits, and they can lead proper lives only when they act in consonance with their respective natures. Any deviation from this course will cause them to surrender their true place on life's map.

A woman's capacities are clearly different from those of a man. This very fact is a proof that the spheres of men and women, in general, are not the same. The man's sphere is basically outside the home and the woman's is within. If both change their spheres of activity, both will lose their respective identities and their ultimate meaningfulness in the context of society. Each, in displacing the other, will have a sense of disorientation.

ENDLESS PROBLEMS

The Lonely Lady, a novel by Harold Robbins first published in the U.S., throws light on one of the weaknesses of the highly developed society of America which causes an unmarried woman to end her life in a state of insufferable loneliness. It is the story of a beautiful, young, American woman who, dazzled by the glamour of the film world, abandons her married life to become an actress. Her perfect femininity helps her to climb the ladder of success and she quickly reaches dizzy heights of fame and wealth. She has a host of fans and is surrounded by luxuries, but the climax of her success does not bring her peace. Now she discovers the bitter truth — that "fame has a way of fading, and friends a way of disappearing when they are most needed."[33]

With a sigh, she says, "Only a woman knows what loneliness is."[34] The main point made by the novel is that a woman cannot afford to find herself in such a situation. Making vast sums of money working in films and securing an independent life may seem very attractive propositions, but as a woman ages, her friends no longer see any charm in her and this, to the woman, proves an unbearable shock.

She may have amassed all kinds of wealth and material objects, but still lacks what she most needs — peace of mind. This is something which can only arise from the stability of a permanent companionship, but now there is no man in her life who could give her just that. Too late, she realizes what it means to possess no family of her own. "Here is a loneliness born of independence, of honest individualism in a society where only dishonesty brings profit."[35]

The system of human life is a web of extremely delicate balances and counter-balances, in which even a minor change can wreak havoc. It is no different from the animal, vegetable and mineral kingdoms in which the secret of success lies in never deviating from the pattern laid down by nature. Achieving the desired result is possible only when the established structure of nature is understood and accepted. But the very people who adhere strictly to this precept as regards the world of matter, forget that this is an eternal truth which applies to their own lives too. Nature's system for men and women takes shape in the institution of marriage. A woman's physique, psychology, familial urges and social relations all demand that she lead a married — and, therefore, moral — life. This is a pattern which has been laid down for her own good.

Being free and independent seems an attractive phrase when applied to a woman, but the practical experience of personal liberty can range from the purely unpleasant to the downright disgusting.

In her youth a woman may easily fall prey to what strikes her — because of her inexperience — as an appealing way of life. But, as she grows older, and goes from one bitter experience to the next, she realizes that she has made a wrong choice. But this dawns on her only when things have gone too far for her to make amends. Now her only alternative is to console herself with her pet dogs, cats, parrots, etc., as it is too late to find a life partner with whom to share the ups and downs of her daily existence. When she finally leaves this world, it is in despair.

THE END OF PLEASURE

Married to John Kennedy (1917-1963), America's 35th President, Jacqueline Kennedy basked in the limelight of her husband, and enjoyed the fame of being America's First Lady. But this did not last for long, because Kennedy was shot dead in November, 1963, just three years after being elected President. Jacqueline was suddenly bereft of all the fame and honor that went with her place in society as wife of the President. But, not long afterwards, the same feminine charm which had attracted John Kennedy in her younger days now brought to her side the Greek millionaire, Aristotle Onassis (1906-1975), whom she subsequently married. At the time of her marriage, she was forty years of age and Onassis was 60. But this marriage was not a success. They soon began to live separately, until after a prolonged illness, Onassis died in 1975. Jacqueline was not even present at his deathbed during the last hours of his life.

Jacqueline found everything but happiness. Her biographer, Kitty Kelly, speaks of her "incurable desire to buy happiness, even if it meant spending as much in one hour as 3,000 dollars."[36]

This shows that even marriage cannot make a woman happy if what her mind is truly set on is not conjugal bliss, but wealth, fame and all the attendant worldly pleasures.

Marilyn Monroe (b. June 1, 1926), one of the most famous women in America, started her career as a photographer's model and soon rose to fame as a film actress. Thanks to her extraordinary attractiveness, she became renowned as the "sex goddess" of the film world. Her films were all a tremendous success in that they never failed to draw crowds.

The last film she made was called *The Misfits* — a title which, in a sense, applied to her own life, because she frequently had a feeling of being out of place. In the midst of even the largest crowds, psychologically, she was alone. Photographs showing her smiling and laughing were regularly published in the newspapers, but, in reality, she was often sunk in depression. Finally, her mental and emotional state became unbearable and, on August 5, 1962, she committed suicide by taking an overdose of sleeping pills. She was just 36 years of age.

Such women appear to be happy on the stage and screen, but in their heart of hearts, they live with a sense of persecution, for they belong to everybody, but nobody belongs to them. They make others happy, but they have always to contend with the feeling deep down inside them that there is really no one with whom they can share their innermost thoughts, no one to whom they can pour out their hearts. At social gatherings they appear to be fulfilled as individuals, but in reality, their lives are empty. The initial spectacular quality of their lives is dimmed, bit by bit, until at the end, life seems little more than a dreary vacuum.

It is a fact that women are temperamentally unfit for solitude. Few women can endure loneliness over long periods of time. But the path along which western civilization pushes a woman can lead to nothing but isolation. Islam, on the contrary, leads a woman to a life where she is never alone, but a member of a united family. The Islamic way is natural, that of the western world quite the reverse.

THE BURDEN OF FAME

Brigitte Bardot (b. 1934), the most famous star in the history of the French cinema, scaled higher peaks of renown than even Marilyn Monroe or Marlene Dietrich. It was said that she brought more currency into France than the Renault Motor Company, and some even declared her to be the most famous Frenchwoman since Joan of Arc. English writer Tony Crawley calculated that by 1958 her photograph had appeared no less than 29,345 times on the covers of European and American magazines.[37]

Film followed film, her popularity soared and, at times, she even gave up trying to go out because the crowds of photographers outside prevented her from doing so. Every day, she was swamped by fan mail, so that it became impossible even to read a selection of the letters which poured in.

Despite all this ostensible glamour, she was so unsatisfied from within that just the fact of being a celebrity became a burden to her. One night, worn out by her own fame, Brigitte swallowed an overdose of tranquillizers. Even at that crucial moment, when her life hung in the balance, photographers forced the ambulance which was rushing her to the hospital to stop halfway so that they could take pictures of her. BB (as she was known in the film world) was once reported as saying that she never really felt at ease in front of the camera.

At the age of 39, after making 48 films, she suddenly ended her career, refusing even to accept the most enticing offers from Hollywood. She sold her Rolls Royce and went to live alone in her house on the Riviera "to cease to be considered a beautiful object and become a human being like any other."

The truth is that to become a heroine in the outside world and attain fame goes against the feminine grain. By nature, a woman is homeloving and at heart she is a housewife. It is, in fact, her birthright. That is why it so frequently happens that women celebrities, who lead artificial lives outside the normal limits of the family, drop everything in favour of living in solitude either somewhere in the middle of their careers, or at the end. Where they finally find peace of mind, after a temporary exposure to bright city lights and glittering society, is in their very own homes, and not in the outside world.

What Islamic law lays down with regard to women is protective of their true nature, and is in no way cruel or repressive, as has been suggested by the uninitiated. When, after experimenting with a life and a career in the outside world, a woman finally realizes that her place is in the home, she has reached the point which Islam encourages every woman of marriageable age to reach at the very outset by way of following her natural womanly inclinations. Islamic law is designed to steer women away from the ordeals of the crassly competitive and brazenly immoral world in which only men can successfully make their way.

AN ENFORCED WITHDRAWAL FROM THE FIELD OF ACTION

Everyone, be it a man or a woman, is rewarded according to his or her abilities and performance. When women in search of equality emerged from their homes, they expected to be able to function in areas which had traditionally been masculine strongholds, and attempted to take up jobs as pilots, drivers, engineers, professors, administrators, police officers, military commanders, etc. But, biologically, women did not have the capacity to perform these tasks, and proved sadly deficient in managerial skills. Their incapability having been demonstrated, the question arose as to what they should do now that they had left domestic life behind them. They began, sooner or later, to enter those spheres in which they could demand a price for their femininity, for instance, in advertising and on the stage, screen and television. But here, again, they were prevented from leading totally satisfactory lives because of an inherently feminine drawback: when a woman began to grow old, she found herself unwanted. In the world of entertainment, only young women were in demand, and the moment they lost their youthful attraction, no further value was attached to them as personalities.

Thanks to "women's lib" having done away with all barriers between men and women in western countries, women now find themselves in the marketplace. It is only those who have obvious feminine charms who attract attention, become popular and manage to make something of their lives as objects of entertainment. Once launched on such a course, they begin to regard marriage as an obstacle to their further progress. They have no further taste for the quiet satisfaction of domestic life, preferring the glamour of the outside world.

But the glitter of such a life is short-lived, for the moment their youth shows signs of waning, these women find themselves cast off like so many rags. Having shirked all domestic responsibilities at an earlier, marriageable age, they can now stake no claim to domestic comfort and bliss. Forgotten and deserted, such women of the western world live on into a forlorn state of decrepitude.

The kind of life that takes shape from being associated with the family is very different from the above example. When a woman begins her life as a wife, she finds herself at the centre of all activity, being in charge of everything and everyone within the domestic sphere. In her own little world, she builds up a reputation for herself as a wife, mother and grandmother. Each day adds to the honor and respect shown to her by her family, and she goes on increasing in worth in the eyes of her husband. If she shone as a young wife, how much greater is her lustre as a mother and grandmother. This position of the woman is quite natural. That is why in the western world itself in circles where the matrimonial fold is still intact, a woman on the strength of nature, comes to acquire the same position. Here is an explicit example from the life of Ronald Reagan, former President of America. According to one American report published in the *Hindustan Times*: "Mr Reagan is known to be deeply attached to his wife, whom he calls 'mommy' away from the public, according to their close associates."[38] Having made the home and the family her whole world, a woman can certainly count on familial support in her middle and declining years. None of the sorrows of solitude for her!

While western civilization supports the liberated woman only for the early years of her life — her youth being her sole attraction — Islamic culture, being family-oriented, attaches value and gives its support to the married woman right throughout her life.

THE EXAMPLE OF JAPAN

In Japan, about 15 million women are employed in offices and factories. Far from enjoying a position equal to that of their male counterparts, they serve as assistants and subordinates.

Two Japanese women were, of course, elected to the Cabinet a few years ago, but that was thanks only to the institution of Women's Year in 1985. Of the 608 diplomats in Japan, only twelve are women. Even to this day, Japan's society is male dominated. It is significant that a woman minister noted in a recent report on the condition of women in Japan that "a bill, yet to be passed by the parliament on ending discrimination against women, is considered by many of its male critics to be reverse discriminatory."[39]

In former times the spheres of men's and women's activities were considered separate. In modern times, however, this clear demarcation has been dispensed with, one of the grounds being that a nation cannot progress if women are not offered equal opportunities in its construction. But the experiment of giving women a free hand has not contributed either to nation-building or to the progress of civilization. In countries where women have already been offered equal opportunities in every field, all of the more important and advanced fields are still dominated by men.

Those who subscribe to the view that a nation will fail to march ahead without the participation of women — who constitute almost half of the population — need only look at the example of Japan, one of the most developed countries of the modern world. They will be forced to change their ideas when they consider that all of the major developments in Japan have taken place without women's involvement as equal in non-domestic activities. Japan's example is the greatest challenge to the feminist view. Its continuing to be a male dominated society clearly shows that the development of a nation does not depend upon equal participation by women — a view erroneously held by feminists the world over. Ms. Sharmon Babior, an American, acknowledging the difference between Japan and America in this matter comments: "I dont't think American women would tolerate the 'Teishukanpaku (the husband is the ruler of his home) behaviour."[40]

Notes

1. *Time,* March 20, 1972.
2. Ibid., p. 26.
3. Ibid., p. 28.
4. Ibid., p. 47.
5. Ibid., p. 47.
6. Ibid., p. 89.
7. Ibid., p. 47.
8. Ibid., p. 47.
9. Ibid., p. 47.
10. Ibid., p. 33
11. Sara M. Evans, "Women in Twentieth Century America: An Overview," *The American Woman 1987-88. A Report In Depth,* Ed. Sara E. Rix (New York: W.W. Norton & Company, 1987).
12. *Time,* op. cit., p. 29.
13. Ibid., p. 55.
14. Ibid., p. 30.
15. Ibid., unnumbered pages following p. 29.
16. Ibid., pp. 70-71.
17. Sara M. Evans, op cit., p. 34.
18. *Time,* op cit., p. 28.
19. Ibid., p. 27.
20. All of the data in this and the following two sections has been taken from two sources: *The American Woman 1987-88. A Report in Depth,* edited by Sara E. Rix (New York: W.W. Norton & Company, 1987), and *The American Woman 1992-93, A Status Report,* edited by Paula Ries and Anne J. Stone (New York: W.W. Norton & Company, 1992).
21. Andrew Cherlin, "Women and the Family," *The American Woman 1987-88, A Report in Depth,* op cit., pp. 74-75.
22. Ibid., p. 76.
23. *Newsweek,* May 18, 1981.
24. *Reader's Digest,* October 1981.
25. *Time,* op. cit., pp. 43-46.
26. Anton Nemilov, *The Biological Tragedy of Woman* (London, 1932), p. 76.
27. Ibid., pp. 194-95.
28. Ibid., p. 77
29. Ibid., pp. 102-103.
30. *The Hindustan Times* (New Delhi), September 21, 1980.
31. *The Times of India* (New Delhi), February 8, 1978.
32. Ibid., November 8, 1981.
33. Harold Robbins, *The Lonely Lady* (London: New English Library, 1976), p. 448.
34. Ibid.
35. Ibid.

CHAPTER 4

The Problems Facing Modern Civilization

PERVERSION IN MUSLIM SOCIETY AND WESTERN CIVILIZATION

A contemporary commentator once observed that of perversion has set in in western society, so also has it taken root in Muslim society. Then how do you regard western civilization as being wrong and Islamic civilization as being right? This objection, if we examine it, will be found to be ill-judged, because our comparison of western and Islamic civilizations makes a judgement on the basis of standards versus behavior. The rot of Muslim society is the result of deviation from Islam, while the rot of western society is the result of putting into practice the very principles in which it believes.

The evils of Muslim societies stem from the gap between principle and practice, whereas the evils of western society are the result of a clash between principles and realities. Western civilization of modern times has formed principles, independent of religious principles, to govern social life, and has maintained that modern principles were superior to older principles. Through colonization and the industrial revolution, etc. the western nations achieved political and material domination over large areas of the world, which placed them in a position to reject the old principles of life and construct a human society based on modern principles of life.

This experiment in ethics has now been going on with the dominance of western nations for more than a century, but practical experiments have failed to verify the new principles. All that has been accomplished is to effectively demonstrate that the new principles favoured by the West are completely incompatible with what nature intends for mankind. The clash between ideals and reality has, in fact, given rise to ever-increasing manifestations of depravity in western life.

While the solution to moral backsliding in Muslim societies lies in a return to the Islamic principles adhered to in the past, this cannot be said about the West. If western society retreats to its past, this return, will be a return to exactly the same principles on which it still adheres to the letter. Those who gave credence to the concept of permissiveness, or those who insisted on the entrance of women in every department of man, or those who advocated that marriage is an unnecessary bond, if they were to return to their past where will they return. This going back will be to the same principles which they still observe and the disastrous consequences which they are now facing. The solution to the perversion of Muslims lies in their going back to the path of Islamic principles which they have left behind, while the rectification of western society lies in renouncing its self-made principles. Here we present some examples to illustrate this point.

REVERSE COURSE

Time magazine, which has a readership of over 23 million, spread over 95 countries, published a revealing report on the condition of women in America. The following is the gist of the report:

> Over the past 25 years there has been an influx of women into the American job market. Some 65% of women of childbearing age now form part of the American workforce and 90% of them have had, or will have children during their careers. This has created a tremendous problem for women: the onerous task of holding down a job and having children at the same time.[1]

One such American woman is Lillian Garland, who worked as a receptionist at the California Federal Savings and Loan Association in west Los Angeles until she became pregnant and left work to have her baby in 1982. Her baby girl was delivered by caesarian section and her doctor prescribed a three-month period of leave. When she returned to Cal Fed, Garland found that her position had been filled. She had lost an $850 dollar job just at a time when, with the birth of her child, her expenses had increased.

Garland filed a suit in the federal court against the company for having discriminated against her in terminating her employment. The lawyers of both parties entered into interminable arguments, and after prolonged litigation — five years to be exact — Thurgood Marshall, former Justice of the American Supreme Court, gave his ruling in January, 1987, that the state requires an employer to provide special job protection for workers temporarily disabled by pregnancy.

This ruling triggered a tremendous controversy. On the one hand, women are happy that they have secured the protection of the law for the bearing and rearing of children. On the other hand, serious American thinkers maintain that this ruling will harm the cause of women.

The debate over pregnancy leave has thus created a deep rift among feminists. One side argues that pregnancy leave, even though it benefits individual women, poses a general danger to female workers because it singles them out for special protection. Historically, they point out, such privileged treatment has eventually led to discrimination *against* women, says Marsha Levick of the National Organization for Women's Legal Defense and Education Fund: "That almost always backfires."

Don Butler, President of the Los Angeles-based Merchants and Manufacturers Association, said that the decision "spells disaster." To this he added: "Larger companies can makeshift to fill a hole, but small ones cannot do that very easily. If I employ ten females, and two or more get pregnant at one time, I might as well file for bankruptcy." Discrimination against women might increase. Many companies "just won't hire women in their childbearing years," says the Chamber's Attorney Lamp.

A well-known feminist, Betty Friedan, said in support of the ruling regarding Garland's case, "Equality does not mean that women have to fit the male model." There is something very incongruous about this argument. When women are so different in their biological structure that they cannot "fit the male model," where is the necessity to bring women into every sphere of life to do the same work as men, and then attempt, by passing laws, to enforce an artificial equality of the sexes.

As economist Sylvia Ann Hewlett puts it: "This decision means that there is recognition at the highest legal levels that, in order to get equal status for women in the workplace, you have to create family supporters." This is an indirect acknowledgement of the rationality and appropriateness of the old traditional system. The concept evolved by modern civilization that woman does not need man as her supporter implies that she should earn and be her own supporter. When this principle was put into practice, it soon became evident that a woman could not do without a supporter. The only difference was in the name. Formerly it was husband,' now it is "the company."

In old, traditional society, when religion was still a positive force, men used to do whatever was required outside the home, while women took care of all indoor work. This was a division of labor which was both practical and natural. But modern civilization has held that this "division" is nothing but sexual discrimination. It is this view which launched the women's liberation movement, and encouraged women to come out of their homes in order to take up employment in offices and factories.

At an early stage it became apparent that under this new arrangement, the path to progress for women was strewn with obstacles. For example, when a woman becomes pregnant and bears a child, she is thereby rendered incapable of tackling jobs outside her own home for a considerable period of time. To remove the disadvantages implied for the woman, a law was passed granting special paid leave to pregnant women and nursing mothers. This was the kind of law which legislators, who were far removed from the situation, could pass with no discomfort to themselves, but whose implementation could not be afforded by those who have to come to grips with the everyday running of a factory or management of an office. This is a situation which has sparked off an unending controversy.

The government so far is supporting women in this conflict in order to maintain the superiority of its cultural principle. But taking sides against reality is hardly practicable. If the government required the managements of all offices and factories to give four months paid leave to women, how many estabishments would be able to afford what would seem to them an unwarranted extravagance? Finding the cost of such a cultural luxury prohibitive, many employers would simply not hire women during their childbearing years, and older women would themselves opt to stay at home. It seems very probable that such negative factors will reinforce the very discriminatory attitudes which the women's liberation movement came into being to end.

WHITHER "WOMEN'S LIB"?

From the 12th to the 16th of January, 1987, a conference was held in Vigyan Bhavan, New Delhi, in which philosophers, scientists, writers and artists from 15 countries participated. This five-day conference was arranged by the Government of India on the topic, "Towards New Beginnings." Many distinguished ladies of the western world, who have now grown old, were among those who participated. They had spent all their lives working for Women's Lib, but their mood was one of frustration. The *Indian Express* cites Germaine Greer of Australia as a case in point:

> They are feminists of different hues — Ms. Germaine Greer, the outspoken, aggressive writer from Australia, and Ms. Gisele Halimi, a Tunisian-born lawyer who spearheaded the women's movement in France along with Simone de Beauvoir and others. But both voice a concern that is troubling feminists in the West today — Whither women's lib? Ms. Greer seems more mellow today: the fire that raged in *The Female Eunuch* is strangely missing. "The movement has solved some problems and left us with a different set of problems," exclaimed Ms. Greer. "Perhaps the problem was that we didn't take our mothers with us. We left them behind, found them antiquated. And now that many of us are mothers ourselves with teenaged daughters, perhaps we understand our mothers better."[2]

"The West has no answers to the problems of inequality between sexes," says the internationally acclaimed writer Germaine Greer. The erroneous belief of western women that the females in veils are unequal and the ones with make-up minus the head-cover are free and liberated has to be rejected. Referring to the prevalance of "wife-beating" even in the so-called civilized West, she asks, how about the unequal treatment meted out to females in the U.S. and England in the areas of wages and jobs? Well, one-fourth of the crimes in England emanate from violence against women. The man-woman relationship understood in the West as an extension of role-models is the primary cause of strain in the sexual relationships. All the western women identify themselves with the *bahu* — the bride — forgetting that the mother-in-law and the sister-in-law are also the specific role-models to be played by females. She feels that child bearing for a woman is a unique investment: "The joys of motherhood fill the blanks that cannot be satiated in the specific husband-wife role models." Known for her non-conformist and non-traditional views, Ms. Greer advocates "coitus interruptus" in the area of birth-control: "The array of occlusive devices, spermicidal creams, quinine pessaries, douches, syringes, abortifacient pills and rubber goods of all shapes and sizes are the ill-effects of a growing consumer-culture. These have achieved nothing but added strain in the sexual relationships."[3]

Ms. Halimi, is more frank. "It is a bad time for the women's movement" she admitted. "It is down at the moment and we are trying to find the reasons for it. Perhaps we got everything women wanted too fast — contraception, abortion, and divorce. And the problems that face women today are not strong enough to give the movement new force and strength." Women have very specific values and morals. "They have a different view of humanity. I am not saying that it is better than that of men, but it is different. And women have to prove that they are women, and not men," she emphasized.[4]

According to religious teaching, the woman's "role model" was that of mother and housekeeper. She was meant to bear and rear children, and manage the home. The modern role model is that of the busy woman executive, functioning on an equal footing with men in every sphere of the professional world. Years of experiment have shown that the latter role is unrealistic. In their old age, the same western women, who had fervently advocated the new role model, are the very ones who are now asking for a return to the status quo ante. Does this leave any room for doubt about the superiority of the role model postulated by religion?

TERRIBLE CONSEQUENCES

Plain Truth, a well-known American magazine with a world-wide circulation of 7,850,000, published an article entitled 'Teen Pregnancy' along with a photograph of Sally, an American teenager. The article included a letter written by Sally, which, though short, is painful and shocking:

> When I was 8 years old I first had sex with a boy of 15. I did it because I lack love and attention from my parents. I need love, and my parents never show me any. Nothing really changed at home, and at 15 I became pregnant. My boy friend blamed me and left. I had nowhere to turn, I was trapped, so I had an abortion. Now I'm afraid to date anyone, and I cry myself to sleep every night.[5]

"For every 1000 girls between 15 and 19 in America," wrote New York correspondent George Gorden, "96 of them are pregnant."[6]

Such are the tragic consequences of deviation from nature. This is the result of deliberately ignoring the fact that when God created men and women, He laid down rules for their relationship with each other: on reaching a sufficiently mature stage of development, they were to marry, have children and, by a process of mutual co-operation, make a home in which to bring up those children, thus providing a stable base for the progress of mankind. But western modernity became so preoccupied with the concept of freedom, that it dispensed with the kind of bonds which held men and women together in a healthy family relationship. The resulting disregard for the institution of marriage gave birth to various kinds of evils in western society, as may be judged from the above-mentioned examples.

The free mixing of men and women, with the sexual liberation it implies, is wholly against nature. In matters of sex, a woman prefers a single partner. It is in her nature to love only one man faithfully. Men, on the other hand, are promiscuous by nature. In a situation, therefore, where freedom of sexual relationships is damaging to faithful sexual partnerships, it is the women who suffer psychologically. Emotionally, they have to pay a very high price for their emancipation.

The famous Australian feminist, Ms. Germaine Greer, has acknowledged, now that she is of a more mature age, that her zeal for the sexual liberation movement in her youth was not realistic. In an interview with the *Indian Express* she lamented over the present state of affairs: "What is worrying today is the results of the sexual liberation movement — the number of teenaged girls who have been on the pill since they were 12 and 13, the number of teenaged girls who get pregnant by the time they are 15 and 16. What is happening to them? Sex means something quite different for men. They can love and leave. When the time comes to go to university, they can take off quite easily. Women have a different sensibility. They love with their heads, hearts and loins. And a broken love affair leaves them quite shattered. I have seen it happen to people close to me. And it is terrible."[7]

In modern times Muslim society has fallen prey to many evils, but the reasons for this having happened are different in respect of the West and Islamic civilizations. In the case of the latter, it is deviation from Islamic principles which has caused the rot to set in, whereas in the former case, it is adherence to a new set of man-made principles which has had so deleterious an effect.

ARTIFICIAL PROBLEMS

The unique Nobel Sperm Bank set up by Dr. Robert Graham, a California millionaire, preserves the sperm of Nobel prizewinners so that women, who wish to produce children of above-average intelligence, may be impregnated with it. Dr. Graham established this bank with the aim of compensating for sterility on the part of husbands. But now, unmarried women — such is the degree of modern, western permissiveness — are coming forward to avail of the bank's facilities. More interested in bearing above-average children, they prefer to ignore the possibilities of marriage, and freely seek the assistance of the bank.

One such unmarried mother is forty-year-old Dr. Afton Blake of California. When she contacted the Nobel Sperm Bank and explained the kind of child she wanted, she was advised that sperm number 28 was what she needed. (Donors of sperm remain unnamed, and are given a code number.) Dr. Blake duly became pregnant with the specially selected sperm, and bore a son whom she named Doron (a Greek word meaning "gift"). His photograph, at age four, appeared in *The Hindustan Times* of September 7, 1986. A *Daily Telegraph* representative, Ian Brodie, who met Dr. Blake at her Los Angeles residence, reports that her happiness is gradually turning to gall, the birth of a child without a father having created a number of problems. Top of the list of such problems is the boy's repeated queries about his father, which he began to make as soon as he could speak.

Dr. Blake told Brodie that "there was one occasion when Doron got angry with me. He said he was going off to live with his Dad." For Dr. Blake, what had started off as an interesting experience, latterly seems to have developed into a series of delicate problems. She now says with regret, "One thing Doron is deprived of is a Daddy."

Deviation from nature has given rise to problems which were hitherto inconceivable.

MARRIAGE VERSUS FORNICATION

"The Big Chill,?" a specially researched *Time* magazine cover story of February 16, 1987, startled the world with horrifying details of a new disease — AIDS. Since AIDS is infectious and fatal, it has produced a new breed of untouchables from whom both men and women flee in fear of their very lives. Publicity on the subject has created such a scare that barber' shops in western countries often display signboards bearing the unlikely legend: "No Shaves Here."

Government officials have described such a reaction as "AIDS hysteria." Barbers, however, maintain that even the AIDS victims' perspiration, or drops of blood from tiny cuts made during shaving, can transmit the virus and that it was, therefore, necessary to keep away from them.[8]

After making detailed investigations, *Time*'s team of experts confirmed that the prime cause of this deadly disease is promiscuity. Since it is transmitted mainly by homosexuals, it has come to be known as the "gay disease." This disease spreads so rapidly that its explosion in the world of today has been geometric. Chilled by the fatality of AIDS, one of its victims exclaimed: "Oh, what will happen in this world, if we have to die when we make love? AIDS is the century's evil."[9]

Promiscuity, euphemistically referred to as "free love" in the western world, has brought down a curse upon humanity. It was estimated that by 1991, 270,000 people will have contracted this disease in the U.S., and that doctors will find it impossible to treat such a large number of patients. The situation will be completely beyond control. The government has started an anti-AIDS campaign whose slogan is "Love carefully." This same advice, differently worded, would read: "Love within the bonds of marriage. Stop loving outside them."

One of the great influences in socially "legitimizing" promiscuity was D.H. Lawrence's novel, *Lady Chatterly's Lover,* first published in 1928. At the time of publication this work was considered obscene and almost immediately banned. Then, with a gradual change of moral climate, permission was given to republish it in 1959. Many young people in America were deeply affected by this novel and, a whole spate of similar literature having followed it, promiscuity began to be the rule rather than the exception. Now, once again, there is a public outcry to ban *Lady Chatterly's Lover* and other such works.

Such a complete about-face has been caused by the devastating effects of AIDS. It has forced the west to re-think the whole question of free sex — a development which seems little short of miraculous. "Swingers of all persuasions may sooner or later be faced with the reality of a new era of sexual caution and restraint."[10]

People had been delighted at having discovered the key to unlimited enjoyment in freeing themselves from the curbs of religion, for, according to divine law, a sexual relationship between a man and a woman was permitted only within the bonds of marriage. But now the realities of nature are finally forcing man to forsake the path of free love and follow the path of sexual restraint. It has taken the fatalities of the final quarter of the twentieth century to convince people that divine law and the law of nature are one. Too late, it has dawned on "free lovers" that promiscuity could be a killer. *Time's* cartoon showing a man and a woman encircled by a deadly snake, epitomizes one of today's major human dilemmas.

It was not without good reason that the Qur'an commanded that sexual relationships should be confined within the bonds of marriage:

> (Lawful to you are), in wedlock, women from among those who believe, and, in wedlock, women from among those who have been given the Book before you — provided that you give them their dowers, taking them in honest wedlock, not in fornication, nor as secret love-companions.[11]

This has been interpreted by Qur'anic commentators as a clear injunction to establish sexual relations only through marriage, and that there should be no extra-marital relationships. Experiments have shown that this is the only right and natural way. Marital relationships and fornication are not just matters of approval or disapproval by religious authorities, but matters of life and death. The married state is a blessing for human society; any other is a curse.

It is significant that the new education plan released by the U.S.[12] government stresses sexual abstinence as a preventive measure. This public exhortation to observe the rules of old-fashioned morality is a clear indication of the superiority of divine law over man-made law.

A believer in divine law, who errs by entering into an illicit sexual relationship, and contracting AIDS in the process, will be considered to have deviated from the principles of divine law. However, one who belongs to western civilization and contracts such a disease as the result of promiscuity will be said to have shown the error of the principle of western civilization itself. The former case proves the error of a man while the latter case proves the error of the principle of a civilization.

THE CONSEQUENCES OF UNNATURAL EQUALITY

"No one who has ever known me can believe what I did," said a 35-year old American whose demeanor suggested innocence and seriousness of mind. He related how he had beaten the wife he loved, choked her till she was unconscious, pushed her face in the mud and held a kitchen knife to her throat.[13] "How could I have done that?" he now wonders. "People know me as a good man. I own my own business. I don't drink, I don't smoke, I don't chase other women." In spite of all such contrary indications, he repeatedly beat his wife.

Reader's Digest gives many instances of wife-beating by Americans in an article entitled, "Why Men Hurt the Women They Love." According to one survey, in America a woman is battered by a husband or boy-friend every 18 seconds. And every year, it is estimated that more than a million of these need medical help. Every day, four die.[14]

Why should the developed and civilized society of America be infested with the evil of wife-beating? A great deal of research has been done on this subject and its findings have been put in a nutshell by Mrs. Susan Schechter, a researcher at the Women's Educational

Institute in New York, when she writes, in her book, *Women and Male Violence:* "It is a pattern of coercive control." Ellen Pence, Director of the Domestic Abuse Intervention Programs says, "Any batterer can tell you why he hit her. He wanted control over her. He wanted his way."[15]

The above statements underline the state of affairs which has resulted from modern western civilization having formulated its own principles of human conduct. Its major mistake was to give its approval to the concept of male-female equality. It opened the doors of the workplace to women, thus giving them the opportunity to earn their own livelihood which, in turn, made them economically independent of men. This made women feel strongly that they were equal to men. They did not realize how artificial this notion was: in spite of the improved economic situation of women, western civilization could not, with all its powers, alter the dictates of nature — that men are the stronger and women the weaker sex.

As a result of this artificial equality domestic life as a whole has met with a contradiction. The women living in these western homes were physically as fragile as ever before, but psychologically (in their temperament, thinking) they had come to consider themselves as equals of men. Men being the stronger of the sexes wanted to hold their control over women. But women due to their artificial/unnatural temper refused to accept their control. The result of this contention proved very bad so far as women were concerned. "You need to feel powerful as a male. I don't know why, but it is true," says Chuck Wilder, a one-time batterer and now a counsellor for men at HAWC (Help Abused Women and their Children) in Massachussets.[16] But women, thanks to their artificially acquired outlook, have refused to go on accepting their control. The consequences of this clash have been universal and are certainly worse for women than for men.

Had men and women been biological equals, sometimes the former and sometimes the latter would have gained the upper hand.

As it is, modern women have become so oppressed as a result of masculine reaction to their sense of total equality, that they cannot even run away to save themselves. According to the *Reader's Digest* report, one woman said, "If you try to leave, your husband may threaten, 'I'll find you and kill you.' Many of the worst injuries — and deaths — happen as women try to get away." The battered woman often feels trapped. "Imagine you are such a woman," suggests Richard Gells, a sociologist and author of *Intimate Violence in Families.* "Right now, leave your job. Leave your wallet, everything on the desk. Take nothing but a one-way ticket to a strange town. Could you do that? Could you also take away the children?"[17]

By nature's division, man was given authority over woman. Now, if attempts are made to change this division artificially, the consequences will be as pictured in the above report. This beating of women in their own homes is just one more symptom of the malaise of modernity. Never before has there been so many instances of male violence against women as there are at present in modern civilization. It is true that there were cases of wife-beating in earlier periods, but these were the exceptions rather than the rule, and occurred mostly amongst the lower classes, who were poor and uneducated. In modern times, even the upper classes are no longer innocent on this score. What was formerly considered uncivilized behavior is now becoming a commonplace amongst so-called civilized members of society. This is a direct consequence of upsetting the natural balance of daily living in the futile quest for unnatural equality.

THE PROBLEM OF MODERN WOMEN

A tourist on a visit to America was once sitting in a club during a dance, when he was suddenly approached by an American girl who said to him, quite sadly, "Mr. Tourist, don't I have any glamour?" "Why, of course you do, replied the tourist. "Then why don't the boys date me?" the girl asked.

"Dating" in western countries refers to the social custom of boys inviting girls to go out somewhere with them. In this way, boys and girls become acquainted with each other before marriage. This practice has become so common in western life that a girl who is not "dated" by one or more boys begins to feel herself of inferior value on the marriage market. In former times, dating, as a system of courtship, was confined to meetings during which conversation could take place. But then morals became so lax that such meetings became occasions for sexual intimacy. The most recent development is to "date" a girl and then forcibly have sex with her — in fact, rape her.

Time magazine has published a revealing report entitled, "When the Date Turns into Rape":

> Susan, now 22 and a college senior, was raped almost three years ago on a first date. She met the man in a cafeteria at summer school and went to his dorm that evening to watch television news and get acquainted. After 45 minutes of chit chat about national affairs, he began pawing and kissing her, ignoring her pleas to stop. "You really don't want me to stop," he said, and forced her to have sex.[18]

Time's report shows how common 'date-rape' has become in western countries: "Date rape," according to some researchers, is a major social problem so far studied mostly through surveys of college students. In a three-year study of 6,200 male and female students on 32 campuses, Kentucky State psychologist Mary Koss found that 15% of all women reported experiences that met legal definitions of forcible rape. More than half those cases were date rapes. Andrea Parrot, a lecturer at Cornell University, estimates that 20% of college women at two campuses she surveyed had been forced into sex during their college years or before, and most of these incidents were date rapes. The number of forcible rapes reported each year — 87,340 in 1985 — is believed to be about half the total actually committed. Says Koss: "You're a lot more likely to be raped by a date than by a stranger jumping out of the bushes." Some feminists argue that the U.S. has a "rape culture" in which males are encouraged to treat women aggressively and women are trained to submit.[19]

Mr. Sri Prakash, former governor of Maharashtra, and India's first High Commissioner in Pakistan, mentions in his memoirs that in 1947 he once asked an Englishman why his countrymen had such a low opinion of Indians. One of the things which the Englishman cited was the number of restrictions there were regarding marriage, which was totally alien to the European concept of the boy and girl choosing one another and then getting married. He obviously despised the "social shackles" which prevented this happening in India.

When women's liberation was launched, the demolishing of such "social shackles" seemed a very attractive idea. But when the lifting of restrictions on the degree of intimacy which could develop between the opposite sexes began to lead with increasing frequency to rape, the pendulum of opinion began to swing back in favor of traditional restrictions as being the healthiest social principles to follow. It has become all too obvious that the path of sexual freedom can lead society only to its own destruction.

A *HADITH*

The prevalent custom of dating, which permits unmarried boys and girls to meet and remain together unchaperoned for unlimited periods in complete seclusion, has been little short of disastrous in its consequences, thus illustrating the meaningfulness of the *shari'ah* in no uncertain manner. The following *hadith,* taking full account of the evil inherent in the situations arising from this custom, gives us a clear injunction prohibiting them:

> One who believes in God and in the Judgement Day ought not to stay with a woman in private while no *mahram* (i.e. a near relative with whom marriage is not permitted, e.g. brother, father, uncle, etc.) is with her, because in such cases the third is Satan.[20]

When an unmarried boy and girl meet alone, Satan immediately grasps this opportunity to tempt them. The presence of a third person, guarantees that such a meeting will not go beyond limits.

THE IMPORTANCE OF VIRGINITY

Sexual permissiveness has become such an all-pervasive feature of modern life that the forming of sexual relationships before marriage has become a commonplace, the current philosophy being that advance experimentation is a better and safer way of choosing one's partner for life. Pre-marital encounters between men and women are, therefore, marked by the same openness and lack of inhibition as those which take place within the sanctity of the marriage bond. This runs counter to nature itself. In fact, deviation from tradition has created problems which have become insoluble in the present-day social set-up. The very intractability of these problems has led to a general reappraisal of sexual permissiveness. Even those who were the greatest champions of permissiveness as a way of life are now beginning to turn against it.

A survey, carried out in America on more than 1400 college students aged 18-19, reveals that young women are more attracted to male virgins than they were 10 years ago.[21] The New York psychologist, Mr Srully Blotnick, whose company carried out the survey, said: "The male virgin may not make the best lover, but usually he's eager to learn — and he's the safest." The safest, that is, from the risk of AIDS and other sexually transmitted diseases. Mr. Blotnick said it was the risk of sexually-related diseases that makes the male virgins so attractive to women. His latest survey showed that 22 percent of college women now want their next lover to be a virgin, compared to just nine percent 10 years ago. This same report was published by the *Hindustan Times* under the title, 'Male Virgins in Vogue."[22]

At the outset of the women's liberation movement, virginity as a condition for marriage was ridiculed, more particularly as it was an obstacle to sexual licence. It was depicted as a preposterous concoction of the religious imagination. But experience showed that such a condition was not the result of a misconception, religious or otherwise, but a biological imperative: insistence on virginity is the only way to ensure that a married couple will be free of deadly communicable diseases. Whereas virginity had before been just a matter of a religious commandment, it has now been reinstated as the sole basis for a healthy marital relationship, what an amazing proof has been provided by human experimentation of religious command-ments having a basis in reality. If, even after this, man does not give the divine *shari'ah* the importance which is due, it will be out of sheer caprice, or willful misinterpretation of the facts rather than a realistic approach.

THE PROBLEM OF CHILDREN BORN THROUGH ARTIFICIAL INSEMINATION

The goal of the feminist movement was to make women equal to men in every respect. But this did not happen in practice. The feminist movement has completely failed in achieving its real objective. An American lady, Ti-Grace Atkinson says: "There is no movement. Movement means going some place, and the movement is not going anywhere. It hasn't accomplished anything."[23]

Due to this experience, feminist extremists in western countries demand a complete withdrawal from dependence on men, including sexual ties. *Village Voice* columnist Jill Johnston, for example, insists that "feminism is lesbianism," and that it is only when women do not rely upon men to fulfill their sexual needs that they are finally free of masculine control.[24]

Living together like husbands and wives is not so simple a matter. Many problems have to be faced. For instance, if the couples want a child, how to find one? Modern medical science has provided the answer in the form of artificial insemination.

Two women from Holland, Paula Deijs and Jeanine Haaksman lived together like husband and wife. Then they felt a desire to have a child. For this purpose they contacted the Lydden Institute of Birth Control. Their first attempt did not succeed, but in the second attempt Paula Deijs became pregnant. Through the semen of an unknown person a child was born to them. The child was named Thomas. But after the birth of the child they realized they again were in need of the same "man" whom they had shunned to become lesbians. The women are sensitive to the fact that Thomas needs men as role models. Uncles, a grandfather, brothers-in-law and male neighbours are encouraged to visit frequently. "We have a good friend not too far from here whom we have chosen to be a father image for Thomas," says Haaksman. "We'll send Thomas over to him for all the technical instructions."[25]

Providing a "father" to Thomas in this artificial way is in no way an alternative to a real father. It is certain that some strangeness must remain between such "sons and fathers." And when Thomas grows up, this unconscious strangeness will turn into conscious strangeness. Thomas will know his mother, but not his father. This vacuum in Thomas's life will produce different kinds of mental complications, which will most probably make it impossible for him to become a useful member of society.

It is as if in the system of lesbianism there is scope for producing girls but not boys. Even then, to produce a girl, lesbians will depend upon the same man whom they had rejected in order to have their own independent ways.

It is easy to deviate from the system of nature but the price that has to be paid for such deviation is too high for an individual or a society.

THE END OF MARRIAGES IN THE WEST

An American magazine, *Better Homes and Gardens,* put a question to its readers: 'Do you think that family life in the U.S. is faced with troubles? Seventy-six percent answered in the affirmative. Eighty-five percent said that their hopes of a happy life had not been fulfilled. Similarly another American magazine, *Newsweek,* published its conclusion after conducting a survey in May 1978. According to its report about half of the marriages in America ended in divorce, then remarriage which again ended in divorce.

A marriage counsellor, Ronald D. Kelly, writes:

> One of the saddest things to me as a marriage counsellor is the many couples who are married, yet strangers to each other in their own homes. They seem to share little in common. Each goes his or her own way, pausing only for occasional conversations — those often arguments about money, child rearing or sex. You wonder how they ever got together in the first place.[26]

With whatever good feelings a marriage takes place, unpleasantness does crop up at one stage or the other. This is generally due to the problems of life, or the loss of sexual attractions. Now if the husband and wife have come together sharing the concept of a "marriage for a purpose," then, keeping in view the purpose they will overlook all such unpleasant circumstances and continue to live together. On the contrary, when the marriage is taken just as a pleasure jaunt (marriage for pleasure) then anything which is not to their liking will take a serious turn. In such a situation they will find no reason to tolerate that unpleasantness and continue to remain together.

ACKNOWLEDGING THE MISTAKE

A book published in the U.S., entitled *Finding Our Fathers,* by Dr. Sam Osherson, shows the beginning of a new age in American family life. In modern civilization the superior standard of life had come to mean that men and women worked in offices and the children were handed over to baby sitters and day-care centers. After the ruination of several generations, Americans have come to understand that there is no substitute for the upbringing and training of children by their own parents. Now more and more parents in the U.S. are taking time off work and other activities to give time to their children.

There is the example of Ken Schuman. He was being offered a high post, but he contented himself with a job at a lower salary. This was because high posts keep people so busy that there is hardly any time left to spend on the upbringing and care of the children. He said that in his present job he couldn't have lunch at high class hotels, nor could he travel first class by air. But he felt happy at his decision, as he had ample time to help his children in their formative stage. Being one of this new breed of fathers, he said, "I'm a convert to this way of life."

Having reached the culmination of his ideology, modern man is acknowledging his mistakes, but due to the powerful domination of previous concepts in modern society, the advocates of this change in thinking do not dare to reveal their names.[27]

THE PROBLEM OF POPULATION

A book published in the U.S., entitled *The Birth Dearth*, has become a hot subject of discussion in various circles. In the light of statistics, the author showed that the population of the U.S. and other western countries had decreased to a dangerous extent. On the other hand the birth rate in the socialist block was increasing. And so far as the third world was concerned, its population will double that of the western world in the next fifty years. Consequently, America in the 21st century will lose its world power status. Similarly the whole western world will acquire second class status in international politics. The solution, according to one critic of the book, lies is slipping back to "the traditional woman as exclusive child-raiser."[28]

The place given to woman in modern civilization bears no true relation to life's realities. Now western thinkers are beginning to feel that in order to have a successful life, the ancient concept of woman shall have to be fully reinstated.

DEPRIVED OF GUARDIANSHIP

A report entitled "Teen Suicide" published in *Time* magazine reveals that the incidence of suicide among the 10- to 20-year age group is rising sharply in the U.S., the annual number having tripled since 1950. In 1985 out of 100,000 people, if there were 60 adults who committed suicide, there were also 60 young people who took their own lives. We reproduce below the impressions of three women concerning the suicide of American children.

"I don't think they think about being dead. They think it's a way of ending pain and solving a problem," says Barbara Wheeler, a suicide-prevention specialist in Omaha. "Everybody is in such a rusk that we don't take the time to listen to our youngsters," states Elaine Leader, co-founder of a teen crisis hotline at Cedars-Sinai medical Centre in Los Angeles. And, Barbara O'Jeary, a hostess at a local diner, says: "When something like this happens, I think about my kids. I have to hope I raised them right. These are the dangerous years. You don't always know what's going on inside their heads."[29]

The American public responded with a spate of letters, selections from which were published by *Time* magazine. One of the letters reads: "My heart bleeds for the families of the teen suicides. I know. My 16-year-old grandson committed suicide by hanging. Our family will spend the rest of our lives wondering why, and we will never know" (Eloise Gradin, Pensacola Beach Florida).[30] What is the reason for this suicidal tendency among the younger generations of the developed countries? One major contributory cause is their being deprived of the kind of guardianship which a united family would hitherto have provided. Another is their development of unhealthy complexes in the absence of the loving care of the family circle. The breaking up of the family as a social unit must ultimately be recognized as the main underlying factor in the suicidal tendencies of the young people of today.

There are two principal reasons for the break-up of the family system in these countries. One is the concentration on pleasure in married life, rather than on responsibility. Couples marry now as if they were on a pleasure-seeking jaunt, so that when no further pleasure is to be extracted from the marital state, they go their separate ways. This has led to an erosion of the sanctity of marriage, and divorce, in consequence, has become common. Any children born to such couples, who subsequently opt to separate, are little better than orphans, though both parents are alive. Another cause of family fragmentation is traceable to the end of the joint family system, the main symptom of which is the increasing number of elderly parents and grandparents being sent to old people's homes, where they live separately from the rest of the family. In the joint family system, grandparents were always present to look after grandchildren, but in western society, their place is no longer in the home.

In a sense, the focus of parental life is likewise no longer in the home, although for different reasons. Formerly, the mother was always at home to look after the children. But now, with both parents working, the children meet them only in the evenings when they are both already too tired to give them their proper attention, or on weekends, when they are generally too concerned with their own recreations. The western child is deprived of his mother because, like his father, she has gone to her office, and he is deprived of his grandparents, because they have conveniently been put away out of sight in old people's homes. It is such children who become so emotionally unbalanced that they see no further point in going on living.

SUICIDE OF A WOMAN SINGER

When the 18-year-old pop singer Yukiko Okada jumped to her death from the roof of a high building in April, 1986, because of an unhappy love affair, she 'inspired' many young people to follow her example. A large number of young people actually threw themselves off high rooftops because they felt sorry for her and wanted to be in heaven with her. A few left suicide notes mentioning the singer by name.[31]

This is the ultimate damage done by making a woman a mere object of the "screen," a mere plaything of the imagination. If a woman devotes her life to managing her home, she becomes the giver of life to the young, whereas when she leaves her home to become a means of entertainment for others, she can do them the greatest injury — even becoming a morbid stimulus to annihilation.

AWAY FROM NATURE

The human baby is the weakest and most tender of all the babies of living creatures. It therefore needs its parents' care and guidance in its physical and mental growth for a more extended period than any other young creature. That is why nature has endowed parents with a special attraction for their offspring.

In the past, the separation of children from their parents was caused only by emergencies such as war, or occasional premature death, and, in normal circumstances, it was taken for granted that the children would enjoy the protection of their parents for as long as they required it.

However, in advanced societies, a prolonged period of guardianship has become the exception rather than the rule, for the simple reason that the modern concept of living has destroyed the sanctity of marriage. Either children are born out of wedlock and are unwanted right from the very beginning, or they find themselves bandied about between parents who have decided to separate shortly after marriage. Their "orphaned" state during their parents' lifetime soon becomes one of social alienation.

The rising incidence of this kind of orphaning is creating complex problems in modern society, one of which goes by the name of "deprivation dwarfism," a disease, according to medical experts, that can cause sleeplessness and severe bowel disorders, and used to kill many children in orphanages. A recent report by western medical authorities says, "Lack of love can stunt children's physical growth, retard their intellect, or even kill them." Pediatricians say that as late as 1915, some 90 percent of the children who died in Baltimore orphanages (in Maryland, U.S.A.) within the first year of admission, did so because of lack of love.[32]

According to Dr. Gardner, studies of human biology have shown that impulses arise from the higher level of the brain. These impulses enter into the bodily system and generate hormones of different kinds which are necessary for physical growth. One of these turns protein into sugar. This natural process in those children who grow up denied of their parents' affection is greatly inhibited. As a result, their bodies are unable to make full use of the available protein necessary for their growth.

This is an example which shows how fatal it is to deviate from the path of nature. Man cannot make another world of his own by deviating from the world created by God. On the contrary, he must live out his life in accordance with this world. If he abandons the path of nature in favour of some other path, this will only end in failure, if not actual disaster.

THE EXPERIMENT OF UNRESTRICTED FREEDOM

On the question of abortion, Americans have now divided themselves into two opposing groups, one unreservedly upholding abortion, and describing themselves as "pro-choice" rather than "pro-abortion," while the other is against abortion and calls itself "pro-life." The American magazine *Newsweek* illustrates the current mood with a photograph of a procession of American women, whose leader, a young woman, is holding aloft a placard bearing in bold lettering the orders: "Keep your laws and your morality off my body."[33]

Modern western thinkers hold their greatest asset to be freedom. But the experiment in the West of having fewer and fewer restrictions on freedom has demonstrated that personal liberty cannot be the highest good. Had it been so, it would never have resulted in the ugly extremes which the above example suggests.

There is no disputing the fact that freedom as a quality of life is something of great value. But, for man, the highest good is freedom within limits, rather than absolute freedom. Personal liberty, however, must never be subject to man-made restrictions, for no man is superior to his fellow men, and no one has the right, therefore, to curtail another's freedom. Restriction is a matter of God, and man must bow to God's dictates when He so wills it.

Every man stands between God and his fellow men. So far as the man-to-man relationship is concerned, every man has his full freedom. But the great, overriding consideration is that man is in complete subjugation to God. As compared to the Almighty, no man has any freedom. This means that in the modern world, man has to use his freedom so that he abides by God's commandments in all circumstances. It is this awareness of the value of restraint which is the greatest guarantee of the proper use of freedom.

THE ACKNOWLEDGEMENT OF AN AMERICAN LEADER

The well-known American novelist and a leader of the feminist movement, Rhoda Lerman, visited India in 1987. *The Times of India* published her interview, which is reproduced here: "I come with very bad news," says Rhoda Lerman. Speaking on the changing role of women in society, she revealed that 77 percent of the poor in America are women and children. The reason she offers is the high wage differential between the earnings of men and women. Women earn 62 percent of what men earn, merely because of the "pink-collared" jobs offered to them. "Equal opportunities and equal pay for equal work are just a myth," she declares. Women have been able to infiltrate only the lower and middle management and are offered innumerable jobs in food chains and the secretarial cadres.

This discrimination, she believes, is due to the male bias which works against women, branding them as 'undependable, since they go in for maternity leave and have children.' Although 96 percent of the working women have children, only 67 percent of them can enjoy maternity leave, without fear of jeopardising their jobs. However, seniority almost always suffers, says Ms. Lerman. "Maternity and child care are the cause of high wage differentials," she adds, "economic reality having nothing to do with spiritual equality." Activists had clamored for sexual equality and abortion rights and won them, without anticipating the economic backlash that would ensue.

With radical feminism accepted as the code, women are treated as equal, without any concessions to their biological differences. For instance, one out of two marriages in America is ending in divorce, with the responsibility of child care devolving on the mother alone. Alimony and maintenance are merely laws, rarely put into practice. A mere 5-10 percent of the men pay maintenance, and that too, only for the first year. For the rest, the burden is borne solely by the mother. Thus, the quality of life of a divorced woman reduces by 73 percent and that of a man increases by 43 percent.

Single households, headed by women trying to play the role of "supermoms," are on the increase, she revealed. In the next ten years, therefore, 40-50 percent of the children will be living in female-headed households, an unhealthy phenomenon, which has its repercussions in increased suicides amongst children. "Due to a lapse in the dependency structure, suicide is becoming endemic amongst children," she said.

Socialist feminism, which takes into account the intrinsic differences between men and women, is the call of the hour, Ms. Lerman believes. We have had an excess of the American dream — of a husband who works, a house in the suburbs, two children, two cars and a mother who stays at home and bakes cookies. With the family structure falling apart, she feels that only government support in the form of day-care centers, maternity leave benefits and subsidies to override the economic limitations of single women can hold the social fabric together. "Otherwise, our victories will be merely Pyrrhic victories,"[34] she predicts, similar, perhaps to the freedom experienced on the funeral pyre.'[35]

The feminist leader has acknowledged that the successes of feminism are little short of Pyrrhic victories. This is the most appropriate word to describe the victory of modern woman. She secured "equality" after a long and hard struggle. In the process, however, of achieving this imaginary equality, she has lost everything. Ms. Lerman feels that only large-scale government support can compensate for the deprivation of western women. This means placing herself under the guardianship of a government, which is completely in the hands of man. Woman was not willing to accept the guardianship of man at home; at her own cost, she has had to come to terms with the guardianship of men in the government.

TWO EXAMPLES

The problems created in western homes by this artificial concept of equality are confined not only to the lower or middle class but have also spread throughout the upper classes and the highly educated classes.

Recently some letters written by Albert Einstein to Mileva Maric (who was to become his first wife) were made public. These reveal the story of their relationship characterized by happiness and sorrow. These letters were found while collecting material for *The Collected Papers of Albert Einstein.* Mileva Maric was four years older than Einstein. His mother was not in favour of this match, which caused him to suffer from depression. Later somehow they got married, a daughter having been born to them before marriage. What happened to her remains unknown. It appears, though, that she never stayed with Einstein. He had met Ms. Maric in 1896 at the Federal Technical Institute in Zurich. Wed in January 1903, their marriage ended in divorce in 1919.[36]

The second example concerns the British heir, Prince Charles: "Prince Charles, heir to the British throne, married the wrong woman," said his biographer, Mrs. Penny Junor in a recent interview with BBC. Charles, she said, was a sad character with the loneliest position on earth. He did not have the support he should have from a wife. Prince Charles and Princess Diana were growing more and more apart. Mrs. Junor said she had drawn her conclusions after talking to people who were close to him. "The palace has seen what I have written and the conclusions I have come to. No one has told me that I am on the wrong lines."[37]

UNDEPENDABLE CHARACTER

In its May 25, 1987, issue *Time* magazine published a report about the Pentagon entitled "Mixing Sex and Secrets." It says: "The Pentagon has been fretting about the sexual practices of the 2.7 million people with Defence Department security clearances. In January (1987) the Pentagon expanded its rules to compel service personnel, civilian workers and contract employees with clearances to divulge whether they had engaged in such sexual acts as adultery, sodomy and incest. The rules were intended to ensure, that those with access to secrets are not vulnerable to blackmail.[38]

Believers in permissiveness hold that sexual relations outside the bond of marriage are simply "sins" in the eyes of God, but are far from harmful as regards human relationships. Experience, however, has shown that one who does not adhere to the limits of the marriage bond in the matter of sexual relationships is not trustworthy. Through such a moral lacuna, an enemy can find an access to our secrets.

THE SCANDAL OF GARY HART

Mr. Gary Hart, the Democratic Party's candidate for the Presidential election of 1987, had every chance of success. An incident, however, took place which set off such a storm of protest that Mr. Hart had to resign from the contest.

Fifty-year-old Mr. Hart was busy in the election campaign, for which he had borrowed one million dollars. During this time he quietly left for Miami on May 1 to spend the weekend there. He spent one day and one night with a 29-year-old actress, Miss Donna Rice. An American newspaper, *Miami Herald,* got an inkling of this, and brought out a sensational story with this heading: "Miami Woman Is Linked to Hart."[39] The news was given priority coverage by radio, television, newspapers and journals. Mr. Hart's photographs along with Miss Donna Rice began to appear on the pages of newspapers. Wherever he went he was asked if he had committed adultery. "He stood in the public dock accused of adultery."[40]

Had the *Miami Herald* published the news that in a certain house Mr. Hart had spent the night with his wife, no one would have cared. But when the news broke of Mr. Hart's spending a night with a woman he was not married to, it caused quite a furor. This incident is a clear indication that establishing sexual relations with a woman, who is not one's wife, is against human nature. Had such an act not been against human nature, the agitators would never have succeeded in their plans.

Mr. Hart did his utmost to overcome this setback. First he refuted the allegation; and, then he started giving evasive answers. Then he persuaded his wife, Lee Hart, to travel 1300 miles from New Hamshire to Denver to give her statement to the press. She said: 'If it doesn't bother me, I don't think it ought to bother anyone else.' When Mr. Hart saw that all his devices had been rendered useless, he finally admitted to the illicit relationship in these words: "Adultery is not a crime. It's a sin. And that is between me and Lee, and me and God."

However, this attempt at justfication failed to satisfy the

American public. Where Mr. Hart's name as future president had topped the list of opinion polls, it now, after the incident, came last on the list. And in the end he found himself alone. According to *Time* magazine, his sexual relationship with the actress amounted to his "political death." The affair was discovered on May 3, and within five days, on May 8, he had to quit saying he was withdrawing from the race, and would then quietly disappear from the stage.[41]

Time magazine[42] rounds off its long article with these words: "Americans now demand the same intimate knowledge about their leaders that once was reserved for the romantic entanglements of Clark Gable or Elizabeth Taylor. Rather than wrestling with the complexities of arms control and a troubled economy, the public tends to look for personalities they can trust, whose judgement and integrity make them feel comfortable."

The same point was made by George Reedy, press secretary of the former American president, Lyndon Johnson, in these words: "What counts with a candidate for President is his character, and nothing shows it like his relationship with women. Here you have a man who is asking you to trust him with your bank account, your children, your life and your country for four years. If his own wife can't trust him, what does that say?"

It is a fact that one who establishes illicit sexual relations only proves that he has no mental discipline. He has no power to control his feelings and emotions. Such a person is not at all trustworthy in respect of his character. There is a strong fear that this psychological weakness might lead him to sacrifice great national interests for the fulfillment of his personal desires. Such a person is not even trustworthy in day to day life, let alone in a high government position.

Experience shows that breaking the limits set by God in matters of sexual relationships is not simply a religious evil. It is not just a sin, but a crime as well — possibly, in terms of its consequences, one of the greatest crimes of all.

SURROGACY

Surrogacy is one of the products of the modern age. The statistics have revealed that 500 children have been born through artificial insemination from 1976 to 1986 in the U.S. There are about one dozen surrogate centers at the moment in the U.S. The number is expected to increase because there are about fifteen percent married people who are infertile.[43]

William Stern and Elizabeth Stern had no issue so they decided to secure one through using the womb of someone on payment. In 1985 they made a contract with Mary Beth Whitehead for $ 20,000 to carry their child. Mr. Stern's sperm was then injected into her womb, resulting in the birth of a baby girl. After carrying the child in her womb for nine months, her motherly instinct was aroused. She refused to hand over the child to the Stern couple. This case was taken to the court which decreed the handing over of the baby to Mr. Stern in view of the contract. After having won the case, Mr. Stern came with five policemen to Mrs. Whithead, who had already escaped through the back door with the child. However she was later traced to another town and finally the child was delivered to the Sterns.

Such cases have set out ethical arguments in the U.S. on the matter of surrogacy. The Bishop of New Jersey commented: Surrogacy exploits a child as a commodity and exploits a woman as a baby-maker.'[44] The woman who bears a child for another person suffers severe psychological complexes. One such woman, by the name of Elizabeth Kane, said: "I miss my baby. I had to suppress those feelings for years." The unnatural concept of sexual freedom results in unnatural problems, the above case being only one of many such examples.

WOMAN AND WAR

When Germany invaded the erstwhile U.S.S.R. in 1941, the Soviet government made emotional appeals to its citizens to treat the saving of their motherland as a sacred duty. Of those who joined the military in response to these appeals, 800,000 were girls between the ages of 15 and 16. A book has recently been published in Moscow entitled *War's Unwomanly Face*[45] which deals with the experiences of these girls. During her four years of research, the authoress travelled to one hundred cities and interviewed 200 women who had participated in the war.

The book reveals many hitherto unknown facts about women's participation in the war, one of which is that many women began to conceal the fact that they had ever had anything to do with the war. "We wanted to become ordinary girls again. Marriageable girls." One of the interviewees, an educated woman by the name of Vera Safronova Davdova, said, "I believe that the women reacted to the war in a completely different way from the men. The men were more matter-of-fact and casual about the experience, whereas the women reacted in an overwhelmingly emotional manner."

In recent times, a great deal of research has been done to discover the true nature of women and their inborn aptitudes. An attempt has been made to understand the female species scientifically. Astonishingly enough, the findings of these researches and investigations corroborate the view of women taken by Islam.

Modern research has shown that woman is sensitive by nature and is more emotional than man. This discovery makes it clear that it is not proper to have women enter those areas where cool and objective decision-making is required, irrespective of the circumstances, and where "manliness" rather than "femininity" is a basic prerequisite.

In the departments of politics, war, international relations, large-scale industrial planning and, not the least important, in the law-courts, mental discipline and dispassionate decision-making are of the utmost importance. In such fields, the decision-makers have to be able to rise above the pressures of the immediate environment. Women, because of their inborn emotionalism, are unsuited to such tasks. Men, on the other hand, being relatively less emotional, are better able to deal with the contingencies of their position.

It is because of this biological difference between men and women that Islam has assigned them separate spheres of influence. This is not a matter of gradation, but of a difference of workplace or field of action. This difference is supported in every way by scientific research. The truth is that it is the champions of feminism who are unscientific by the standards of today, and not the upholders of traditional Islamic attitudes.

DEGRADATION INSTEAD OF PROGRESS

The 29th December, 1986, publication of *Time* was a special number which was titled, "A Letter to the year 2086." This issue covered the happenings in the following century in the U.S. One part of it related to the state of the family as could be foreseen for the next century. A part of it is reproduced here: "The American family, not 50 years ago the rock on which the country built its church, has fractured into atoms with separate orbits. The American woman, having shunned motherhood and house-wifehood 15 years ago to establish herself in the labor market, now seeks to balance all three lives like dinner plates on sticks. The American man finds himself in new and scary territory and scrambles for adjustment. When the American man and woman part company, as half the newly married couples are expected to do these days, the American child is suddenly stranded, growing taller without a structure."[46]

As they near the close of the twentieth century the American intellectual class are acknowledging that what they thought of as the ladder of progress, at the beginning of the 20th century, has turned out to be the ladder of destruction. Taking women out of their homes has only resulted in the total disruption of the American family system. The rosy plan of liberating woman has, in practice, resulted in so many social evils.

Now new thinking is emerging from a revision of past errors, but modern woman is not ready to go back to her former role as a housewife, even if the life adopted by her of necessity involves her bearing the burdens of both the home and the workplace. What kind of progress is it which culminates in destruction? How strange is this freedom which, in practice, has turned into a new kind of bondage.

Notes

1. *Time*, January 26, 1987.
2. *Indian Express* (New Delhi), January 14, 1987.
3. *The Hindustan Times* (New Delhi), January 12, 1987.
4. *Indian Express* (New Delhi), January 14, 1987.
5. *Plain Truth,* September 1986.
6. Ibid.
7. *Indian Express* (New Delhi), January 14, 1987.

8. *The Times of India* (New Delhi), February 19, 1987.

9. *Time*, February 2, 1987.

10. Ibid.

11. Qur'an, 5:5.

12. *The Times of India* (New Delhi), March 19, 1987.

13. *Reader's Digest,* March 1987.

14. Ibid., p. 135.

15. Ibid., p. 142.

16. Ibid., p. 140.

17. Ibid., p. 137.

18. *Time*, March 23, 1987.

19. Ibid., p. 35.

20. Ahmad ibn Hanbal, *Masnad,* 3/446.

21. *The Times of India,* March 18, 1987.

22. *The Hindustan Times,* March 19, 1987.

23. *Time*, March 20, 1972.

24. Ibid., p. 30.

25. Ibid., August 10, 1987, p. 25.

26. *Plain Truth,* June 1987.

27. This information has been derived from *Span,* an American magazine, in its issue of September 1987. The article is titled: "Putting Kids First. The New generation of American fathers is balancing the demands of careers and children."

28. Ben J. Wattenberg, *The Birth Dearth* (1987), p. 48.

29. *Time*, March 23, 1987, pp. 18-19.

30. Ibid., April 13, 1987.

31. *The Times of India,* (New Delhi), March 30, 1987.

32. *Evening News* (New Delhi), June 27, 1984.

33. *Newsweek,* January 21, 1985.

34. The word "Pyrrhic" has come from a Greek king, Pyrrhus (295-272 B.C.) who invaded Italy in the third century B.C. to aid Tarentun against Rome. After a protracted battle, in which he sustained heavy losses, Pyrrhus won a victory over Rome, finally to be defeated at Beneventum in 275. Hence "Pyrrhic victory" has come to be associated with a victory which brings disaster in its wake.

35. *The Times of India* (New Delhi), April 30, 1987.

36. Ibid., May 5, 1987.

37. *Time*, May 11, 1987.

38. Ibid., May 25, 1987.

39. *Miami Herald,* May 3, 1987.

40. *Time*, May 18, 1987.

41. Ibid.

42. Ibid.

43. Ibid., January 19, 1987.

44. Ibid.

45. S. Alexiyerich, *War's Unwomanly Face,* Progress Publishers, Moscow.

46. *Time*, December 29, 1986.

CHAPTER 5

Position of Woman in the Islamic *Shari'ah*

QUR'ANIC VERSES

The Qur'an and Hadith give detailed commandments regarding women, and also lay down clear guidelines for the relationship between men and women. The following quotations from the Qur'an and Hadith highlight the most important aspects of feminine virtue and the standing which a woman should have vis-à-vis her husband and father:

Treat them with kindness; for even if you dislike them, it may be that you dislike a thing which Allah has meant for your own abundant good.[1]

Women shall with justice have rights similar to those exercised against them, although men have a degree (of advantage) above women. Allah is mighty and wise.[2]

Men shall have a share in what their parents and kinsmen leave; whether it be little or much, it is legally theirs.[3]

And among His signs is this, that He created for you mates from among yourselves, that you may dwell in tranquillity with them, and He has put love and mercy between your (hearts).[4]

Those that do evil shall be rewarded with like evil; but those that have faith and do good works, both men and women, shall enter the Gardens of Paradise and receive blessings without measure.[5]

But the believers who do good works, whether men or women, shall enter the gardens of Paradise. They shall not suffer the least injustice.[6]

We shall reward the steadfast according to their noblest deeds. Be they men or women, those that embrace the faith and do what is right We will surely grant a happy life: We shall reward them according to their noblest actions.[7]

The true believers, both men and women, are friends to each other.

They enjoin what is just and forbid what is evil; they attend to their prayers and pay the alms-tax and obey Allah and His Messenger. On these Allah will have mercy. He is mighty and wise.[8]

Their Lord answers them, saying: "I will deny no man or woman among you the reward of their labor." You are the offspring of one another. Those that fled their homes or were expelled from them, and those that suffered persecution and fought and died for My cause, shall be forgiven their sins and admitted to gardens watered by running streams, as a reward from Allah: it is He who holds the richest recompense.[9]

WORDS OF THE PROPHET MUHAMMAD

The first four of the following sayings of the Prophet Muhammad, upon whom be peace, stress the high standard of conduct which a man is meant to maintain in his relations with women:

Only a man of noble character will honor women, and only a man of base intentions will dishonor them.[10]

The best among you is he who is best for his family. For my family, I am the best of all of you.[11]

No believing man should hate a believing woman, for if there is any habit of hers that displeases him, there will be some other habit of hers which pleases him.[12]

The most perfect man of religion is one who excels in character. The best among you is he who gives the best treatment to his womenfolk.[13]

According to Abu Hurayrah, the Prophet considered a woman good if she was a delight to her husband's gaze, obeyed his wishes when something had to be done for him, and placed her person and her wealth entirely at his disposal.[14]

The following traditions give a clear indication of the position that a woman occupies in Islam.

Everything in this world is a piece of propety, or a possession. The best possession in the world is a pious woman.[15]

Shall I not tell you what the best form of wealth is? It is a pious woman who is a delight to her husband's eyes, who obeys when asked to do anything, and who looks after his interests when he is away.[16]

When it was revealed in the Qur'an that punishment awaited those who heaped up gold and silver, certain of the Companions said that if they could find out which form of wealth was better, they would accumulate that instead. At this the Prophet said, "The best thing one could have is a tongue which expresses remembrance, a heart which gives thanks and a believing woman who helps one to be more steadfast in one's faith."[17]

Next to piety itself, the best thing that a believer can find is a pious wife. She should be such that if he asks her to do anything, she obeys, and when he looks at her she should make him happy. When she swears upon him, she should fulfill her pledge and, in the absence of her husband, she should devote herself earnestly to keeping his wealth and preserving her chastity.[18]

They have found all the good of this world and the hereafter who are in possession of these four things: a heart that gives thanks, a tongue that remembers God, a body which is patient when persecuted, and a wife who can be trusted to remain chaste and refrain from misusing her husband's wealth.[19]

Treat women well, for they have been created from a rib. The rib is most curved in its upper part, so that if you try to straighten it out, it will break, but if you leave it as it is, it will remain intact. Therefore, follow my advice on giving women fair treatment.[20]

Women are the other half of men.[21]

Fear God in respect of women.[22]

Heaven lies beneath the feet of mothers.[23] (That is, those who serve their mothers well are deserving of Paradise.)

One who brings up three daughters, teaches them good manners and morals, arranges their marriages and treats them with fairness, deserves to be ushered into Paradise.[24]

If a man to whom a girl is born neither buries her alive, humiliates her, nor gives his sons preference over her, he will be allowed to enter heaven by God, as a reward.[25]

Shall I not tell you what the best object of your charity is? It is your own daughter who has returned to you as a widow, or a divorcee, and who has no one to earn for her except you.[26] (That is, to spend on a daughter in need is the best form of charity.)

When a man is tested through his daughters by God, and he treats them well, his actions will guard him from hellfire.[27]

THE QUALITIES OF A BELIEVING WOMAN

Umm Salmah, the Prophet Muhammad's wife, once remarked to the Prophet, "I hear of God mentioning men but not women." It was in this context that the following verse was revealed to the Prophet:

I will deny no man or woman among you the reward of their labors.
You are members, one of another.[28]

This makes it clear that, although males and females differ from one another biologically, they are equal in terms of human status, they have a definite partnership with one another, and there is no distinction made between them as regards their respective rights. They are, in fact, each other's lifetime companions.

THE PRINCIPLE OF THE DIVISION OF LABOR

Within the social framework, however, Islam — to the extent that it is both natural and practical — has adopted the division of labor in respect of the sexes, the man's field of activity being basically external to the home, while the woman's is domestic. This division, however, has never been intended as a form of discriminatory treatment. Its main purpose has always been to preserve the distinctive characteristics of both sexes, while deploying their respective talents and skills in the most socially useful manner. This enables both sexes to make the best use of their innate capabilities without causing any undue disruption in the family or in society. In modern parlance, this is a form of managerial optimization rather than sexual discrimination. For this principle to be effective, the spheres of activity of men and women have had to be quite different and, of course, separate from each other. That is to say that the man's field of activity is in the outside world, while the woman's is in the home. This traditional distinction has been so often cited by feminists as an inhibiting factor in women's lives that the true meaning of equality has been lost sight of. After all, it will be the very same virtues in thought, word and deed which will be prerequisites for both sexes to enter Paradise. If the qualities of piety, humility, honesty, patience and compassion are demanded of men, they will in like measure be demanded of women. The fact that men and women function in different spheres has no bearing whatsoever on the ultimate equality — equality in the eyes of God.

BASIC ATTRIBUTES OF MEN AND WOMEN

The characteristics of true believers, both men and women, are depicted in the Qur'an in the following words:

Men and women who have surrendered,
believing men and believing women,
obedient men and obedient women,
truthful men and truthful women,
enduring men and enduring women,
humble men and humble women,
men and women who give in charity,
men who fast and women who fast,
men and women who guard their chastity,
men and women who remember God in abundance —
for them God has prepared forgiveness and a great reward.[29]

These then are the basic attributes which both men and women must cultivate if they are to endear themselves to God and become His favored servants:

ISLAM. The initial step to be taken is to embrace Islam, which means that one should willingly obey God, leading one's life within the bounds of God's commandments.

IMAN (faith). Islam begins really to take root with the conscious discovery of God, which is known as *iman* (faith). When *iman* is genuine, the men or women concerned cannot but surrender themselves to God. Discovering God as their Creator causes them to treat Him as an object of worship and to mold their thinking upon the truth. They control their desires and dedicate their wealth to the cause of God. They even stop eating and drinking the whole day throughout the month of Ramadan in obedience to God's will. Their consciousness of their servitude to God makes them remember God constantly, on all occasions and at all times.

QUNUT (sincere obedience to God). This entails the adoption of the path of piety as shown by God and His prophet. It means the fullest concentration of the heart and mind on the will of the Almighty.

SIDQ (truthfulness) means living an honest, straightforward life in the sense of saying plainly what one is going to do, and then actually doing as one has said. In other words, it means leading a life of principle.

SABR (patience) is a quality which enables one never to deviate from religious teachings, even if one is faced with difficulties and persecution. It is the quality one needs if one is to follow the path of truth, surmounting all obstacles which have been placed there either by the self or by Satan. It is the virtue which will keep one from abandoning the divine path and succumbing to worldly temptations.

KHUSHU' (apprehension, fear) is a powerful emotion which engenders an attitude of humility and submission. One comes to this state through a realization of God's greatness and His absolute power, which is in stark contrast to man's total powerlessness. The fear of God completely engulfs the believer, making him bow before his Maker. In consequence, he becomes kind to and humble towards other human beings.

SADAQAH (alms-giving, charity) is the duty of acceding to others the right to a share in one's wealth. It makes one aware that if one's own needs require the expenditure of money for their satisfaction, so also do the needs of others. One is never then oblivious to the needs of others.

SAWM (fasting) must be practised for the sake of God. By fasting, man contrasts his own helplessness with God's omnipotence, and thanks God for the food and drink which He has bestowed upon him.

IHSAN (chastity). It is important as it keeps one pure and guards one against shameful behavior. The sense of shame which God has given man acts as a natural deterrent against permissiveness.

DHIKR (remembrance of God). One of the most important virtues is the frequent remembrance of God. It is not enough to have made the discovery of the Creator and Sustainer of mankind: truly virtuous men and women must remember God at all times. One who has truly found God will always have Him in his thoughts and will always have His name on his lips.

The 66th chapter of the Qur'an, entitled "Prohibition," mentions three more qualities of believing men and women: penitence, devoutness and obedience.

TAWBAH means feeling penitent about having committed a sin and then turning away from sinfulness. This is a very special attribute of believing men and women. In this world of trial one does make mistakes from time to time — dominated as one is by the self — but the effect of one's wrongdoing will not be irreversible if one at once turns to God and repents one's misdeeds. This repentance acknowledges God's greatness as compared to man's insignificance. Those who are truly repentant find the greatest favor in God's eyes.

'IBADAH (worship). This is the act perfomed to acknowledge supernatural exaltedness. It is familiarly known as worship, and its object should be none other than the Almighty. Believing men and women worship God and God alone.

SIYAHAH (itinerancy). The virtues of undertaking journeys for God's cause are best explained in the *hadith* recorded by Abu Dawud: "According to Abu Umamah, a certain individual once asked the Prophet's permission to become a dervish. The Prophet replied that the dervishism of his *ummah* (community) meant struggling in the path of God."[30]

Travelling for the cause of God includes, according to Imam Raghib Asfahani, taking such action for His sake as necessitate moving about from one place to another. Examples of such travel are: covering long distances in order to acquire a knowledge of religion; emigrating for the sake of religion; visiting scenes of natural beauty or placces of historical interest which have some lesson for mankind; and, especially, undertaking journeys in order to convey God's message to His creatures.[31]

These qualities, separately enumerated above, when taken together constitute an ideal, not just for men, but for both sexes. These are the qualities that form the basis of Islam, and are the true means of salvation in the world to come.

THE EXAMPLE OF MUSLIM WOMEN

Just as men function on different planes of religiosity, so do women have their own separate spheres of religious effectiveness.

Let us first consider their everyday level of existence in which adherence to their religion broadly means paying the dues of God and men in purely personal matters. In particular, it means true belief in God and the carrying out of His commandments; strict adherence to justice in all worldly transactions; withstanding the temptations of the self as instigated by Satan; paying what is due to God in terms of one's wealth and life; giving the hereafter priority over the present world; being guided by Islamic ethics in dealing with one's family, relatives and friends; invariably dealing with all matters in the manner approved of by Islam.

Next in importance to these feminine duties is the training and nurturing of children. Most women become mothers, and the relationship between mother and child is of the utmost importance, because the mother's influence can be used for ends which may be good or evil depending upon the mother's own proclivities. As a Muslim of course, it is clearly her duty to use her maternal influence to bring her children up as moral beings. If they have deviated from the path of moral rectitude, it is her duty to reform them. Everything that she does, in fact, should be for their betterment.

Another domestic imperative is that the woman who is both wife and mother should organize her own and her family's lives in such a way that they are free of problems. She herself should never create difficulties for her husband and children. In many cases, knowing "what not to do" is more important than knowing "what to do." In such matters, women are liable to err because they are more emotional by nature. By creating unnecessary problems for their husbands and children, they destroy the peace and quiet of home life. Sometimes they unwittingly slip into wrong ways of thinking: they have all the necessities of life, but these things, perhaps because they have been attained without a struggle, gradually cease to please them. Then they begin to feel that there are so many things lacking in their lives and their own dissatisfaction begins to vitiate what had formerly been a healthy, familial atmosphere. Regardless of whatever else a woman does, if she can simply refrain from creating problems of this nature, she will to a large extent have succeeded in creating a wholesome, domestic atmosphere and a happy family circle.

On a higher plane, it is possible for talented women to further the cause of religion when the right opportunity presents itself. There are innumerable examples in Islamic history of such work having been successfully carried out by women.

A notable example is that of 'Aishah, an extremely intelligent woman who was one of the Prophet's wives. Being much younger than he was, she survived him by about fifty years, and, with her excellent, almost photographic memory, was able to continue to communicate in great detail everything that she had learned from him during their very close companionship, so that for about half a century she was able to fulfill a highly informative role. In short, she became a living cassette recorder for the *ummah*. 'Abdullah ibn al-'Abbas, a Companion of great stature, and one of the Qur'an's best commentators, was one of 'Aishah's pupils. The greater part of his knowledge of religion was learned from her. Similarly, many other *Sahaba* (Companions of the Prophet) and *Tabi'un* (companions of the *Sahaba*) acquired their religious knowledge from her. So here we have the very fine example of a Muslim woman imparting to others the religious knowledge which she had imbibed directly from the Prophet.

Another example of a woman making a signal contribution to the spread of religious learning is that of the daughter of Imam Abu Ja'far Tahavi (229-321 A.H.), the famous traditionist whose book, *Sharh Ma'ani al-Athar*, is regularly included in the syllabuses of Arabic schools. He dictated his book of traditons to his daughter and, as he read out the *hadith*, he would explain its finer points to her and then she would write it all down. The whole book was prepared in this way. This is one of the finest examples of a woman helping her family members in matters of religion.

The above examples show the nature and extent of the contribution which can be made by believing Muslim women to the cause of Islam.

WOMANHOOD IN ISLAM

Fear of God and honoring one's fellow men — this is the twin foundation of Islam laid down in the Qur'an in these words:

> Mankind, fear your Lord who created you from one soul and created man's mate from the same soul, from these two scattering on earth many men and women. Fear God, in whose name you entreat one another, and be careful not to sever your ties of kinship. Allah is watching over what you do.[32]

The words, "and created man's mate from the same soul" have been explained as meaning that first Adam was created from earth; then a rib was taken from his body, out of which Eve — his mate — was formed. But there is nothing in the Qur'an to support this theory. It is a biblical explanation, not a Qur'anic one. Here is what the Book of Genesis has to say about the creation of Eve:

> And the Lord God caused a deep sleep to fall upon Adam, and he slept: and he took one of his ribs, and closed up the flesh instead thereof;

> And the rib, which the Lord God had taken from man, made he a woman, and brought her unto the man. And Adam said, This is now bone of my bones, and flesh of my flesh: she shall be called Woman, because she was taken out of man.[33]

From this biblical tradition comes the theory that Eve was created from Adam's rib. This story has been given credence by some commentators of the Qur'an, who have used it to explain Eve's creation "from the same soul as Adam." But this notion does not stand up in the face of established fact, and it has been proven that, over the centuries, the Bible has been subjected to alterations and additions. Its present form is no longer as the prophets originally taught it. Along with prophetic inspiration, it has received a fair injection of human interpolation. For this reason, one cannot rely on explanations given in the Bible, nor is it proper to explain verses of the Qur'an in the light of biblical statements.

Neither in the verse of the Qur'an quoted above, nor in any other verse of the Qur'an, is there any mention of Eve having been created from Adam's rib. The Qur'an says only that Eve was created from "it." What this "it" refers to is the point in question. Most of those commentators who have penetrated deep into the meaning of the Qur'an have taken "it" to refer to "species": Eve was created — not from Adam himself — but from the same species as Adam. This is the explanation given — among others — by Abu Muslim Asfahani, and it is this explanation that fits in with other verses of the Qur'an.

In several verses of the Qur'an the word for "soul" (nafs) has been used to mean "species." Such verses provide a clear elucidation of the verse quoted above. A selection of them is given here:

> God has created for you spouses, of your own kind.[34]

> And of His signs is that He has created for you — of your own kind — spouses, that you might take comfort in them.[35]

Creator of the heavens and the earth: He has made for you spouses of your own kind, and the cattle He has also created in pairs.[36]

From a perusal of these verses, one can see that the same word has been used for the spouses of ordinary human beings as was used for Adam's spouse in the verse quoted above. Just as Eve was created from Adam's *nafs*, so other women have also been created from the same *nafs* — or kind — as their male counterparts.

Clearly there is no question, in these other verses, of inferring that every female spouse has been created from the body of the male. There is no alternative but to take the word *nafs,* occurring in these verses, as meaning 'kind.' God has created for you spouses of your own kind, the Qur'an is telling us, in order that they may provide you with true companionship in your journey through life.

To summarize, women and men are from the same species. Biologically speaking, women have not been extracted from the bodies of their male counterparts. God fashioned them according to His Will, just as He fashioned men in accordance with His Almighty Will and Power.

SAYINGS OF THE PROPHET

Now we come to certain sayings attributed to the Prophet Muhammad, in which the Arabic word *dil'* has been mentioned for the word "rib." The first thing that has to be remembered here is that these traditions are about ordinary women, and do not refer to the creation of Adam and Eve. It is the manner of every woman's creation that is being dealt with, not specifically that of Eve. One of the relevant sayings is as follows:

Treat women well, for they have been created from a rib.[37]

Now this cannot be taken to mean that women have actually been created from a rib, for this has no connection with the point conveyed in the rest of the sentence, which is that women should be treated well. A correct interpretation of the word 'rib' has to be one that fits in with the underlying purpose behind the Prophet's statement.

The statement, "women have been created from a rib," should be taken metaphorically, not literally. What the Prophet wished to convey was this: "Women are akin to a rib and should be treated with due consideration." There is another tradition which explains what this means. "A woman is like a rib," said the Prophet, "if you try to straighten it, it will break."[38]

This saying of the Prophet Muhammad, related in the *Sahih* of both Bukhari and Muslim — the most authentic collections of traditions — makes it clear that women are like ribs; they are not actually created from ribs. The allusion is figurative not literal. Light is also cast on the meaning of the metaphor. Ribs break when one tries to straighten them. So it is with women. Rather than try to straighten them, it is better to let them be.

"Women have been created from ribs," and "Women are like ribs," are just two different ways of saying the same thing. There is a difference in the mode of expression of the two statements, but there is no difference in meaning. It is common in every language for metaphors to be expressed directly, without the use of the words "like" or "as." For instance, if one wishes to pay tribute to a person's bravery, one can say that he is like a lion. But there is not as much force in saying that a person is "like a lion" as there is in saying that he "*is* a lion." Examples of such usage abound in every language, including English. A notable one is to be found in the poem, "Morte d'Arthur," by the celebrated poet, Alfred Lord Tennyson:

> ... More things are wrought by prayer
> Than this world dreams of, wherefore, let thy voice,
> Rise like a fountain for me night and day
> For what are men better than sheep or goats
> That nourish a blind life within the brain,
> If knowing God, they lift not hands of prayer
> Both for themselves and those who call them friend?
> For so the whole round earth is every way
> Bound by gold chains about the feet of God.

In this last line the poet does not mean that the world is physically tethered to the feet of God by chains, but merely wishes to indicate the unbreakable bonds that exist between God and this world. In referring to the chains as "golden," he suggests the very great beauty and value of these bonds. By referring to the "feet" of God, rather than any other part of Him, he suggests the humble position of man in God's divine scheme. It is, indeed, a very rich metaphor. To return to the metaphor of the rib, in saying that if one tries to straighten a woman one will break her, the Prophet was referring to her delicate nature. Physically, women are weaker than men: psychologically, they are more highly strung, more prone to emotional upset. This is a fact of life which everyone realizes, irrespective of whether he is educated or not. A father, for instance, will not be as hard on a daughter as he might be on his son, for he knows that boys are made of sterner stuff than girls. The latter tend to break under severe pressure. For this reason females are more prone to suicide than males. Sometimes a trivial matter can drive a woman to suicide, or cause her to have a nervous breakdown. In likening a woman to a rib, the Prophet was expressing this fact of life in metaphorical terms. Ribs have a slight curve in them. There is good reason for them to be made that way. They should be left in their natural state. No attempt should be made to straighten them.

The Prophet used a parable to explain the delicacy of women's nature, pointing out that they should be treated in accordance with their nature. Their delicate emotional constitution should always be borne in mind. God has created them that way, and He has done so for good reason. They should be treated kindly. If they have to be told something, it should be done tactfully, in a gentle tone. Abruptness and severity will break them, as a rib is broken by any attempt to straighten it. Once, when the Prophet was on a journey, he saw some women riding on a camel. The man leading the camel made to drive the animal on faster, forgetting that this would cause undue discomfort to his passengers. So the Prophet said to the camel driver: "You have glass cases there. Be gentle with them."[39]

MODERN RESEARCH

In recent times, it has been accepted as fact, on a purely academic level, that fundamental, inborn differences do exist between men and women. A detailed article on the status of women in the *Encyclopaedia Britannica* includes a section on "Scientific Studies of Male-Female Differences." Here the author points out physical differences in the respective constitutions of the male and female of the human species. "With respect to personality traits," he writes, "men are characterized by greater aggressiveness, dominance and achievement motivation, women by greater dependency, a stronger social orientation, and the tendency to be more easily discouraged by failure than men."[40]

And there are a number of latter-day scientific experiments to back this up. Researchers have found greater dependence and docility in very young girls, greater autonomy and activity in boys. One such experiment was conducted in the U.S. When a barrier was set up to separate youngsters from their mothers, boys tried to knock it down; girls cried helplessly.

There are personality differences between the sexes too. Some distinctions turn up remarkably early. At New York University, for example, researchers have found that a female infant stops sucking a bottle and looks up when someone comes into the room; a male pays no attention to the visitor.

Scientific researchers almost unanimously agree that hormones help determine how people feel and act. Thus the male-female differences are entirely genetic in nature. The passivity found in women is due to the particular nature of the female hormones. Differences between male and female hormones exist from birth: they are not acquired later, as would be the case if they stemmed from differences in environment.

The tenets of Islam are based wholly on nature. This is because Islam is the religion of nature. The laws Islam requires us to follow are, in fact, our own instinctive human requirements expressed in legal terms. And the teachings of Islam with respect to women are no exception. They too are based on nature. Modern, psychological, biological and anatomical research proves women to be more passive than men. This is the way their Maker has fashioned them. The nature of their womanhood, the special part they have to play in society, demand that they should be just as they have been made — that is, relatively delicate as compared to men.

It is this fact of nature on which Islamic teachings have been based. Because of women's delicate constitution, Islam teaches men to be gentle with them. That way they will not lose heart or become too despondent to perform their special duties in life. Women are not like iron and steel ribs: they are fragile and delicate. It is best to let them be, in their natural state. If one treats them as though they were tough metal, one will only break them.

REMARK OF THE CHIEF JUSTICE

Giving his verdict in the Muhammad Ahmad-Shah Bano case, Mr. Y.V. Chandra Chud, Chief Justice of the Indian Supreme Court, has written a special note in which he says:

> Some questions which arise under the ordinary civil and criminal law are of a far-reaching significance to large segments of society which have been traditionally subjected to unjust treatment. Women are one such segment. *"Na stree swatantramarhati"* (The woman does not deserve independence), said Manu, the law giver. And, it is alleged that the "fatal point in Islam is the degradation of woman." To the Prophet is ascribed the statement, hopefully wrongly, that "woman was made from a crooked rib, and if you try to bend it straight, it will break; therefore treat your wives kindly."[41]

I would like to make it clear that the phrase in this passage, "hopefully wrongly," does not mean that this saying has been wrongly attributed to the Prophet. It means rather that although the Prophet said that woman is born of a "crooked rib," those who want to establish equality between man and woman should take heart, as this saying of the Prophet was contrary to the fact. This phrase of the Chief Justice is meant to deny the statement itself and not the attribution.

Only a man of law can give a final opinion as to the relevance of this remark of the Chief Justice from the purely legal point of view, but it is certainly not correct from the academic point of view. He has quoted this saying of the Prophet to support his claim that Islam advocates the unjust treatment of a segment of society, whereas, on the contrary, this saying enjoins men to treat women with justice. The remark of the honorable Chief Justice does apply to Manu's statement, but it does not apply at all to the sayings of the Prophet.

When it has been clearly stated that women should be treated gently, how can it be claimed that unjust and unfair treatment of women was advocated in a saying of the Prophet (as it clearly was in Manu's dictum)?

So far as a woman's being like a rib is concerned, mention of this is made only to support fair treatment of women rather than the reverse. It has been clarified above that this was only an example. In view of the particular psychology of women, it was cited to show that if she was subjected to rough treatment, it would go against her nature and would result in perversion rather than reform.

In this saying of the Prophet the likening of woman to the rib was a simple metaphor. The misunderstanding arose because of the biblical statement brought in to explain it. While this saying had nothing to do with the biblical conception of woman, what has been said in the above *hadith* is a natural fact which has often been expressed in different ways, as in the words of Matthew Arnold: "With women the heart argues, not the mind."

CORRESPONDENCE

In response to the remark made by the former Chief Justice, Mr. Chandra Chud, in his verdict on the Muhammad Ahmad-Shah Bano case, we sent him a letter which is reproduced on the next page.

As is clear from the preceding discussion, this remark of the Chief Justice is wholly baseless from the academic point of view. But what is stranger still is the fact that when we drew his attention to this by this letter, he did not care to reply. We sent him this letter for the first time on 17 April, 1986, by registered post. Having received no reply we sent a copy of this letter to him again on May 14, 1986, but again he did not respond. Then, after trying several times, we succeeded in contacting him on the telephone. We asked for an appointment with him, so that we could discuss this matter with him, but he excused himself and refused to comply with our request. Now we have no choice but to publish this letter without his reply.

SUMMARY

God "created man's mate from the same soul" means simply that women are of the same species as men. God created them that way so that there should be harmony between the two sexes. If men and

Mr. Y.V. Chandrachud   May 14, 1986
Ex-Chief Justice
A-503 Som Vihar
R.K. Puram
New Delhi 110 022

Dear Mr. Chandrachud,

I am taking the liberty of addressing myself to you because, on going through your verdict on the Muhammad Ahmad-Shah Bano case, I find that one of the statements you make casts unfair aspersions on Islam. You allege that women have been "traditionally" subjected to unjust treatment, and that the "fatal point in Islam is the degradation of woman." To support this, you quote Manu as having stated that woman did not "deserve independence," and the Prophet of Islam as having said, "Woman was made from a crooked rib, and, if you try to bend it straight it will break; therefore, treat your wives kindly."

While Manu's dictum bears out your statement, I must point out that you have badly misquoted the Prophet. Nowhere in the Hadith is it stated that woman was made from a crooked rib, this being an ancient biblical version of God's creation of human life. The word "rib" was used by the Prophet in a purely metaphorical sense and his actual words were: "Woman is like a rib, if you try to straighten her out, she will break, so treat her kindly."

The *Encyclopaedia Britannica* states: "With respect to personality traits, men are characterized by greater aggressiveness, dominance and achievement motivation, women by greater dependency, a stronger social orientation and the tendency to be more easily discouraged by failure than men" (19/907).

Presumably the Prophet, with his great understanding of human nature, had a fine intuitive grasp of the fundamental, biological and psychological differences between men and women, particularly the latter's fragility and passivity — and, for this reason, found it necessary to admonish lesser men to treat their wives kindly.

I fail to see how "the degradation of women" can ensue from such an injunction. It would be fitting, to say the least, if you were now to retract, or amend, your statement, now that this point has been clarified.

I remain,

Yours faithfully,

Wahiduddin Khan
President, The Islamic Centre

women had been derived from different species — if one had been
made from fire, for instance, and the other from earth — then the
two would have been unable to get on together. Family life would
have lacked peace and harmony: men and women would have been
unable to struggle hand in hand to build a better world.

As for the saying of the Prophet likening women to a rib, it is
a parable illustrating the need to treat women gently on the basis of
their particular, natural constitution. The Prophet Muhammad
delivered this advice time and time again, in different words, and it
is something that he himself practiced throughout his life.

In the time of the Prophet, women used to attend the night prayer,
and sometimes they used to take their small children along with them.
The Prophet used to pay special attention to strict and full observance
of prayer. Yet so great was his consideration for women that
sometimes, when he heard babies crying, he would cut short the
prayer. He once said: "Sometimes I stand up for prayer, my intention
being to make it a long one. Then I hear a baby crying. So I cut
short prayer, not wanting to make things difficult for the child's
mother."[42]

THE STATUS OF WOMAN

In Islam, a woman enjoys the same status as that of a man. In the
words of the Qur'an, "You are members, one of another."[43] There
is no difference between man and woman as regards status, rights
and blessings both in this world and in the hereafter. Both are equal
participants so far as the carrying out of the functions of daily living
is concerned. If Islam stresses the division of labor between the sexes
rather than sexual equality, it is because it does not countenance the
idea of either sex suffering from the feelings of degradation and
inferiority resulting from any imitation of the opposite sex. As the
Prophet once observed: "Those men are cursed who try to resemble
women, and those women are cursed who try to resemble men."[44]

The biological division of human beings into male and female
is the result of purposeful planning on the part of the Creator. And
there can be no human progress without constant respect being shown
for this division. Any attempt to cross the dividing line laid down

by the Almighty is akin to breaking down the whole system of nature, a procedure which can lead only to destruction.

Man and woman in the eyes of Islam are not the duplicates of one another, but the complements, there being in each quite incontrovertible, biological differences which lead to the natural separation of sphere and occupation. This division of labor permits the shortcomings of one sex to be compensated for by the strengths of the other.

Islamic precepts for men and women are based on their respective, natural constitutions. It is now an established biological fact that there is a difference in their physiological structure, a difference which gears men to work which is external to the home, and women to a life led mainly indoors within the home. This biological difference has not only been the determining factor in the societal division of labor, but has also necessitated the framing of special Islamic laws to ensure justice for both sexes.

THE CONTRACT OF LIFE

The relationship formed by marriage in Islam is described in the Qur'an as a "firm contract."[45] It is exactly the same as any ordinary contract in that it is bilateral in nature: where it differs is in its spelling out of the rights and responsibilities which bind a man and a woman together in a vital partnership, making them companions for life. There is a saying of the Prophet Muhammad on this subject: "Beware, your women have rights over you and you have rights over your women."[46]

WOMAN — SOURCE OF GOODNESS

Here are some verses from the Qur'an and some traditions which elaborate this point.

> Live with them on a footing of kindness and equity. If you take a dislike to them, it may well be that you dislike a thing which God has meant for your own abundant good.[47]

This verse draws our attention to the fact that nothing is perfect in this world and that apparent imperfection may conceal some virtue. If in certain respects a woman is imperfect, there will be other respects in which she is perfect: it is her plus points, rather than her minus points, on which attention should be focussed. Only those can succeed in the outside world who have learned this lesson at home, that is, seeing light where there is darkness and discovering plus points along with minus points. Therein lies the secret of success in the modern world.

MOTHER IS MORE HONORABLE

According to Abu Hurayrah, a man once came to the Prophet and asked him:

> "O Messenger of God, who rightfully deserves the best treatment from me?"
> "Your mother," replied the Prophet.
> "Who is next?" asked the man.
> "Your mother," said the Prophet.
> "Who comes next?" the man asked again.
> "Your mother," replied the Prophet.
> "Who is after that?" insisted the man.
> "Your father," said the noble Prophet.[48]

The projection of woman as the most honorable human being in the form of a mother makes it quite clear what sort of a society Islam wants to create. It is one in which a woman is accorded the maximum honor and respect. A member of such a society, who shows full respect to a woman as a mother will, of necessity, become more and more caring in regard to other women. With the creation of such a mentality, women in general will share the status accorded to a mother at home.

FREEDOM OF EXPRESSION

There were several examples of Muslim women's intervention in religious matters, one of which occurred in the time of 'Umar ibn al-Khattab, the second Caliph. It concerned the amount of money or goods which had to be given as dower (given by the husband to the wife at the time of marriage as a token that he will meet all her expenses in future). In the Prophet's lifetime this had been a very nominal amount, but with the increase in resources after the conquest of other countries, people had begun to apportion more substantial dowers. Feeling that this was an unhealthy trend, 'Umar once addressed an assembly of his people from the pulpit, saying that he did not know who had increased the amount of dower to more than 400 *dirhams*. 'The Prophet and his Companions handed over 400 *dirhams* or even less. Nobody should fix a dower of more than 400 *dirhams*. If it comes to my knowledge that anyone has exceeded this amount, I will confiscate the excess amount for the State Treasury."

When he had had his say, a woman got up from one corner of the gathering and said, "O Chief of the Faithful, is the Book of God (Qur'an) to be followed or what you have to say?" 'Umar replied that it was certainly the Book of God that was to be followed. The woman then retorted, "You have just forbidden people to increase the amount of dower, whereas God says in His book: 'O believers, it is unlawful for you... to force them to give up a part of what you have given them...'"[49]

The woman had actually misquoted the text, but 'Umar did not choose to assert himself and simply said, "Everyone knows more than 'Umar."[50] With these words he relented on the question of the dower.

Here was a common woman criticizing the ruler of an empire, and the latter withdrawing his words. The right of absolute freedom of expression as we find in this incident, is a clear indication that woman has been granted her full rights in Islamic society.

HOME MANAGEMENT IS NOT AN INFERIOR TASK

A certain woman called Nasibah once came to the Prophet Muhammad and said: "O Messenger of God, Men have excelled in meriting the rewards of the Hereafter. They join the Friday prayer, attend congregations and perform *jihad*. Then what is left for us women to do?" The Prophet replied, "O Nasibah, if your manner of living with your husband is proper and obedient, such conduct in itself is equal to all the actions performed by men, which you have just mentioned."[51]

In modern times, as a result of perverted thinking, managing a home is considered inferior to work done outside the home. But Islam gives the same place of honor to both kinds of work, it being a fact that both are equally important. On this score, neither man nor woman need have a superiority or an inferiority complex.

THE IMPORTANCE OF WOMAN IN THE CONSTRUCTION OF SOCIETY

According to Jabir ibn 'Abdullah, the Prophet once observed: "The throne of Iblis (Satan), the chief of the devils, is situated above the seas, whence he sends his bands to lead human beings astray. To Iblis, the most worthy of the devils is the one who causes the greatest wickedness. The devils visit him as their chief to report their deeds to him, and Iblis gives a hearing to all of them. On one occasion, Iblis remained unimpressed with their achievements, until one of the devils came and told him that he had pursued a husband and wife until he managed to separate them. He had achieved this by causing them to have doubts and misgivings about one another. Iblis was so overjoyed to hear this that he drew him to him in a close embrace, saying, "Yes, you did it," meaning that he had really managed to lead human beings astray."[52]

This *hadith* shows that Satan's greatest weapons in perverting human society are the conflict and discord which he creates between a husband and wife, resulting in their separation.

In ancient times, this phenomenon was not widespread, only a very limited number of people being afflicted by the evil of separation. However, in modern times the whole human race has come to be affected by exposure to new and misguided ideas about the freedom of woman and unnatural equality of the sexes. It is as a result of these artificial concepts that the marital state has come to be looked down upon in developed societies, and men and women have begun to opt increasingly for divorce, even on the most minor provocations. In the wake of such divorces, a number of evils have followed, not the least of which is their baneful effect on the children, who, in a state of bewilderment at the separation of their parents, often join gangs of criminals. Then the discarding of family bonds has given rise to a general atmosphere of permissiveness, which in turn has resulted in the spread of fatal diseases. The widespread loosening, or even destruction of family bonds has become the greatest problem afflicting modern societies.

When the rot of perversion sets in at home, the whole of society is affected and, ultimately, it is the entire nation which has to bear the brunt of it. The only reason for this widespread moral degeneration is the violation of the sanctity of marriage, which has come to be regarded as an unwelcome bond.

WOMEN IN POSITIONS OF POWER

A film called *Kisses for My President*, made in Hollywood in 1964, tells the story of a married American woman who is elected the U.S. President. She almost immediately becomes pregnant and finds herself faced with so many problems because of this that she decides to leave the presidential home and go and live in her own home. Finally she resigns from the office of president. Even the modern world still finds it unimaginable that a woman should be given a high government office. In a poll taken in 1972, the majority of American voters said that they would rather have a black man than a woman as president. The idea of a woman president was ridiculed. Someone joked: "When the lady president delivers her child, the hospital bulletin will have to announce that 'the President and baby are doing well.'"[53]

Opinion polls were conducted on this particular issue in 1987 in the U.S. Reuter reported from Washington that according to a poll conducted for a women's rights group, nearly one third of American voters believed men to be better suited than women to the role of U.S. President. The study released by the National Women's Political Caucus (NWPC) said only 8 percent of those polled believed a woman could do better than a man in the White House, 40 percent said there was no inherent difference between the sexes, and 31 percent believed men made better presidents. The poll, conducted by the Washington-based Hickman-Maslin political research firm, showed that women were credited with being more capable of dealing with social issues, such as poverty, health care, education, drug abuse, and civil rights.[54]

The Persian emperor Chosroes died during the life of the Prophet. His courtiers crowned Chrosroes' daughter queen. On hearing this news, the Prophet said: "A nation which makes a woman its ruler will not make progress."[55]

The researches of the modern age now testify to the truth of this time-honored principle laid down by Islam. Fourteen hundred years ago, Islam held that a woman was not fit for so high a position as that of a sovereign. While until very recently this could have been regarded as a mere assertion made a very long time ago, today it is accepted as a scientific fact. What the Prophet had said as a matter of inspiration has now been established, after a long period of study and research, as a reality. This is clear proof that Islamic principles are based on facts of nature and not just on supposition and conjecture.

THE TESTIMONY OF WOMAN

The testimony of two women is regarded as equal to that of one man. While dealing with matters of debt, the Qur'an says:

> When you contract a debt for a fixed period, put it in writing. And call in two male witnesses from among you, but if two men cannot be found, then one man and two women whom you judge fit to act as witnesses; so that if either of them forgets, the other will remember.[56]

Recent research has testified to this law mentioned in the Qur'an as being perfectly natural. A UPI report quotes a Soviet scientist as saying that men have a greater ability to memorize and process mathematical information than women, but females are better with words. Speaking to the Tass news agency, Dr. Vladimir Konovalov said, "Men dominate in mathematical subjects due to the peculiarities of their memory. The stronger sex shows greater difficulties in processing and adapting language material."[57]

As indicated in the Qur'anic verse initially quoted, whenever there is to be any delay in payment after the conclusion of a business transaction, there must be witnesses to this, either two men, or one man and two women. The phrase "so that if either of them forgets the other will remember" makes it quite clear that in such credit dealings, what has to be considered next in importance to justice is memory. When biological studies have shown a woman's memory to be weaker than a man's, it is quite in accordance with the facts of nature to stipulate that there should be two female witnesses in place of one man. This command thus sets a value upon memory per se. This is a matter of practical requirement, and does not discriminate against women or grant superiority to men.

AN ADDITIONAL, NOT A SUPERIOR QUALITY

Here is a verse of the Qur'an which reads: "Men are the protectors and maintainers of women, because God has made some of them to excell others."[58]

Fadilah is the Arabic word used in the scriptures to indicate the additional, masculine quality of protectiveness. For a household to be properly run, it should, of necessity, have a guardian. Guardianship is rightly entrusted to the family member who is best qualified to undertake this responsibility — namely, the husband, for protectiveness is a virtue which has been granted by nature in greater measure to men than to women. Far from mentioning absolute masculine superiority, the above-quoted verse only implies that man is the master in the home because of the additional attributes with which he has been endowed by nature.

Faddala ba'dahum 'ala ba'd is an Arabic expression meaning "excelled some on other," which occurs several times in the Qur'an. For instance, various kinds of crops and fruits grow from the same soil and water. Of this the Qur'an says: "And in the land, there are adjoining plots: vineyards and corn fields and palm-groves, the single and the clustered. Yet We make some excel others in taste. Surely in this there are signs for men of understanding."[59]

The following is an excerpt from a commentary on this verse by 'Abdullah Yusuf 'Ali, well known Commentator on the Qur'an: "The date palm, the crops of food grains, and the grape-vine are all fed by the same kind of water: yet how different to all vegetation. The fruit or eatable produce may vary in shape, size, colour, flavour, etc. in endless variety."[60]

All Commentators on the Qur'an have placed emphasis on this difference and variety, rather than on some fruits being superior, in an absolute sense, to some others. That is to say, each fruit has some particular quality to it as regards color, and taste, which is not found in other fruits. Similarly there are differences between men and women. Just as women have uniquely feminine qualities, so also do men have uniquely masculine qualities.

That is why God enjoins us not to be jealous of others' qualities:

Do not covet the favors by which God has exalted some of you above others. To men is allotted what they earn, and to women what they earn.[61]

That is, each has been blessed with different sets of attributes. So what others have should not make one jealous. On the contrary, one should avail of whatever talents have been bestowed upon one and, in the processs, make a positive contribution to family and social life.

It is a fact that women are not physically as strong as men, but their physical weakness in no way implies their inferiority to men. The eyes are the most delicate parts of our body, while the nails by comparison are extremely hard. That does not mean that the nails are superior to the eyes.

Just as two different kinds of fruit will differ in color, taste, shape and texture, without one being superior or inferior to the other, so also do men and women have their different qualities which distinguish the male from the female without there being any question of superiority or inferiority. If men and women have been endowed with different capacities, it is so that they will play their respective divinely predetermined roles in life with greater ease and effectiveness. Certain feminine abilities will be superior to certain masculine abilities, and vice versa simply because their natural spheres of application are different. Success in life for both men and women can be attained only if they devote themselves to the particular set of activities which has been preordained for them in God's scheme of things.

MUSLIM WOMEN

Women, throughout the history of Islam, have played significant roles and, by their feats, have demonstrated not only the vast arena which Islam affords them for the performance of noble and heroic deeds, but also the exaltedness of the position accorded to women in Islamic society.

Within the sphere of Islam, 'Aishah, the daughter of Abu Bakr and wife of the Prophet, stands out as a woman of notable intelligence, whose intellectual gifts were fittingly utilized in the service of Islam. Very young in comparison with the Prophet, she survived him by almost half a century, during which period she became a great and authentic source of religious learning for the *ummah* (community). This was largely thanks to the accuracy with which she had preserved in her memory the speeches, conversations and sayings of the Prophet. In all, she related about 2210 of his sayings and was extraordinarily gifted in being able to formulate laws from them. It is said that no less than one quarter of the *shari'ah* injunctions have been derived from her narrations. Her knowledge and deep perception in religious matters was so established that whenever the Companions of the Prophet found themselves in disagreement over any religious matter, they would come to her to seek her assistance. According to Abu Musa 'Ashari, whenever they were in any doubt as to the meaning of any part of the *hadith*, they would turn to 'Aishah. It was seldom that she was unable to solve their problems.[62]

Although the *Encyclopaedia Britannica* mentions her as 'Aishah, the third wife of the Prophet Muhammad, who played a role of some political importance after the Prophet's death,'[63] her real importance is not that of her own individual superiority in Islamic history, but the indication her position gives of the high status women were accorded within the sphere of Islam, and of the vastness of the field in which their talents might honorably be used. It was owing to the distinctive character of Islam that she was able to render such important social and political services.

We present below some additional examples of women who played an effective role in Islam.

TWO REMARKABLE WOMEN

When the Judaic era was drawing to a close, a woman had to be singled out who would in every way be fit to become the mother of one so miraculous in nature as the Prophet Jesus, on whom be peace. God had ordained that the final prophet of the Jewish people was to be born without a father: the character of his mother had, therefore, to be one of irreproachable innocence and chastity. Mary, who subsequently became known as the Virgin Mary, was found to have lived her life according to this exacting standard, and, by her extraordinary chastity, had proved herself fit to be chosen as the mother of Jesus.

In one of the most authentic collections of the *hadith* by Bukhari, the Prophet is recorded as saying, "The best woman out of all of them (the Jewish people) was Mary (mother of Jesus), the daughter of 'Imran, and the best woman out of all of my own people was Khadijah bint Khuwaylid."[64] (This saying was passed on by 'Ali, the Prophet's cousin and son-in-law.) The special historical status that both Khadijah and Mary enjoyed was due to their both having given themselves up entirely to God: they both subordinated their own wills to that of the Almighty.

In the case of Khadijah, she was chosen by God to be the life partner of the final Prophet, Muhammad, because the circumstances of his life were such that he needed someone of superlative virtue, who would put herself and her property entirely in his hands without ever raising her voice in complaint. She did, indeed, give up everything — her life, her property, her leisure and her comfort — for the sake of the Holy Prophet. Although her life, as a result, was one of severe affliction, she was never heard to protest. It was these qualities then that made her worthy in the eyes of God to become the life companion of His Final Prophet. What was the underlying cause of her superiority? Here are two parts of the *hadith* which throw some light on this.

'Aishah says that the only other wife of the Prophet that she ever felt envious of was Khadijah, even though she was not a contemporary of hers. "Whenever the Prophet sacrificed a goat," says 'Aishah, "he would tell me to send some meat to Khadijah's friends." One day I became annoyed, "Oh no, not Khadijah again!" I exclaimed, whereupon the Prophet replied, "I have been intoxicated with her love."[65]

According to 'Aishah, the Prophet would not leave home without praising Khadijah. "One day when he mentioned Khadijah, I became annoyed and said, 'She was just an old woman. In her stead, God has given you one who is better.' This angered the Prophet, who said, 'God knows, He has given me no better than her. She believed when others disbelieved. She had faith in me when others rejected me. She supported me with her wealth when others left me in the lurch. And God gave me children by her, which He has not given me by any other wives.'"[66]

In every age, there is a need not only for men but also for women to devote themselves to the mission of Islam. Ideally, they should be individuals who are willing in the way that Khadijah was, to involve themselves unstintingly in the scheme of God. Such people are like small cogs which revolve strictly according to the motion of a larger wheel — in this case, the will of God. This is undoubtedly a trying task; but it is also one that carries a great reward. To perform this task is "to help God." There can be no doubt about the excellence and superiority of those whom God chooses to enlist as His helpers.

THE IDEAL LIFE COMPANION

One of Khadijah's most significant contributions to the furtherance of Islam was the reassurance which she gave to the Prophet on the occasion of his receiving the first divine revelation in the solitude of the Cave of Hira from the Archangel Gabriel. This was an experience which left the Prophet awestruck and trembling with fear. When he returned to his home, he was still overwhelmed by a feeling of dread and, as he entered, he asked Khadijah to wrap him in a blanket. After some time, when in some measure he had regained his mental equilibrium, he related the entire experience to her, expressing his fears that his life was in danger. She hastened to reassure him, and comforted him by observing, "It cannot be. God will surely never forsake you. You are kind to your kin; you always help the weak; you solace the weary; you take care of whoever crosses your threshold; you speak the truth."[67]

Then it occurred to Khadijah that she had best make enquiries of some learned Christians who, well-versed as they were in the scriptures, were bound to have knowledge of revelation and prophethood. She went first to a *rahib* (hermit) who lived near Mecca. On seeing her, the priest asked, "O noble lady of the Quraysh, what has brought you here?" Khadijah replied, "I have come here to ask you about Gabriel." To this the *rahib* said, "Glory be to God, he is God's pure angel. He visits prophets: he came to Jesus and Moses." Then Khadijah went to another Christian called Addas. She put the same question to him, and he too told her that Gabriel was an angel of God, the very same who had been with Moses when God drowned the Pharaoh. He had also come to Jesus, and through him God had helped Jesus.[68]

Then Khadijah hastened to Waraqah ibn Nawfal, a Christian convert who had translated part of the Bible into Arabic. When she had finished telling him of what Muhammad had seen and heard, Waraqah exclaimed, "Holy, holy! By the Master of my soul, if your report be true, O Khadijah, this must be the great spirit who spoke to Moses. This means that Muhammad must be the Prophet of this nation."[69] On a subsequent visit, Khadijah brought Muhammad to meet Waraqah ibn Nawfal. Muhammad related the events exactly as they had taken place and, when he had finished, Waraqah said, "By the Master of my soul, I swear that you are the same Prophet whose coming was foretold by Jesus, son of Mary." But then Waraqah sounded a note of warning: "You will be denied and you will be hurt. You will be abused and you will be pursued." He nevertheless immediately pledged himself to the Prophet: "If I should ever live to see that day, I should surely help you."[70]

ABSOLUTE FREEDOM

Zihar was an old pagan custom among the Arabs which permitted a husband to nullify his wife's right to consider herself his lawful spouse. All he had to do was utter the words, *"anti'alayiya ka zahr ummi,"* meaning, "be to me as my mother's back." He was then free of conjugal responsibilities, but the wife was not thereby set free to leave her husband's home or to contract a second marriage.

It happened once in Medina that a Muslim by the name of Aws ibn as-Samit cast off his wife, Khawlah bint Tha'labah, by uttering the fateful words. This was particularly hard on Khawlah, who loved her husband and had little children to support. She lacked the means to provide for her children, but, according to the convention of *zihar,* she could not claim any support from her husband. She came, therefore, to the Prophet, laid the whole case before him and urged him to assist her. But, since up to that point no revelation had been made to the Prophet on this subject, he could only reply that she was no longer the lawful wife of her husband.

On hearing this, Khawlah began to lament the ruin of her home and the penury into which she and her children would sink. She also told the Prophet that her husband had not expressly stated that he was divorcing her. But the Prophet could give her no positive answer because he thought that by Arab custom, the separation must already have taken place. Then Khawlah could only weep and pray to God to save her from ruin.[71]

It was on this occasion that the *surah* 58 of the Qur'an entitled, *al-Mujadilah* (She Who Pleaded), was revealed. It begins with these words:

> God has indeed heard the statement of the woman who pleads with thee concerning her husband, and carries her complaint to God. And God always hears the argument between both sides among you, for God hears and sees all things.[72]

On the basis of this revelation, the justice of her plea was recognized, and this iniquitous custom, based as it was on a false set of values, was finally abolished.

Much later, when Khawlah was an old woman, she once met 'Umar ibn al-Khattab, who had by that time become the Caliph of the Islamic Empire. 'Umar greeted her and she returned his greeting. Then she said: "O 'Umar, there was a time when I saw you in the marketplace of 'Ukaz. Then you were called 'Umayr[73] and you would set your goats to grazing with a stick in your hand. Then, the times changed and you came to be called 'Umar. Later you became the Chief of the Faithful. Be God-fearing in dealing with your subjects and remember, that for one who fears God's chastisement, a distantly related man is like a close relative; and one who does not fear death risks the loss of all that he seeks to gain."

One Jarud Abdi, who was in the company of 'Umar at that time, exclaimed, "O woman, you have been impudent to the Chief of the Faithful!" But 'Umar immediately silenced him by saying, "Let her speak. You know who she is. She is the one whose plea was heard above the seventh heaven. She, above all others, deserves to be heard out by 'Umar."[74]

DIVISION OF LABOR

Islam has assigned separate spheres to men and women, the former having the management of all non-domestic, external matters, and the latter being completely in charge of the home. The ensuing division of labor is justifiable in terms not only of biological and physiological differences, but also of the social benefits which stem therefrom. One important benefit resulting from men and women functioning in different spheres is that they can see each others' lives objectively, without that sense of personal involvement which tends to cloud their judgement and lead to a damaging emotionalism. They are better able to counsel each other wisely, to give moral support at critical moments, and to offer the daily encouragement with which every successful union should be marked. Experience has repeatedly shown that when one is confronted by a serious problem, one is often initially incapable of arriving at a well-reasoned, objective judgement of the situation. It is only when there is some sympathetic adviser present, who is personally uninvolved in one's predicament, that solutions begin to present themselves. With men and women having their activities in separate spheres, they are in a better position to bring objective opinions to bear in such difficult situations, and can give truly helpful advice in an unemotional and coolly detached way.

In Islamic history, there are many examples of women who have helped their husbands when faced with critical situations. One of the most notable was Khadijah, who successfully brought the Prophet back to a state of normalcy after his experience in the Cave of Hira.

Similarly, when the Prophet entered into the Treaty of al-Hudaybiyyah, he felt severely afflicted by his own people's display of dissatisfaction with the terms of the Treaty, which, in their opinion, made far too many concessions to their enemies, the Quraysh. The Companions felt, in fact, that in accepting humiliating peace terms, they were bowing to the enemy. However, even in the face of such sentiments, the Prophet ordered his people to sacrifice the animals they had brought with them, and to shave their heads.[75] No one got up to obey his order. The Prophet repeated his order three times, but no one stirred from his place. This was extremely disconcerting, for never had an order given by the Prophet been deliberately ignored.

The Prophet, dismayed at the resentment shown by the Muslims, returned to his tent and to the company of his wife, Umm Salmah. Seeing him look so grieved, she asked him what ailed him. The Prophet then told her of this unprecedented refusal to obey his order. Umm Salmah then said, "O Messenger of God, if you are convinced that your judgement is right, you should go outside, and, without a word to anyone, slaughter your animal and shave you head."[76]

The Prophet did exactly as she had suggested. He went out, sacrificed his animal and shaved his head. When the people saw what he had done, they immediately began to follow suit.

Their anguish was so great that it seemed they would cut one another's heads as they began to shave them after the sacrifice.

The reason that Khadijah and Umm Salmah were able to arrive at a correct judgment in such delicate situations was that they were detached from them and, therefore, in a position to offer objective opinions. If they too had been seriously involved, they might have been too subjective in their thinking.

WOMAN — AS A SOURCE OF KNOWLEDGE

There is a famous saying of the Prophet that the acquisition of knowledge is the duty of all Muslims.[77] In this saying, the word *muslim* is in the masculine form, *muslimah* being the feminine form, but the work of scholars carried out on the traditions makes it clear that *muslimah* may be legitimately inferred. That means that the acquisition of knowledge is likewise the duty of Muslim women.

In the biographies of the narrators of Hadith literature, mention is made of the academic services of women, which is a clear indication that during the first era of Islam, there was a strong tendency among women to acquire knowledge. The benefits ensuing from their efforts were far-reaching. For example Imam Bukhari, whose *al-Jami' as-Sahih* is by far the most authentic source of Hadith learning, set off, when he was 14 years of age, to acquire knowledge from far distant scholars: if he was in a position to appreciate the lessons given by the great teachers of the time, it was because his mother and sister had given him a sound educational background at home. It is said that Imam ibn Jauzi, the famous religious scholar, received his primary education from his aunt. Ibn Abi Asiba's sister and daughter were experts in medicine — the lady doctors of their time. And among the Hadith teachers of Imam ibn Asakir, several women teachers are mentioned.

During the first era of Islam, academic activity related mostly to work on the Hadith and *athar*.[78] We find, in this age, that a number of the Prophet's Companions were women, and that they contributed in large measure to the narration and preservation of the traditions of the Prophet. The Prophet's wife, 'Aishah, herself handed down to posterity a substantial proportion of what comprises the vast whole of Islamic knowledge. The next generation of women in their turn handed down the traditions which they had heard at first hand from the Prophet or his Companions. Many of them acquired their knowledge from religious scholars to whom they were related, and carried on the good work of passing it on to their successors.

ISLAM GIVES COURAGE

Tumadir bint 'Amr ibn ath-Tharid as-Sulamiyya (d.24 AH), a poetess, later known as Khansa, who was born into a noble family (her father was the Chief of the Banu Salim tribe of Mudar), lost her two brothers in a war fought prior to the advent of Islam. Their deaths were a great shock to her. Before this tragedy it had been her wont to compose just two or three couplets at a time, but now, after her bereavement, the verses simply flowed from her heart as the tears flowed from her eyes. The elegies she wrote in memory of her brothers, particularly Sakhr, were heart-rending: she continued to write and lament until she became blind in both eyes.

After the fall of Mecca, she came to the Prophet with her tribe and accepted Islam. It is related that when she read out some of her verses to the Prophet, he was very moved, and asked her to continue reading.

In her youth, she had been unable to bear the tragedy of her brothers' deaths, but she derived such strength from Islam that, in her old age, she sacrificed her own sons in the path of God. She had four sons, all of whom she persuaded to fight in the battle of Qadsiya. They all fought bravely and were finally martyred. When she received the news of the deaths of all of her sons, she neither wrote elegies, nor did she bewail their passing. Instead, she heard the news with great calm and fortitude, and said: "Thank God who has awarded me the honor of their martyrdom. I hope God will bring us together in the life Hereafter."[79]

PATIENCE FOR PARADISE

It is related that in the early days of Islam, the Prophet was once passing in the vicinity of Yasir and his family in Mecca when they were being subjected to the violence of the Quraysh. When Yasir set eyes on the Prophet, the only question he asked him was, "O Prophet of God, is this all there is to the world?" The Prophet replied, "O family of Yasir, be patient, for you have been promised heaven."[80] Yasir and his wife Summaiyah were the first to succumb to persecution by the Quraysh. Yet, even after seeing the painful fate which his parents had suffered, 'Ammar, their son, being strong of will, did not flinch from his faith. It is said that 'Ammar ibn Yasir was the first Meccan Muslim to have built a mosque in his home. It is believed that it is he who is referred to in this verse of the Qur'an:[81]

> Can he who passes his night in adoration, standing up or on his knees, who dreads the terrors of the life to come and hopes to earn the mercy of his Lord, be compared to the unbeliever? ...Truly, none will take heed but men of understanding.[82]

IN THE FIELD OF ACTION

The general lot of women in the early days of Islam was frequently a hard one, but they bore themselves with remarkable fortitude and adapted themselves to whatever conditions they found themselves in. One shining example is that of Abu Bakr's daughter Asma', who was born 27 years before the Emigration. When she accepted Islam in Mecca, the Muslims were just 17 in number.

When Abu Bakr emigrated to Medina, he possessed 6000 *dirhams,* all of which he took with him. When his father, Abu Qahafa, heard of this, he came to his family to console them and said, "I think that Abu Bakr has not only given us a shock by leaving you alone, but I suppose he has also taken all the money with him." Asma' then told her grandfather that he had left them well provided for. She thereupon collected some small stones and with them she filled up the niche where Abu Bakr had formerly kept his money. She covered the pile of stones with a cloth and then placed her grandfather's hand on it. Having gone blind in his old age, he was easily taken in by this trick, and thought that the niche was full of *dirhams*. "It is a good thing that Abu Bakr has done. This will suffice for your necessities." Asma' then confessed that her father had not left them a single *dirham* and that it was only to comfort her grandfather that she had conceived of this idea.[83]

Before the advent of Islam, Asma's father had been one of the richest merchants of Mecca, but when Asma' emigrated to Medina with her husband, Zubayr, they had to live in the harshest of conditions. Bukhari has recorded Asma's account of how her own existence was eked out from day to day:

When I married Zubayr, he had neither wealth nor property, nor anything else. He had no servant, and there was only one camel to bring water and only one horse. I myself brought the grass for the camel and crushed date stones for it to eat instead of grain. I had to fetch the water myself, and when the water bag burst I would sew it up myself. As well as managing the house, I had also to take care of the horse. This I found the most difficult of all. I did not know how to cook the bread properly, so whenever I had to make it, I would knead the flour and take it to the Ansar women in the neighbourhood. They were very sincere women and they would cook my bread along with their own. When Zubayr reached Medina, the Prophet gave him a piece of land which was two miles away from the city. I used to work on this land, and on the way back home I would carry a sack of date stones on my head.

One day, when I was returning like this with a sack on my head, I saw the Prophet mounted on a camel going along the road with a group of Medinan Muslims. When he saw me, he reined in his camel and signed to me to sit on it, but I felt shy of travelling with men, and I also thought that Zubayr might take offence at this, as he was very sensitive about his honor. The Prophet, realizing that I was hesitant, did not insist, and went on his way.

When I came home, I told Zubayr the whole story. I said that I had felt shy of sitting with the men on the camel and that I had also remembered his sense of honor. To this Zubayr replied, "By God, your carrying date stones home on your head is harder for me to bear than that."[84]

Such instances of how women toiled during their stay in Medina are numberless. At that time women worked not only in their homes, but outside as well. This was because their menfolk were so preoccupied with preaching Islam that there was little time left in which to discharge their household responsibilities. It was left to the women then to deal with both internal and external duties. They even tended the animals, did the farming and worked in the orchards.

THE VIRTUE OF BELIEVING WOMEN

When this verse was revealed in the Qur'an — "They who hoard up gold and silver and spend it not in the way of God, unto them give tidings of a painful doom"[85] — then the Prophet said: "Woe to gold, woe to silver." When the Companions of the Prophet learned of this they were upset. They began to ask one another what things they were going to store then. At that time 'Umar ibn al-Khattab was with them. 'Umar said, if they liked, he could put this matter to the Prophet. Everyone agreed, so 'Umar went to the Prophet and said, "The Companions are saying, 'Could we but learn which kind of wealth is better, we would store that and no other.' The Prophet said: 'Everyone should possess a tongue which remembers God, a heart that thanks God and a wife that helps him in his faith.'"[86] Another version has used the word "Hereafter" for faith.

WOMEN IN EVERY FIELD

Once Umm Salmah was having her hair combed when she heard the sermon starting in the mosque. The Prophet began with the words, "O people..." On hearing this she told the woman who was combing her hair to braid it just as it was. The woman asked her why she was in such a hurry. Umm Salmah replied, "Are we not counted among 'people'?" And so saying, she promptly braided her hair herself, went to the corner of the house nearest the mosque and listened to the sermon.

In all, Umm Salmah related 378 traditions and used to lay down laws. Ibn Qayyim writes that if her decrees were to be compiled, they would take up a whole book.

Out of all the Prophet's wives, 'Aishah was the most intelligent. About 2210 traditions of the Prophet were related by her, and these were passed on by about one hundred of the Prophet's Companions and their close associates. Among her pupils were such eminent scholars as 'Urwah ibn Zubayr, Sa'id ibn Mussayyib, 'Abdullah ibn 'Amir, Mashruq, 'Ikramah and 'Alaqamah. A jurist of high calibre, she used to explain the wisdom and background of each tradition that she described. To take a very simple example, she explained that the prescribed bath on a Friday was not just a matter of ritual, as had been maintained by Abu Sa'id al-Khudri and 'Abdullah ibn 'Umar, but was meant as practical advice for people who had to travel from far-off places to say their Friday prayers in the Prophet's mosque.[87] While travelling, they perspired and became covered in dust: the Prophet had, therefore, told them to take a bath before attending prayers.[88]

When the Prophet was preparing to set off for Khaybar to engage in *jihad,* some women of the Banu Ghifar tribe approached him and said, "O Prophet of God, we want to accompany you on this journey, so that we may tend the injured and help Muslims in every possible way." The Prophet replied, "May God bless you. You are welcome to come."[89] Umm 'Atiyah, a Medinan woman, said that she had been present on seven expeditions: "I looked after the emigrants, cooked their food, bound up the wounds of the injured and cared for those who were in distress."

During the battle with the Jews in Medina, the Muslim women and children were gathered on the roof of a fort with Hassan ibn Thabit as their guard. Safia, the daughter of Abdul Muttalib, who was also present on the roof, describes how she saw a passing Jew taking a round of the fort: "At that time the Banu Qurayza (a Jewish tribe) were doing battle with the Muslims, which is why the road between us and the Prophet was cut off, and there was no one to defend us from the Jews. The Prophet and all his Companions, being on the battlefront, were in no position to come to our assistance. In the meanwhile, the Jew was coming nearer to the fort, and I said, 'O

Hassan, look! This Jew who is walking all around our fort is a danger to us, because he might go and inform the Jews of the insecure position we are in. The Prophet and his Companions are in the thick of battle, so it is your duty to go down and kill him.' But Hassan replied, 'By God, you know I am not fit for such a task.'"

At this, she tied a cloth round her waist, picked up a stick, went down to the outside of the fort and beat the man to death. "This done, I came back inside the fort and asked Hassan ibn Thabit to bring the things the Jew had on him, as I, a woman, did not want to touch him. Hassan ibn Thabit replied, 'Daughter of Abdul Muttalib, I have no need of his possessions.'"[90]

THE SUCCOR OF GOD

In the sixth year of Hijrah, a 10-year peace treaty was concluded at al-Hudaybiyyah, one article of which specified that anyone emigrating to Muhammad's camp without the permission of his guardian would have to be returned to Mecca; whereas any Muslim emigrating from Muhammad's camp to Mecca would not have to be returned.[91] This was adhered to in the case of men, one notable instance was that of Suhayl ibn 'Amr's son, Abu Jandal, who in spite of having walked 13 miles from Mecca to al-Hudaybiyyah in a badly injured condition with his feet in shackles, was promptly returned to his persecutors. Similarly, other Muslims having managed to free themselves from Quraysh were returned one after another.[92] This pact, however, was not regarded as covering the case of Muslim women. This verse of the Qur'an was revealed on this occasion:

> Believers, when believing women seek refuge with you, test them. Allah best knows their faith. If you find them true believers, do not return them to the infidels.[93]

Many incidents have been recorded of women managing to free themselves from the clutches of the Quraysh, coming to Medina, and then not being returned to the Quraysh in spite of the latter invoking the terms of the peace treaty. For example, when Umm Kulthum bint 'Uqbah ibn Abu Mu'ayt escaped to Medina, she was not returned even when two of her brothers came to take her back.[94] The Quraysh considered this refusal a violation of the pact and quickly seized this opportunity to defame the Prophet. It is remarkable, however, that they soon ceased to protest on this score and, considering that they were the Prophet's direst enemies, it is difficult to understand how this came about. No satisfactory answer is to be found in the books of *Sirah* and Commentaries on the Qur'an. Qadi Abu Bakr ibn al-'Arabi writes that the Quraysh ceased to protest because God had miraculously silenced their tongues.[95] There can be no doubt about it: it was one of God's miracles. (Although not in the usual sense of the word).

It is perhaps easier to arrive at the truth by examining the wording of this particular condition of the pact. Here we quote Bukhari's version, which may be taken as the most authentic: "You will have to return any of our men who come to you, even if they have accepted your faith."[96] The expression "any of our men" (*rajul*) obviously gave Muslims a loophole by which to exclude women from the application of this condition. This condition of the pact had not been put forward by them, but by the Meccans, and the actual wording had been dictated by the delegates of the Quraysh. It seems that when one of them, called Suhayl ibn 'Amr, was dictating, he was thinking of both men and women, but that the actual word he chose in order to convey "any person" (inclusive of both men and women) was *rajul*, which in Arabic is actually used only for men. Most probably this was why the Prophet could legitimately refuse — according to Imam Zuhri — to hand over Umm Kulthum bint 'Uqbah to her brothers when they came to him to demand her return. Razi is another annalist who records the Prophet on this occasion as having explained that "the condition applied to men and not to women."[97]

Thus God, by means of a single word, saved virtuous Muslim women from the humiliation of being returned to their oppressors.

WORKING OUTDOORS

According to 'Abdullah ibn Mas'ud, when Abu ad-Dahdah, one of the Prophet's Companions, heard the revelation of this Qur'anic verse: "Who will give a generous loan to God? He will pay him back two-fold and he shall receive a rich reward,"[98] he asked the Prophet, "O Messenger of God, does God want a loan from us?" When the Prophet replied in the affirmative, Abu ad-Dahdah took him by the hand, and said, "I hereby lend my orchard to God."

Abu ad-Dahdah's orchard was a sizeable one with six hundred date palms and, at the time he donated it to the cause of Islam, his wife, Umm ad-Dahdah, was staying in it with her children. Nevertheless, having made his pledge to the Prophet, Abu ad-Dahdah came to the orchard, called his wife and told her that she would have to leave, as it had been loaned to God. Umm ad-Dahdah's reaction was that he had made a good bargain. That is, that God would reward him many times over in the hereafter. So saying, she left the orchard with her children, taking with her all her bags and baggage.[99]

From this incident we can gather that Umm ad-Dahdah worked on the date orchard. There are many such incidents in the early phase of Islam (the exemplary phase) which show that certainly women were not confined indoors. They certainly went out in order to attend to many necessary outdoor duties. However, one point should be made clear: these outdoor activities of women were not engaged in entertainment but as a matter of necessity. They were meant to build up the family on proper lines and were in no sense intended to establish women's equality with men in the outside world.

WOMEN'S POSITION

The honorable position accorded by Islam to woman is symbolically demonstrated by the performance of the rite of *sa'i,* as an important part of the pilgrimage to Mecca, made at least once in a lifetime as a religious duty by all believers who can afford the journey. The rite of *sa'i* is performed by running back and forth seven times between Safa and Marwah, two hillocks near the Ka'bah. This running, enjoined upon every pilgrim, be they rich or poor, literate or illiterate, Kings or commoners, is in imitation of the desperate quest of Hajar (Hagar), Abraham's wife, for water to quench the thirst of her crying infant when they arrived in this dry desert country, four thousand years ago, at God's behest, long before there was any such city as Mecca. (God's aim in leading Abraham and his wife and child to this barren, inhospitable land was to bring into being a live community which, free of all superstitions and all other corruptions of civilization, would play a revolutionary role led by the last Prophet.) The performance of this rite is a lesson in struggling for the cause of God. It is of the utmost significance that, this was an act first performed by a woman. Perhaps there could be no better demonstration of a woman's greatness than God's command to men, literally to follow in her footsteps.

IN THE LIGHT OF EXPERIENCE

The position of women in Islam, as expounded so far in the pages of this book, is a matter neither of conjecture, abstract theory nor of ancient history. Nor is it purely a concept gleaned from readings of the Qur'an, the Hadith and the history of Islam. It is a matter of actual fact, to which I myself am a witness.

I give the example of the women of my own family who, in times of dire distress, were totally Islamic in their conduct. (I restrict myself to examples taken from my own family, because Islamic precepts do not favor a fuller acquaintance with women outside one's own family circle). Their nobility of character, under the severest of strains, is something to which I can testify, having seen it with my own eyes. The way in which they have come through certain ordeals in life is a clear proof that, *within the limits prescribed by Islam*, women can be positively constructive not only within their own domestic sphere, but also much further afield: they can indeed be a powerful and beneficial influence upon others.

I intend in my autobiography to give a fuller account of these experiences, but here I shall record only such details as are relevant to the role played by my mother. The daughter of Khuda Bux, she was born towards the end of the nineteenth century in the town of Sanjarpur (Azamgarh, U.P., India), and was given the name of Zaibun Nisa. When she passed away in Delhi on the 8th of October, 1985, she was about 100 years of age. The type of education she had permitted her to read only the Qur'an and a little Urdu: she was a religious woman in the fullest sense of the word. Never to my knowledge did she tell a lie, or act in a way which could be described as unethical. She was punctual in her prayers and fasting and also had performed Hajj. Spending her entire life in *hijab*, she was a woman of fine, upstanding character and unbending principle.

My father, Fariduddin Khan, died when I was very young — on December 30, 1929, to be exact. He was the biggest landlord in that part of the country, with lands spread over several villages. One day, on a routine visit to his farm in Newada, he suffered a paralytic stroke, fell unconscious and had to be carried home on a bedstead. There could be no words of final parting, for he passed away the next day without having regained consciousness. My mother, quite suddenly, found herself a widow. I had two brothers and two sisters. My elder brother, Abdul Aziz Khan, was barely 8 years old, I was 5 and my younger brother was just one year old. My sisters were older, but not even in their teens. Both of my sisters died during my mother's lifetime. By the grace of God my younger brother and I are still alive. My elder brother died in June 1988.

The death of our father at that time was a great blow, not only because we had lost a loving parent, but because of the treatment we received at the hands of certain members of our joint family. After father's death, these relatives took over the management of the entire family property. My grandfather, under the joint family system, was the person who had actually been entrusted with the management of the farm. But he was so honest that he would not take a single penny more than what was actually required to meet the barest of necessities. After his death, those who then took charge of the orchard exceeded all limits of injustice in their treatment of us. From being landowners of some substance, we suddenly found ourselves landless. There was no easy way out of our problems.

Our family home had been very commodious, but after father's death, we found ourselves in a disused, half-ruined stable. We lacked even the basic necessities of life, and were unable even to find enough money to buy food. At this juncture, people began to advise my mother to remarry, or return to her parents' home, or go to court to recover the land which was lawfully hers. But mother refused to follow any of this advice. Like the brave Muslim woman that she was, she resolved to face up to those circumstances on her own. This decision was backed up by just two things: faith in God and hard work.

Although my mother's parents owned a vast tract of land, 20 acres[100] of which had been willed to her by her father, she never demanded her share of the land, nor did she seek any help from the members of her family. She depended upon God alone: her sturdy independence was a shining example to us all.

I have seen how she would get up early every morning, say the prescribed prayers and then work right throughout the day without once stopping to rest. When she went to bed, it was always late and only after having said the *'isha* prayer. The tasks on which she spent her entire day included looking after poultry, goats, etc. In this way, I too found the opportunity to graze the goats, a *sunnah* (practice) of the prophets.

In addition to this work, she voluntarily stitched clothes for people in the neighborhood. Although she did not accept any money for this, her neighbors would send her grain and other comestibles in return for her good offices. This work was by no means easy for her, because it was done in the days before sewing machines had become popular, i.e. she did it entirely by hand. She also managed to keep a buffalo, and in our broad, open courtyard, she grew vegetables and planted fruit trees, like papaya and banana, which gave us a good yield. In those early days of penury, a woman passerby once remarked, "I see you have kittens to look after." We did indeed look like scraggy little kittens in those days, and if my mother had not made such extraordinary sacrifices in order to look after us, our fate might well have been no better than the little, stray, motherless kittens one sees wasting away in the streets.

My eyes are witness to my mother's total commitment over a prolonged period to our proper upbringing. But it would really take a whole book to do justice to her, and I have at my disposal just these last few pages.

How straitened were the circumstances in which we were living in those days can be judged by my not even having one paisa to buy a small piece of rubber for a catapult I was making. Hearing of this, one of our acquaintances kindly gave me the money for it. It was galling to think that once having been the biggest landowning family in the area, we had now come to such a sorry pass.

To be quite honest, after our father's death we had not even the smallest pittance to call our own. The hardships my mother faced at that time are now barely imaginable. It is greatly to her credit that she bore up as well as any man. And from within the confines of the four walls of her home — such as it was — she contrived to influence the external world. She gained the upper hand over her circumstances where such circumstances might well have proved too overwhelming. The most remarkable feature of her attainments is that she succeeded in achieving, within the limits set for her by Islam, all those objectives for which it is now considered necessary to make women emerge from the Islamic fold — in the process, divesting themselves of their essentially feminine virtues.

Whatever she did, she did in the true spirit of Islam. Instead of turning to man, she turned to God. Instead of thinking in terms of the world, she focussed her attention on the hereafter. All her actions were perfectly in consonance with traditional religious thinking. She had received no such higher education as would have lead her to consider the philosophical implications of the course she took. But now, at the mature age of 60, when I look at her strivings through the eyes of a scholar, I see in them the manifestations of human greatness. Even if she had left her home in quest of such higher education as would have fitted her for a post in some secular organization, I do not think she could have done any better for us than she did. Even to imagine her taking such a course of action is quite meaningless.

My mother's sacrifices made it possible for her not only to give us a satisfactory upbringing, but also to demonstrate what the Islamic bent of mind — positive thinking and a realistic approach — is capable of achieving. My brothers and I were greatly influenced by the example she set. In fact, this was the greatest gift that she could have bestowed upon us. In giving us this awareness of the virtues of Islam, she fulfilled the duties of both father and mother.

I can still recall that after my father's death, a maternal uncle, Shaikh Abdul Ghafur, used to pay us frequent visits. A great expert in legal matters, he insisted that my mother should file a suit to recover the land which had been willed to her by her father, but which relatives by marriage were unwilling to relinquish. He assured her that all she had to do was to append her signature to the legal documents relevant to her claim on the land and that he would do whatever else was required. He promised her that she would soon have control of all the land of which she was the rightful owner. He continued to pay her visits over a long period of time and went on in the same vein each time, but my mother refused to allow herself to be persuaded by him.

Being deprived of the property from our father's side, to which we were legally entitled, did, of course become a source of great provocation, and we increasingly felt the urge to fight for our rights. Ultimately, it was through the intervention of others that we were given some tracts of land, but this hardly improved our situation, for, human nature being what it is, it was all the arid and unproductive land which fell to our lot. This niggardly treatment had the effect of making us want to plunge into the fray to do battle with the other party, but my mother staunchly adhered to her policy of patience, often admonishing us to exercise greater self-control. On such occasions she would recite to us this line of poetry:

Patience is the price of eternal paradise.

Our family circumstances which, it appeared, could be improved only by resorting to litigation, were certainly such us to lead us all into negative thinking. Litigation meant a number of families all being drawn into the quarrel, with the inevitable series of unpleasant confrontations. It could even mean the loss of valuable lives, for such situations bring out the most baneful characteristics in all of us. Had our mother not chosen to adopt the only attitude which could be considered positive under the circumstances, we might, at that early formative stage, have fallen prey to unreasoning destructiveness. Each of us would have become permanently tainted by hatred and the desire for revenge.

It was really mother's single-mindedness in remaining patient that altered the entire course of our lives. She taught us that it would be wrong to fight against those who deprived us of our rights, and inculcated in us the belief that the only course for us to adopt was to improve our lot in life by dint of sheer hard work. She encouraged us to turn our eyes away from what had been denied us and, instead, to give our full attention to that which we still enjoyed, namely, our God-given existence.

Today, my evaluation of this attitude is a rational, conscious process, but in our youth, our positive mental adaptation to negative circumstances was, as it were, an unconscious process stimulated by my mother's training. This capacity for detachment having become a permanent trait in all of us, we were able to steer clear of confrontations, and chose instead a course of action which should be free of disputes. We three brothers may all have followed different paths, but our basic attitude remained unaltered. That is to say that we studiously ignored the injustice of our immediate environment, and endeavored to pursue a morally correct course of action in the broader spectrum of the outside world. If we were deprived by man, we would seek from God. My elder brother, Abdul Aziz Khan, went into business when he grew up, "emigrating" to the town of Azamgarh in 1944. At the outset, he had a long, hard struggle, for he never borrowed, never accepted credit. Only after 40 years of strenuous effort, did he attain the position of Chairman of the Light & Company Ltd., an Allahabad firm which produces electrical goods. From being considered the least important member of our very large family after father's death, he became its most respected member. He even succeeded in having his share of the family lands restored to him by having the property re-divided in a just manner. The most noteworthy feature of this redistribution is that he caused it to come about without once resorting to litigation.

My younger brother, who opted for scientific studies, received his degree in engineering from the Benaras Hindu University. He later entered the Department of Technical Education run by the Government of Uttar Pradesh, from which he retired as Deputy Director. By virtue of his hard work, faultless character and principled life, he commanded the respect of his whole department.

As for myself, I was interested in religious education, having been initially educated in an Arabic school. I later worked hard to learn the English language and made a thorough study of whatever academic literature was available to me in English. Now, by the grace of God, I am able to work in a positive and constructive manner, as I am sure the readers of my works will confirm.

One special aspect of my work — the call to Muslims to rise above negative thinking and become more positive in their approach — has found an effective vehicle in the *Al-Risala* monthly which I started in 1976. *Al-Risala*'s mission has, by the grace of God, assumed the form of a powerful movement all over the Muslim world. I frequently receive oral or written comments from academic circles which acknowledge that *Al-Risala*'s is the first Islamic movement in modern times which has attempted to steer Muslims resolutely away from negative activities, and set their feet on the path of positivism.

I thank all those who have been good enough to encourage me; but the real credit for my achievements must go by rights to that devoted Muslim woman called Zaibun Nisa. In this material world of ours, if there is anyone who may be fittingly called the initial founder of this modern, constructive movement, it is certainly my mother. She had never heard of "Women's Lib," being very far removed in space, time and culture from such activities, but it is worthy of note that she needed none of the philosophizing of the women's liberationists to be able to perform what she regarded as her bounden duty in the eyes of God. Whereas my brothers and I set about our tasks in life in a reasoned, conscious manner, for her it was all a matter of instinct, prayer and faith.

I know more than one of my own relatives who, having lost his mother at an early age, became destructive in outlook. We must never underestimate the role of woman as mother. It is perhaps her greatest role in human affairs. In Islamic history, there are numerous examples of the strong and decisive influence of mothers upon their families. A notable example is Maryam Makani, the mother of the Emperor Akbar. When Akbar was harsh in his treatment of Shaikh 'Abdun Nabi, a great religious scholar of his time, she convinced him of the error he was making, and persuaded him to stop what amounted to persecution.

I cannot but imagine that if I had been deprived of my mother in early childhood, or if I had the kind of mother who kept urging me to fight our "enemies," my life would have taken an entirely different, and downward course. Undeniably it is the grace of God which has saved me from an ill-fated existence and caused me to become a medium of expression of the truth. But in this world of cause and effect, the human purveyor of God's will was a lady, a mother, a housewife — one who was Islamic to her very fingertips.

Notes

1. Qur'an, 4:19.
2. Qur'an, 2:228.
3. Qur'an, 4:7.
4. Qur'an, 30:21.
5. Qur'an, 40:40.
6. Qur'an, 4:124.
7. Qur'an, 16:97.
8. Qur'an, 9:71.
9. Qur'an, 3:195.
10. *Kanz al-'Ummal*, 16/371.
11. Ibn Majah, *Sunan, Kitab an-Nikah*, 1/636.
12. Muslim, *Sahih, Kitab ar-Rada'*, 2/1091.
13. At-Tirmidhi, *Sahih, Abwab ar-Rada'*, 2/1091.
14. An-Nasa'i, *Sunan, Kitab an-Nikah*, 6/68.
15. Ibid., 6/69.
16. Abu Dawud, *Sunan*.
17. At-Tirmidhi, *Sahih, Abwab at-Tafsir*, 11/238.
18. Ibn Majah, *Sunan, Kitab an-Nikah*, 1/596.
19. Al-Haythami, *Majma' al-Zawa'id wa Manba' al-Fawa'id, Kitab an-Nikah*, 4/273.
20. Al-Bukhari, *Sahih, Kitab an-Nikah*, (*Fath al-Bari*, 9/206-207).
21. Abu Dawud, *Sunan, Kitab at-Taharah*, 1/61.
22. Ibn Majah, *Sunan, Kitab al-Manasik*, 2/1025.
23. Jalaluddin al-Suyuti, *Al-Jami' as-Saghir fi Ahadith al-Bashir an-Nadhir*, 1/536.
24. Abu Dawud, *Sunan, Kitab al-Adab*, 4/338.
25. Ibid., 4/337.
26. Ibn Majah, *Sunan, Kitab al-Adab*, 2/1209-10.
27. At-Tirmidhi, *Sahih, Abwab al-Birr was-Silah*, 8/105.
28. Qur'an, 3:195.
29. Qur'an, 33:35.
30. Abu Dawud, *Sunan, Kitab al-Jihad*, 3/5.
31. Qur'an, 22:46.
32. Qur'an, 4:1.
33. Bible, Genesis, 2:21-23.
34. Qur'an, 16:72
35. Qur'an, 30:21.
36. Qur'an, 42:11.
37. Al-Bukhari, *Sahih, Kitab an-Nikah* (*Fath al-Bari*, 9/207).
38. Ibid., 9/207.
39. Al-Bukhari, *Sahih, Kitab al-Adab*, (*Fath al-Bari*, 10/454).
40. *Encyclopaedia Britannica* (1984), 19/907.
41. Criminal Appeal No. 103-1981 — dated April 23, 1985.
42. Al-Bukhari, *Sahih, Kitab as-Salah*, (*Fath al-Bari*, 2/160).
43. Qur'an, 3:195.
44. Al-Bukhari, *Sahih, Kitab al-Libas*, (*Fath al-Bari*, 10/273).
45. Qur'an, 4:21.
46. Ibn Majah, *Sunan, Kitab an-Nikah*, 1/593.
47. Qur'an, 4:19.
48. Al-Bukhari, *Sahih, Kitab al-Adab* (*Fath al-Bari*, 10/329-330).
49. Qur'an, 4:20.
50. Al-Baihaqi, *as-Sunan al-Kubra, Kitab as-Sudaq*, 7/533.
51. *Kanz al-'Ummal*, 16/411.

52. Muslim, *Sahih, Kitab Sifat al-Munafiqin wa Ahkamihim,* 4/2167.
53. *Time,* March 20, 1972.
54. *The Times of India* (New Delhi), August 14, 1987.
55. Al-Bukhari, *Sahih, Kitab al-Maghazi, (Fath al-Bari,* 8/104-105).
56. Qur'an, 2:282.
57. *The Times of India* (New Delhi), January 18, 1985.
58. Qur'an, 4:34.
59. Qur'an, 13:4.
60. 'Abdullah Yusuf 'Ali, *The Holy Qur'an: Text, Translation and Commentary,* p. 587.
61. Qur'an, 4:32.
62. At-Tirmidhi, *Sahih, Abwab al-Manaqib,* 13/257.
63. *Encyclopaedia Britannica* (1984), 1/167.
64. Al-Bukhari, *Sahih, Kitab Ahadith al-Anbiya', (Fath al-Bari,* 7/104-105).
65. Muslim, *Sahih, Kitab Fada'il as-Sahabah,* 4/188.
66. Al-Haythami, *Majma' al-Zawa'id wa Manba' al-Fawa'id, Kitab al-Manaqib,* 9/224.
67. Ibn Kathir, *As-Sirah an-Nabawiyah,* 1/386.
68. Ibid., 1/408-409.
69. Ibid., 1/404.
70. Ibid., 1/399.
71. Ibn Sa'd, *at-Tabaqat al-Kubra,* 8/378-380.
72. Qur'an, 58:1.
73. 'Umayr is a diminutive of 'Umar.
74. Al-Qurtubi, *Al-Jami' li Ahkamil Qur'an,* 17/269-270.
75. The animals were to be sacrificed after the performance of Hajj. However, the Quraysh did not allow the Muslims to enter Mecca. The terms of the treaty were humiliating. The Muslims were so disconcerted at not being allowed to make the pilgrimage that they were in no state of mind to follow the Prophet's command.
76. Ibn Kathir, *As-Sirah an-Nabawiyah,* 1/386.
77. Ibn Majah, *Sunan, Al-Muqaddimah* 17, 1/81.
78. Sayings and deeds of the Prophet's Companions.
79. Az-Zarkali, *Al-A'lam* (Beirut, 1979), 2/86.
80. Ibn Kathir, *As-Sirah an-Nabawiyah,* 1/494.
81. Ibn Sa'd, *At-Tabaqat al-Kubra,* 3/250.
82. Qur'an, 39:9.
83. Ibn Kathir, *As-Sirah an-Nabawiyyah,* 2/236.
84. Bukhari, *Sahih, Kitab an-Nikah, (Fath al-Bari,* 9/264-265).
85. Qur'an, 9:34.
86. Ibn Kathir, *Tafsir,* II/352.
87. Ibn Hajar al-'Athqalani, *Fath al-Bari fi Sharh al-Bukhari,* 2/284-288.
88. Bukhari, *Sahih, Kitab al-Jumu'a,* 2/307.
89. Ibn Sa'd, *Tabaqat al-Kubra,* 8/292.
90. Ibn Kathir, *Al-Bidayah wa an-Nihayah,* 4/108-109.
91. Ibn Kathir, *As-Sirah an-Nabawiyah,* 3/321.
92. Ibid., 3/321-335.
93. Qur'an, 60:10.
94. Ibn Hajar al-'Athqalani, *Fath al-Bari,* 7/366.
95. *Ahkam al-Qur'an,* Edited by 'Ali Muhammad al-Bajawi (Beirut, 1987), 4/1786.
96. Bukhari, *Sahih, Kitab ash-Shurut fi al-Jihad wa al-Musalah (Fath al-Bari,* 5/262).
97. Ibn Hajar al-'Athqalani, *Fath al-Bari,* 9/345.
98. Qur'an, 57:11.
99. Ibn Kathir, *Tafsir,* 4/308.
100. One acre is equivalent to 4840 square yards, or 4047 square meters.

CHAPTER 6

The Rights of Husband and Wife

The Qur'an states: "They (women) are your garments. And you (men) are their garments."[1] These words from the holy scriptures define how men and women relate to each other — like body and its garments. Without garments a body is meaningless, and without a body garments are meaningless. The two must go together, for apart they have little reason to exist. This symbolizes the closeness of the two sexes in the material and spiritual senses.

How beautiful a bird appears with its feathers, but if all the feathers are to be removed, it would be totally disfigured. The importance of the feather to the bird is similar to the importance of the garment to a man. A man without a garment is just like a bird without its feathers.

This example of garments shows the great importance men and women have for each other, for, without each other, they are incomplete. They are the closest of companions — a relationship which is both natural and inevitable. Each derives strength from the other, and each acts as a shield for the other. They are described by a commentator of the Qur'an as "fitting into each other as a garment fits the body."[2] Men and women were created to find sexual attraction in one another. The Qur'an makes this point in these words:

And among His Signs is this, that He created for you mates from among yourselves, that you may dwell in tranquility with them, and He has put love and mercy between your (hearts): Verily in that are Signs for those who reflect.[3]

It is in the context of this natural relationship that men and women are attracted to each other. This attraction finds expression in the free mixing of men and women. But this goes against the human grain. A man would normally want whatever belonged to him to be reserved for him alone. Free sexual relations are therefore at variance with human nature.

It is often said, with justice, that man is a social animal. But more important is the fact that man is an ethical animal. There may be a physical resemblance between human beings and animals, but, from the moral standpoint, man is in a class by himself, animals knowing none of the self-imposed, ethical constraints which govern human lives. It is this ethical sense in man and other civilizational demands which require members of the opposite sex to refrain from establishing free sexual relations. The natural urge to procreate must, according to the *shari'ah,* be confined within the bonds of wedlock. Men and women are enjoined by the *shari'ah* to marry (barring certain close relations) and to lead a family life. The Qur'an says:

> Except for these (prohibited) all others are lawful, provided you seek (them in marriage) with gifts from your property, desiring chastity not lust.[4]

Sexual attraction between men and women is the result of a natural biological urge. It was to give this relationship legal sanction that the institution of marriage (*nikah*) was established. Human psychology, biological realities and social considerations all demand that sexual relationships between men and women should be regularized and placed on a stable basis. And for such organization, there is no better solution, than marriage. The human way is the way of marriage: free mixing is inhuman.

LIFE PARTNER

What fundamentally determines the rights and duties of men and women in the roles of husbands and wives is the fact that they are partners for life. This basic principle is derived from the verse of the Qur'an which says that men and women are part of one another.[5]

In this respect the difference between the tenets of modern civilization and the rulings of the *shari'ah* is that, the former hold men and women to be equals, while the latter hold men and women to be lifelong partners.

It is this difference which shows that the two systems are poles apart.

A RELIGION OF NATURE

Islam being a religion of nature, its teachings are based on simple principles of nature. When these principles are earnestly adhered to, the family becomes a cradle of peace and amity.

Many details have been formulated by the jurists of Islam regarding the relationship between men and women. Here we are not concerned with legal details. I would like here to state only those basic principles which are laid down in the Qur'an and the Hadith, which serve as the basis of the Islamic way of life. (Legal details are available in all the standard books, which may be consulted by anyone who is interested in the legal aspects of marriage.)

THE POSITION OF MAN VIS-À-VIS WOMAN

When a man and a woman enter into the marital bond, they bring into existence a social unit called the family. Like any other social unit, this requires an organizer or supervisor. For this special role, Islam has chosen man.

> Men are the protectors and maintainers of women, because God has made some of them to excell others, and because they support them from their means.[6]

Making man the maintainer in no way indicates that man is superior to woman. This choice is based on man's capacities for management rather than on his superiority. In a democratic system, everyone has been granted an equal status yet when a government is formed, one particular individual is entrusted with supreme political power. This does not mean that this possesser of power is superior to other citizens. In a democratic system, the president or the prime minister has one vote like all the other citizens. Even then, in the interest of good management authority is entrusted to a single individual.

Except for man's role as manager, man and woman have completely equal status. For instance, if a woman kills a man, and the crime is proved, the woman will be required to pay the penalty (Qur'an, 2:178). Similarly, as a *hadith* tells us, if a man kills a woman, after the crime is proved, "Verily the man will be killed for having killed a woman."[7]

There is no legal discrimination in the eyes of the *shari'ah* between woman and man. The laws applicable to men are also applicable to women.

DOWER

After *nikah* the first obligation upon a man in regard to his wife is to give her the *mahr* fixed at the time of marriage:

And give the women (on marriage) their dower as a free gift.[8]

The *mahr* is in no way a payment for conjugal rights. Conjugal rights are far too precious to be equated with what is normally given as mahr. The amount of mahr is, in actual fact, a token sum of money, which symbolizes, in material form, the responsibility that a man has to fulfill in regard to his wife till his last breath.

What is this responsibility? It is that man will maintain and protect his wife for life. In the family organization the *shari'ah* has basically entrusted the woman with looking after the house, bringing up and training the next generation. This task is not a profitable one. That is why a woman's maintenance is entrusted to her husband. If a woman had to shoulder both the responsibility of looking after the house as well as making money, she would not be able to perform either of the two duties properly. That is why her economic maintenance has been entrusted to her husband so that the proper upkeep of the home and family is guaranteed. At the beginning of marital life a man makes this pledge symbolically by giving the woman a sum of money in the form of *mahr*.

MAINTENANCE

The specific monetary form of the symbolic pledge is called "maintenance." Each office brings with it responsibility, that of a man being the upkeep of his wife.

In the home, man is the protector (the head). This is because man is by birth the stronger sex in the physical sense. This in no way means that he is superior to woman in the absolute sense. Whatever superiority he has relates only to those traits which make a man deserving of the office of maintainer. The wording of the above mentioned verse (4:34) means that everyone is superior to others in some particular respect. The distinguishing features required for becoming a maintainer (*qawwam*) are more numerous in men than in women, that is why he has been selected as the *qawwam* of the house. Conversely, the distinguishing features required for maintaining the home, for the bringing up and training of new generations are more numerous in women than in men. It is due to this kind of superiority in women that they have been entrusted with the internal affairs of the home.

A woman has a legal right to maintenance, which devolves upon her husband. If he fails in this regard, the woman can receive it through the court. The amount of maintenance will, however, be fixed in relation to the man's means. If his income is low, the amount of maintenance will be reduced, and if it is high, the rate of maintenance will go up.

PROPER BEHAVIOR

Man has been bound at all events to treat women kindly:

> Live with them on a footing of kindness and equity. If ye take a dislike to them it may be that ye dislike a thing and God brings about through it a great deal of good.[9]

This shows that man has been bound to behave gently with women not only in pleasant, but also in unpleasant circumstances. This is an absolute injunction applying to all situations. A man has to be kind to his wife, whether or not she is to his liking.

The injunction on gentle behaviour with women is so important that this is held to be the essential condition for having more than one wife. That is the permission to have more than one wife is given only to those who can treat all of them with perfect justice. The Qur'an says: "But if you fear that you shall not be able to deal justly (with them) then only one."[10]

The Qur'anic injunction of "gentle behavior"[11] covers all those things human nature demands, and whatever is considered necessary, by reason or by the *shari'ah*. This fair treatment is considered so important in Islam that the Prophet said: "The best among you is one who is best for his family."[12]

THE RESPONSIBILITIES OF A WOMAN AS A WIFE

How should a woman or a wife live with her husband? This has been instilled into the woman by nature itself. If a woman is of a really serious cast of mind, her inner nature will suffice to guide her in this matter. This has been expressed in the following verse of the Qur'an:

> Therefore the righteous women are devoutly obedient, and guard in (the husband's) absence what God would have them guard.[13]

The responsibilities of woman as regards man described by the Qur'an and *sunnah* are in complete accord with this feminine nature. If a woman's nature is alive and she wishes to lead her life as a realist, she will not find any strangeness in the teachings of Islam; rather she will accept them as if they were the voice of her own heart. Here I would present these teachings of Islam in brief under different headings.

OBEDIENCE

The Qur'an says that "the righteous women are devoutly obedient."[14] The word *qanitat* (obedient women) has been interpreted by 'Abdullah ibn 'Abbas as meaning women who are obedient to their husbands.[15] That is, the righteous women in the eyes of God are those who are obedient to their husbands.

It is natural for a man who has been entrusted with the maintenance of family life to expect obedience from his wife. Without that, the division of labor would be meaningless. The husband is just like the ruler of a country who can function as such only when the public is ready to obey him. In the face of public disobedience, even the best of rulers will have no control over the running of the country.

The same is also true of the internal workings of the home. The home is the basic unit of the vaster organization of the nation. It is only when the smaller units are in order, that the larger unit can function successfully. It is, therefore, absolutely essential that the home should be marked by an atmosphere of obedience and conformance. Of course, the woman enjoys the right to dissent and to give advice. But once the man has come to a decision, it becomes incumbent upon the woman to abide loyally by that decision.

Having more experience of the outside world, a man is somewhat more broad-minded than a woman. His thinking is more realistic. A woman's thinking, on the contrary, is often marked by limitations. She easily falls prey to emotion. She inherits this as part of her nature, and so far as her sphere of home-based activity is concerned, her limitations or emotions are in no way a deficiency. However, a woman must be aware of her natural shortcomings. She can advise the man, but inflexible insistence on her part is not proper.

The system of the house is similar to a miniature democracy. But every democratic system has a leader. And according to *shari'ah* the leader of the democracy at home is the man.

THE GUARDING OF THE SECRET

Another right of man over woman has been described in the Qur'an in these words: "...and guard in (the husband's) absence what God would have them guard."[16]

Woman is man's garment. Just as a garment is closest to man so a woman is closest to man. A husband and a wife are the only companions between whom there is no secret even of hidden parts.

Due to this close relation a woman comes to have access to all of man's secrets. She comes to learn the most private and concealed facts of his life. This is a delicate state of affairs. Every man has his secrets. He dislikes their being brought to the knowledge of others. But a man cannot hide these things from his wife. So he makes no effort to do so. Such an attempt would neither be useful nor practically possible.

The solution offered by the Islamic *shari'ah* is to make it binding upon the woman to guard the man's secrets. In no circumstances may she reveal them to others. If she shows carelessness in this regard, she should fear God for revealing her secrets to others. If God unveils her in the next life, no one will ever be able to come to her rescue.

It is a fact that when two people live together, it is inevitable that differences and complaints will arise. Keeping this fact in mind, the Qur'anic injunction on the guarding of man's secrets specifies that, even if a woman bears her husband a grudge it will still be unlawful for her to reveal his secrets. Even if she has differences with her husband she is not at liberty to disclose to others matters which he wishes to have kept in strict confidence.

A woman is man's secret-keeper. She is bound to remain so till the end of her days.

THE MANAGEMENT OF THE HOME

Addressing women, the Qur'an says: "Stay in your homes."[17] The commentators of the Qur'an have explained that in this verse a woman's staying at home means that her sphere of activities should be her home.[18]

In modern times a woman has become an external show-piece, whereas according to the scheme of Islam a woman should stay at home and look after the internal responsibilities. Housekeeping, family requirements, management of all affairs at home, looking after the children — all are the woman's responsibility: "staying at home" covers it all.

Looking after a home is like looking after a state, even if it is on a much smaller scale. It is certainly as important and respectable a task as that carried out by a head of state: a woman should, therefore, engage herself in domestic affairs with the same zeal and energy as a genuine head of state, devoting her full potential to making her home an ideal one. She should nurture and cherish it as a gardener does his garden. As one of the *hadith* puts it: 'The woman is the guardian of her husband's home and she is accountable for it.'[19]

Proficiency in domestic matters is woman's greatest ornament. A woman so equipped is the perfect woman, one deserving of honor and success in the life hereafter.

THE BEST WOMAN

The Prophet Muhammad was once asked who of all women was the best. He replied, "One who makes her husband happy when he sees her, who obeys her husband when he asks her for anything and who does not do anything against his will as regards either herself or his wealth."[20] This *hadith* very aptly points out a woman's duties towards her husband.

After facing the hardship of the outside world the man comes back home. Now the best wife is one who can bring him comfort and cheer. She should become a regular source of solace to her husband. Even when, on occasion, he asks her to do something without explaining all the pros and cons, she should — if she is a successful life partner — create no trouble over this at home, but do her utmost to see that her husband's plans come to fruition. Her husband should also be able to trust her personally in her conduct, and rest assured that all his belongings will be properly looked after by her. The loyal wife then becomes the husband's trustee in the fullest sense of the word.

As well as being a comfort to her husband, she has to act as his deputy at home. The best kind of woman is one who fulfills both these responsibilities. There is a *hadith* which very aptly says: "Of the worldly goods, there is nothing better than a virtuous wife."[21]

GIVING IMPORTANCE TO THE INWARD
RATHER THAN THE OUTWARD

On the subject of their wives, the Qur'an enjoins men: "Treat them with kindness; for even if you do dislike them it may well be that you may dislike a thing which God has meant for your own good."[22]

The same point has been made in a *hadith:* "No believing man should hate a believing woman. Even if he does not like one of her habits, another of her ways will be of his liking."[23] To put it differently, this teaching means that even if outwardly unpleasant, a wife should not cause aversion, because God has not made anyone imperfect in all respects. All men and women, if deficient in some respects are gifted in other respects.

Once, a newly married man found when he brought his wife home that she was not gifted with feminine graces. Instead of having a slender figure she was stout like a man. He was put off by her not being slim as he would have liked. But events soon took a strange turn. Having met with an accident, he was not able to work hard. Now his stout wife decided to support her husband and worked hard to make money. Being sturdy, she succeeded in earning money as well as looking after the home. In this way the family suffered no setback. Now the husband realized that the woman he had taken as a curse was indeed a blessing in disguise. Although his wife was not gifted with slimness, she had been blessed with another quality which had proved so precious at his time of need.

It is this aspect of life which has been emphasized in the Qur'an in these words:

> Take in marriage these women among you who are single and those of your male and female slaves who are virtuous. If they are poor, God will enrich them from His own abundance.[24]

There is a *hadith* to the same effect: 'God Himself has taken charge of helping three types of person. Those who marry in their desire to preserve their chastity, and those slaves (*mukatib*) who want to be free by paying the money they owe to their masters, and those who want to fight in the cause of God."[25]

BALANCED EDUCATION

When there are two parties in any undertaking, it is common for both parties to concentrate on their own personal gain. It is less common for each to think of the other's good. In the latter case, one's attention is fixed on one's responsiblities, while in the former it is on one's rights. The latter leads one to a higher moral plane while the former leads to evil.

When a man's eyes are on his rights, he holds the other party responsible for everything. As a result, he is always in a frustrated state and wants to revenge himself on the other party. Failing to do his duty himself, he merely wants the other party to keep giving him all that is due to him.

Conversely, when one's eyes are on one's own responsiblities, one's critical faculties are focussed on oneself. One is keen to know one's own short-comings. As a result, the psychology of self-reckoning is aroused and one becomes serious-minded. All one's strength is diverted from destruction to construction. Such action makes the other party serious too, so that he feels compelled to fulfill his responsibilities in like manner.

This is the Islamic way. If one party is weaker, Islam enjoins him to remain patient, while exhorting the other party, the stronger, to tread the path of justice and fair play.

The guidance of Islam regarding the relationship between husband and wife, is, in some respects, based on this principle. From the physiological standpoint, the woman is the weaker and the man the stronger party. That is why in its guidelines Islam keeps this difference in mind, so that more and more harmony and cooperation may build up between the two, and the task of home building may proceed smoothly and without any hindrance.

While Islam enjoins women to become obedient to their husbands, the Qur'an says that virtuous women are already obedient to their husbands.[26] 'Abdullah ibn 'Abbas has interpreted this verse in these words: "women obedient to their husbands."[27]

What is intended by making women obedient to their husbands is to cultivate in them the kind of fine temperament that will make them true partners to their husbands. This will result in a positive and constructive atmosphere at home rather than one of confrontation and discord. An obedient wife wins the heart of her husband and thus gains the upper hand. Hers is the highest place at home. A disobedient wife, on the contrary, keeps quarrelling with her husband so that her whole life in consequence is marred with bitterness.

So far as men are concerned, Islam aims at cultivating fair mindedness on all occasions. Being the maintainer of the house, the man should not lose sight of the fact that after death he will be faced with the greatest of the Lords and Masters. There he will not be able to justify himself for being hard to those who were under him in the world, while those who were kind to people under them will be given kind treatment by God. Here is a *hadith* to this effect, related by 'Aishah: The Prophet said, "The best of you is one who is best for his family, and I am best of all of you for my family."[28]

According to this *hadith* home is not a place for ruling, but a place for training. One who does well in the system of his home, will prove to be good for the whole of society and the nation. On the other hand one who is bad for his home will be bad for the whole of society and the nation. The former is a blessing for the vaster humanity while the latter is a curse.

The rights of men and women, in reality, are not a matter of legal lists, but rather it is a matter of good living. The points or the lists mentioned here are not exhaustive. They are only pointers to what makes for a good life at home. In such matters one cannot make a complete list of "do's and don'ts."

Islam wants both the man and the woman to acknowledge natural realities. Both should keep their eyes on their responsibilities rather than on their rights. Both should attach real importance to the common goal (the proper maintenance of the family system) rather than on their own selves, and should be ever willing to make any personal sacrifice aimed at this goal.

A good home is made by people of a good temperament. A good family can be brought into being by those men and women who have succeeded in cultivating an awareness within themselves. The secret of success in married life depends more on an awareness of 'life's realities' than on any list of "do's and don'ts." Those who are aware of life's realities will never be a failure, while those who do not know life's realities will never meet with success in this world.

Notes

1. Qur'an, 2 : 187.
2. 'Abdullah Yusuf 'Ali's commentary of 2:187.
3. Qur'an, 30:21.
4. Qur'an, 4:24.
5. Qur'an, 3:195.
6. Qur'an, 4:34.
7. Bukhari, *Sahih, Kitab ad-Diyat, (Fath al-Bari*, 12/180).
8. Qur'an, 4:4.
9. Qur'an, 4:19.
10. Qur'an, 4:3.
11. Qur'an, 4:19.
12. Ibn Majah, *Sunan, Kitab an-Nikah*, 1/636.
13. Qur'an, 4:34.
14. Qur'an, 4:34.
15. Ibn Kathir, *Tafsir*, 1/492.
16. Qur'an, 4:34.
17. Qur'an, 33:33.
18. Ibn Kathir, *Tafsir*, 3/483.
19. Bukhari, *Sahih, Kitab al-Jumu'ah, (Fath al-Bari*, 2/304).
20. An-Nasa'i, *Sunan, Kitab an-Nikah*, 6/68.
21. Ibn Majah, *Sunan, Kitab an-Nikah*, 1/596.
22. Qur'an, 4:19.
23. Muslim, *Sahih, Kitab ar-Rada'*, 2/1091.
24. Qur'an, 24:32.
25. Ibn Majah, *Sunan, Kitab al-'Itq*, 2/842.
26. Qur'an, 4:34.
27. Ibn Kathir, *Tafsir*, 1/491.
28. Ibn Majah, *Sunan, Kitab an-Nikah*, 1/636.

CHAPTER 7

Polygamy and Islam

In terms of the birth rate, men and women are almost equal in number. But subsequently, for a variety of reasons, the number of men in society decreases, leaving an excess of women. Now the question arises as to what should be the solution to this problem. In view of the inevitability of this imbalance, how is a healthy relationship between the sexes to be established? The choice for us, therefore, is not between monogamy and polygamy, but rather, between the lawful polygamy of Islam or the illicit polygamy of non-Islamic peoples.

One of the commandments given in the Qur'an as a matter of social organization concerns polygamy, that is permission for a man to marry up to four women:

> If you fear that you cannot treat orphans with fairness, then you may marry such women (widowed) as seem good to you : two, three or four of them. But if you fear that you cannot do justice, marry one only.[1]

This verse was revealed after the Battle of Uhud (Shawwal 3 A.H.) in which seventy Muslims were martyred. Suddenly, seventy homes in Medina were bereft of all male members, and the question arose as to how all these widows and orphans were to be cared for. This was an acute social problem. It was solved by the revelation of this verse asking the people who could afford it to take care of the orphans, by marrying the widows and keeping their orphaned children under their guardianship.

The background and wording of this verse appear to express a commandment which should be only temporary in effect. That is to say that it applied only to a particular state of emergency when, due to loss of men in battle, the number of women exceeded the number of available men. But the Qur'an, despite its having been revealed at a particular time and place, is universal in its application. One of the great characteristics of the Qur'an is that it describes eternal realities, with reference to temporal issues, this commandment being typical of this special quality of the Qur'an.

One point greatly in need of clarification is the fact that in the matter of marrying more than one woman, the initiative does not lie solely with any individual man. There is always the condition — an inescapable one — that whatever the society, the women should outnumber the men. Suppose the earth were inhabited by one billion people out of which 500 million were men and 500 million were women. It would not then be possible in such a situation for a man to have more than one wife. A second, third or fourth wife would be obtained only by force. But in Islam, a forced marriage is not considered lawful. According to the shari'ah the willingness of the bride-to-be is a compulsory condition.

Looked at from a practical angle, the above commandment of the Qur'an can be complied with only if that particular situation exists in society which existed in Medina after the Battle of Uhud — that is, there is a disproportion in the ratio of men and women. In the absence of such a situation, this commandment of the Qur'an would be inapplicable. But studies of human society and its history have shown that the situation in ancient Medina was not one which existed only at a particular point in time. It is a situation which had almost always been prevalent throughout the entire world. That situation of emergency is, in fact, the general situation of mankind. This commandment is yet another proof of God's omniscience. His commandment, seemingly elicited by an emergency, became an eternal commandment for the whole of our world.

THE INEQUALITY IN NUMBERS

Records show that male and female births are almost equal in number. But a study of mortality shows that the rate is higher for men than for women. This disparity is in evidence from early childhood to extreme old age. According to the Encyclopaedia Britannica: "In general, the risk of death at any given age is less for females than for males."[2]

The proportionately higher numbers of women in society can be traced to a variety of causes. For instance, when war breaks out, the majority of the casualties are men. In the First World War (1914-18) about 8 million soldiers were killed. Most of the civilians killed were also men. In the Second World War (1939-45) about 60 million people were either killed or maimed for life, most of them men. In the Iraq-Iran war alone (1979-1988), 82,000 Iranian women and about 100,000 Iraqi women were widowed. All in the space of ten years.

Another drain on the availability of men in society is imprisonment. In the U.S., the most civilized society of modern times, no less than 1,300,000 people are convicted daily for one crime or another. A number of them — 97% of whom are men — are obliged to serve lengthy prison sentences.[3]

The modern industrial system too is responsible for the lower proportion of men in society, death by accident having become a matter of daily routine in present times. There is no country in which accidents do not take place every day on the streets, in the factories and wherever sophisticated, heavy machinery is handled by human beings. In this modern industrial age, such accidents are so much on the increase that a whole new discipline has come into being — safety engineering. According to data collected in 1967, in that year a total of 175,000 people died as the result of accidents in fifty different countries. Most of these were men.[4]

In spite of safety engineering, casualties from industrial accidents have increased. For instance, the number of air accidents in 1988 was higher than ever before. Similarly, experimentation in arsenals continues to kill people in all industrialized countries, but the death toll is never made public. Here again, it is men who have the highest casualty rate.

For reasons of this nature, women continue to outnumber men. This difference persists in even the most developed societies, e.g. in America. According to data collected in 1967, there were nearly 7,100,000 more women than men. This means that even if every single man in America got married, 7,100,000 women would be left without husbands.

We give below the data of several western countries to show the ratio of men to women.[5]

Country	Male	Female
Austria	47.7%	52.93%
Burma	48.81	51.19
Germany	48.02	51.89
France	48.99	51.01
Italy	48.89	51.01
Poland	48.61	51.30
Spain	48.94	51.06
Switzerland	48.67	51.33
Soviet Union	46.59	53.03
United States	48.58	51.42

THE WILLINGNESS OF WOMEN

The presence of a greater number of women in a society is not the only prerequisite for polygamy. It is, in addition, compulsory that the woman who is the object of the man's choice should be willing to enter into the married state. This willingness on the woman's part is a must before a marriage can be lawful in Islam. It is unlawful to marry a woman by force. There is no example in the history of Islam where a man has been allowed to force a woman into marriage.

The Prophet Muhammad's own view that "an unmarried girl should not be married until her permission has been taken"[6] had been recorded by both Bukhari and Muslim. 'Abdullah ibn 'Abbas, one of the Prophet's Companions and a commentator on the Qur'an, narrates the story of a girl who came to the Prophet complaining that her father had her married off against her wishes. The Prophet gave her the choice of either remaining within the bonds of wedlock or of freeing herself from them.[7]

Another such incident narrated by 'Abdullah ibn 'Abbas concerns a woman called Burairah and her husband, Mughith, who was a black slave. 'Abdullah ibn 'Abbas tells the story as if it were all happening before his very eyes: "Mughith is following Burairah through the paths of Medina. He is crying and his tears are running down his beard. Seeing him, the Prophet said to me, 'O 'Abbas, are you not surprised at Mughith's love for Burairah and Burairah's hate for Mughith?' Then the Prophet said to Burairah, 'I wish you would take him back.' Burairah said to the Prophet, 'Is that a command?' The Prophet replied, 'No, it is only a recommendation.' Then Burairah said, 'I don't need your recommendation.'"[8]

There was an interesting case of polygamy which took place during the Caliphate of 'Umar ibn al-Khattab. A certain widow, Umm Aban bint 'Utbah had four suitors for marriage. All four — 'Umar ibn al-Khattab, 'Ali ibn abi Talib, Zubayr and Talhah — were already married. Umm Aban accepted the proposal of marriage made by Talhah and, of course, refused the other three, whereupon she was married to Talhah.[9]

This happened in Medina, the capital of the Islamic State. Among the rejected suitors was the reigning Caliph. But no one expressed even surprise or dismay, the reason being that in Islam, a woman is completely free to make her own decisions. This is a right that no one can take away from her — not even the ruler of the day.

These incidents show that the Islamic commandments giving permission to marry up to four women does not mean having the right to seize four women and shut them up inside one's home. Marriage is a matter of mutual consent. Only that woman can be made a second or a third wife who is willing to be so. And when this matter rests wholly on the willingness of the woman, there is no cause for objection.

The present age gives great importance to freedom of choice. This value is fully supported by Islamic law. On the other hand, the upholders of "feminism" want to turn freedom of choice into restriction of choice.

THE SOLUTION TO A PROBLEM RATHER THAN A COMMANDMENT

The above discussion makes it clear that the difference in number of men and women is a permanent problem existing in both war and peace. Now the question arises as to how to solve this problem. What should those women do to satisfy their natural urges when they have failed to find a husband in a monogamous society? And how are they to secure an honorable life in that society?

One way — hallowed in Indian tradition — is for widows to

burn themselves to death, so that neither they nor their problems survive. The alternative is to allow themselves to be turned out of their homes on to the streets. The state of Hindu society resulting from adherence to this principle can be judged from a detailed report published in *India Today*[10] entitled "Widows: Wrecks of Humanity."

Now there is no need to discuss this further, because it is inconceivable that in present times any sensible person would advocate this as a solution.

The other possible 'solution' to be found in the 'civilized' society of the West is the conversion of unwillingness to become a second wife into willingness to become a mistress, often of more than one man.

During the Second World War, in which several western countries such as Germany, France, Britain, etc. took part, a large number of men were killed. As a result, women far outnumbered men at the end of the hostilities. Permissiveness then became the order of the day, to the extent that boards with such inscriptions as "Wanted: A Guest for the Evening" could be seen outside the homes of husbandless women. This state of affairs persisted in western countries in various forms, even long after the war, and is now largely prevalent because of industrial and mechanical accidents.

UNLAWFUL POLYGAMY

People who would outlaw polygamy have to pay the price. That is, they are forced to tolerate men and women having illicit relations, which is surely a much more unsavory state of affairs. Failure to control a natural process whereby the male population dwindles, leaving "surplus" women, coupled with the outlawing of polygamy, has given rise to the evil of the "mistress" (defined by Webster's Dictionary as "a woman who has sexual intercourse with and, often, is supported by a man for a more or less extended period of time without being married to him; paramour"). This, in effect, sets up a system of illegal polygamy.

The system of keeping a mistress is prevalent in all those countries, including India, where there are legal constraints on polygamy or where polygamy is looked down upon socially. In such a situation, the real problem is not whether or not to adopt polygamy. The real problem is whether or not to legalize its adoption. The problem of surplus women in society can be solved only by polygamy, whether we choose to consider it legal or not.

THE ISLAMIC WAY

The solution to this problem in the Islamic *shari'ah* is the giving of permission to men, under special conditions, to marry more than one woman. This principle of polygamy, as enshrined in the Islamic *shari'ah* is designed, in actual fact, to save women from the ignoble consequences mentioned above. This commandment, although apparently general in application, was given only as a solution to a specific social problem. It provides an arrangement whereby surplus women may save themselves from sexual anarchy and have a proper stable family life. That is to say, it is not a question of adopting polygamy rather than monogamy. The choice is between polygamy and sexual anarchy.

If the commandment to practice polygamy is seen in the abstract, it would appear to be biased in favor of men. But when placed in the context of social organization, it is actually in favor of women. Polygamy is both a proper and a natural solution to women's problems.

The permission to practice polygamy in Islam was not given in order to enable men to satisfy their sexual urges. It was designed as a practical strategy to solve a particular problem. Marrying more than one woman is possible only when there are more women than men. Failing this, it is out of the question. Is it conceivable that Islam, just to satisfy man's desires, would give us a commandment which is neither possible nor practical?

The *Encyclopaedia Britannica* (1984) aptly concludes that one reason for adopting polygamy is the surplus of women. Among most peoples who permit or prefer it, the large majority of men live in a state of monogamy because of the limited number of women.[11]

To have more than one wife is not an ideal in Islam. It is, in essence, a practical solution to a social problem.

CONCLUSION

In terms of the birth rate, men and women are almost equal in number. But, subsequently, for a variety of reasons, the number of men in society decreases, leaving an excess of women. Now the question arises as to what should be the solution to this problem. In view of the inevitability of this imbalance, how is a healthy relationship between the sexes to be established?

By following the principle of monogamy, hundreds of thousands of women fail to find husbands for themselves and are thus denied an honorable place in society. Monogamy as an absolute principle may seem pleasing to some, but events show that this is not fully practicable in the world of today. The choice for us, therefore, is not between monogamy and polygamy, but rather between the lawful polygamy of Islam and the illicit polygamy of non-Islamic peoples. The latter system leaves "surplus" women to lead lives of sexual anarchy and social destruction. The former, on the other hand, permits them to opt on their own free will for marriage with anyone who can give fair treatment to more than one wife.

Notes

1. Qur'an, 4:3.
2. *Encyclopaedia Britannica* (1984), vol. 7, p. 37.
3. Ibid, vol 14, p. 1102:
4. Ibid, vol. 16, p. 137.
5. Figures taken from *Encyclopaedia Britannica* (1984).
6. Al-Bukhari, *Sahih, Bab la Yunkihu al-Ab wa Ghairuhu al-Bikra wath-Thayyiba illa bi Ridaha (Fath al-Bari, 9/157).*
7. Abu Dawud, *Sunan, Kitab an-Nikah,* 2/232.
8. Ad-Darimi, *Sunan, Kitab an-Nikah,* 2/170.
9. Ibn Kathir, *Al-Bidayah wa an-Nihayah,* 7/153.
10. *India Today* (New Delhi), November 15, 1987.
11. *Encyclopaedia Britannica* (1984), 8/97.

CHAPTER 8

Concerning Divorce

When a man and a woman bind themselves together by tying the knot of marriage, they cherish the hope of living together for the whole of the rest of their lives. Then, when nature blesses their union with a child, it strengthens the bond of marriage, providing a guarantee of its greater depth and stability. On the basis of data collected in western countries, the *Encyclopaedia Britannica* of 1984 confirms this with the statement that "childless couples tend to have a higher divorce rate than couples with children."[1]

A divorce court judge in the West holds that "every little youngster born to a couple is an added assurance that their marriage will never be dissolved in a divorce court."[2]

Inspite of these apparently favorable psychological factors and natural, traditional attachments of parents and children, the rising incidence of divorce is a new and observable phenomenon of the modern world. One of the most important contributing factors is the ease with which women can now make a living. On this the *Encyclopaedia Britannica* says: "Industrialization has made it easier for women to support themselves, whether they are single, married, divorced, or widowed. In this connection, it is interesting to note that the Great Depression of the 1930s stopped the rise in the number of divorces in the United States for a time."[3]

In the modern age, western civilization has been beset by many problems, many of which are more artificial than real. In many things western civilization has adopted unnatural ways, thus giving rise to unnatural problems. The matter has further been worsened by attempts to solve them unnaturally. Problems have thus gone on increasing instead of decreasing. The problem of divorce is one of them. The initial stimulus of the women's liberation movement in the West was not wrong, but its leaders did not care to define its limits. In a bid to make a free society, their efforts culminated in the creation of a permissive society. Affairs between men and women knew no limits and this had the effect of weakening the marriage bond. Men and women were no more husbands and wives. In the words of the Prophet, they became sensual, pleasure-seeking people. This state of affairs was given a boost by industrialization, as a woman could easily procure an independent livelihood for herself. This had never before been possible. Because of this, she has frequently refused to live under the guardianship of men which, in consequence has created a large number of social problems leading to greatly increased rates of divorce.

The western philosophers who wanted to check divorce advocated legal curbs upon men, which would legally bind them to provide maintenance to the wife after the divorce. This maintenance sum was fixed according to western living standards, so that, in most cases, divorce meant that the man had to part with a fair amount of his hard earned money for the whole of the rest of his life.

A victim of this unnatural state of affairs was Lord Bertrand Russell, one of the most intelligent and outstanding intellectuals of his time. Soon after his marriage, he discovered that his wife no longer inspired any feelings of love in him. Although realizing this incompatibility, he did not seek an immediate separation. In spite of severe mental torture he tried to bear with this situation for ten years. He refers to this period as one of "darkest despair." Finally he had to separate and remarry, but he was not satisfied even with the second match and he married for a third time. Two divorces were a costly bargain. According to English law, the amount of alimony and maintenance he had to pay his wives upset him greatly. He writes in his Autobiography:

> ... the financial burden was heavy and rather disturbing: I had given Pounds 10,000 of my Nobel Prize cheque for a little more than Pounds 11,000 to my third wife, and I was now paying alimony to her and to my second wife as well as paying for the education of my younger son. Added to this, there were heavy expenses in connection with my elder son's illness; and the income taxes which for many years he had neglected to pay now fell to me to pay.[4]

Such a law had been passed in order to ensure justice for women who had to resort to divorce. But when people began to realize that divorce inevitably led one into financial straits, the marriage bond began to be dispensed with altogether. Men and women simply started to live together without going through the formality of the marriage ceremony. Now more than fifty percent of the younger generation prefer to live in an unmarried state.

It was only natural that a reaction should have set in against a law which so patently disfavored men and brought corruption, perversion and all kinds of misery in its wake. Children — even newborn babies — were the greatest sufferers.

Now take the situation prevailing in Hindu society, in which the extreme difficulty of divorce acts as a deterrent. Obviously this was a bid to reform, but this has served only to aggravate the matter. The ancient Indian religious reformers held that separation was illegal: they even prohibited women from remarrying, so that they would be left with no incentive to seek divorce. The laws were made in such a way that once marriage ceremonies were finalized, neither could a man divorce his wife, nor was it possible for a woman to remarry after leaving her former husband.

But such reformations were unnatural, and have been generally detrimental to individuals in Hindu society. When a man and a woman are unable to satisfy one another, the whole of their lives is passed in great bitterness because of there being no provision for remarriage. They are doomed to continue to live a tormented life alongside partners with whom they have nothing in common. I shall cite here only one of the hundreds and thousands of such instances which are reported in newspapers almost everyday, leaving aside those cases which go unreported. Manu, 25, was a cousin of Khushwant Singh. He has written in detail about her tragedy in his "Malice" column.[5] Manu had a flourishing business selling ready-made garments in Los Angeles. As she did not want to marry a foreigner, she decided to come to India to find a husband and return with him to the States. She found her own husband in a tall, handsome, powerfully built Hindu boy who was anxious to go abroad. The marriage took place with all pomp and splendor in a five-star hotel. It took her some months to arrange for her husband's visa, during which time she maintained him and paid for his passage. The marriage was a disaster.

The boy turned out to be an alcoholic, prone to violence and averse to doing any work. Manu sought her parent's consent to wind up her business, divorce her husband and return to India. Her parents travelled to America and tried to persuade her not to be hasty. A few days after her mother returned to Delhi, Manu's husband strangled her and dumped her body in a deserted spot. He collected all he could in the house and was planning to flee the United States when the police caught up with him. He is now in jail on a charge of murder.

It is obvious that Manu was not careless in selecting her partner. She travelled from America to find a suitable match in her birth place. But all that glitters is not gold. Our human limitations make it impossible for us to understand every facet of a person's character before entering into a relationship with him. The question arises if, after such revelations, one should feel forced to respect a marriage bond even at the cost of one's life? When society considers separation taboo, or the laws on this show no human leniency, the only alternative left for such incompatible couples is either to commit suicide, or waste away the whole of their lives in the "darkest despair." Even when one dares to surmount the hurdle of divorce, it is very difficult to get remarried in societies where divorcees are looked down upon. One can at best marry someone beneath one's social status. But in Islam remarriage is not a taboo: the Prophet himself married a widow. The provisions of Islam are thus a great blessing to couples who realize only too late that they have erred in making their choice of a partner. Islam provides for them to separate amicably, in a spirit of goodwill.

Just think of couples wasting away the whole of their lives in mental torment only because the conditions of separation and its consequences are hard to meet. It is as unnatural as anything can be.

Islam is a natural religion. Such a situation has not developed in Muslim communities because Islamic law on marriage and divoice provides for all, or almost all, eventualites. For example, when a woman wishes to divorce her husband, she has to put her case before a religious scholar, or a body of religious scholars. This facility is available to her in all the great Arabic schools in India. They then give consideration to her circumstances in the light of the Qur'an and the Hadith, and, if they find that there are reasonable grounds for separation, they decide in her favor. The reason that the woman must have scholars to act on her behalf is that women are more emotional than men — as has been proved by scientific research — and it is to prevent hasty and ill-considered divorces taking place that she is thus advised. If we seldom hear of Muslim women committing suicide, or being murdered by their in-laws, it is because they have the alternative — separation.

Separation, of course, is strongly advised against in the case of minor provocations. Are we not commanded by God to be tolerant and forgiving? It is meant only as a last resort, when it has become truly unavoidable.

Islamic law is thus fair to both husband and wife, unlike occidental law, which places an undue burden on the man, while Hindu society forces the woman into familial rejection, destitution and social ostracism.

"THE MOST HATEFUL OF ALL LAWFUL THINGS"

While marriage is the rule of life, and divorce only an exception, the latter must also be accepted as a reality. Indeed there already exist commandments to deal, accordingly, with such cases in both divine and human laws.

The only true, authentic representation of divine law now exists in the form of the Qur'an, it having been preserved in its entirety by God and free, therefore, from all human interpolations. In the Qur'an, and in the Hadith, there are various commandments regarding divorce, the main point being that divorce should be sought only under unavoidable circumstances. The Prophet spoke of it as being the most hateful of all the lawful things in the eyes of God, and said that when it does take place, it should be done in an atmosphere of good will. In no way should one harbor ill-will against the other.[6]

THE MEANING OF PROVISION

In Islamic jurisprudence, the material arrangements which a man makes for his divorced spouse are termed "divorce provision." There is a consensus among Muslim scholars that this provision in no way means life-long maintenance, there being absolutely no basis for this in the divine scriptures. The concept of maintenance for life is, in fact, a product of modern civilization. It was never at any time enshrined in divine laws, either in Islam, Judaism or Christianity. In material terms 'provision' simply takes the form of a gift handed over by the man on parting, so that the woman's immediate needs may be catered for, and in all cases, this is quite commensurate with his means.

But the Qur'an makes it explicit that the parting must above all be humane and that justice must be done: "Provide for them with fairness; the rich man according to his means, and the poor according to his. This is binding on righteous men. Do not forget to show kindness to each other... reasonable provision should also be made for divorced women. That is incumbent on righteous men."[7]

When divorce takes place before the settling of the dowry and the consummation of the marriage, even then the man must give the woman money or goods as a gesture of goodwill. In this instance the question of his repaying dowry money does not arise. The Qur'an is also quite explicit on this — "Believers, if you marry believing women and divorce them before the marriage is consummated, you have no right to require them to observe a waiting period. Provide well for them and release them honorably."[8]

This "waiting period" (iddah) actually applies to a woman who has been married for some time and who may, subsequent to the divorce, discover that she is pregnant. This statutory waiting period of three months makes her position clear and then the man is required to pay her additional compensation if she is expecting his child. But again there is no question of maintenance for life, for the Qur'an seeks a natural solution to all human problems. It would, therefore, be wholly against the spirit of the Qur'an for a woman to be entitled to life maintenance from the very man with whom she could not co-exist. Such a ruling would surely have created a negative mentality in society. The Qur'an again has the answer: "If they separate, God will compensate each of them out of His own abundance: He is Munificent, Wise."[9]

The munificence of God refers to the vast provision which God has made for his servants in this world.

In various ways God helps such distressed people. For example, when a woman is divorced, it is but natural that the sympathy of all her blood relations should be aroused. And, as a result, without any pressure being put on them, they are willing to help and look after her. Besides, a new will-power is awakened in such a woman and she sets about exploiting her hidden potentialities, thus solving her problems independently. Furthermore, previous experiences having left her wiser and more careful, she feels better equipped to enter into another marital relationship with more success.

DIVORCE IN ISLAM

Nature demands that men and women lead their lives together. The ideal way of leading such a life is, according to the *shari'ah*, within the bonds of marriage. In Islam, marriage is both a civil contract entered into by mutual consent of the bride and groom, and a highly sacred bond to which great religious and social importance is attached. As an institution, it is a cohesive force in society, and worth protecting and preserving for that reason. To that end, detailed injunctions have been prescribed to maintain its stability and promote its betterment.

However, in the knowledge that an excess of legal constraints can lead to rebellion, such injunctions have been kept to a realistic minimum and have been formulated to be consistent with normal human capabilities. Moreover, their enforcement is less relied upon than the religious conditioning of the individual to ensure the maintenance of high ethical standards and appropriate conduct in marital affairs and family life.

The state of marriage not only lays the foundations for family life, but also provides a training ground for individuals to make a positive adjustment to society. When a man and woman prove to be a good husband and a good wife, they will certainly prove to be good citizens in the broad spectrum of their social group. This has been aptly expressed in a *hadith*: "The best of you is one who is best for his family."[10]

The family being the preliminary unit for the training of human beings, its disintegration has an injurious effect on the society to which those human beings must individually make a positive contribution, if collectively they are to form a good and just nation. If the family no longer exists, it is the whole of humanity which suffers.

Once a man and a woman are tied together in the bonds of matrimony, they are expected to do their utmost, till the day they die to honor and uphold what the Qur'an calls their firm contract, or pledge.[11] To this end, the full thrust of the *shari'ah* is levelled at preventing the occurrence of divorce; the laws it lays down in this regard exist primarily, therefore, as checks, not incentives.

Islam regards marriage as an extremely desirable institution, hence its conception of marriage as the rule of life, and divorce only as an exception to that rule. According to a *hadith,* the Prophet Muhammad said, "Marriage is one of my *sunnah* (way). One who does not follow it does not belong to me."[12]

Although Islam permits divorce, it lays great emphasis on its being a concession, and a measure to be resorted to only when there is no alternative. Seeing it in this light, the Prophet Muhammad said, "Of all things permitted, divorce is the most hateful in the sight of God."[13]

When a man and a woman live together as husband and wife, it is but natural that they should have their differences, it being a biological and psychological fact that each man and each woman born into this world are by their very nature quite different from each other. That is why the sole method of having unity in this world is to live unitedly in spite of differences. This can be achieved only through patience and tolerance, virtues advocated by the Prophet not only in a general sense, but, more importantly, in the particular context of married life. Without these qualities, there can be no stability in the bond of marriage. According to Abu Hurayrah, the Prophet said, "No believing man should bear any grudge against a believing woman. If one of her ways is not to his liking, there must be many things about her that would please him."[14]

It is an accepted fact that everyone has his strengths and his weaknesses, his plus points and his minus points. This is equally true of husbands and wives. In the marital situation, the best policy is for each partner to concentrate on the plus points of the other, while ignoring the minus points. If a husband and wife can see the value of this maxim and consciously adopt it as the main guiding principle in their lives, they will have a far better chance of their marriage remaining stable.

However, it sometimes happens, with or without reason, that unpleasantness crops up, and goes on increasing between husband and wife, with no apparent indication of their being able to smooth things out by themsleves. Their thinking about each other in a way that is conditioned by their maladjustment prevents them from arriving at a just settlement of their differences, based on facts rather than on opinions. In such a case, the best strategy according to the Qur'an is to introduce a third party who will act as an arbiter. Not having any previous association with the matters under dispute, he will remain dispassionate and will be able to arrive at an objective decision acceptable to both parties.

For any arbiter to be successful, however, the husband and wife must also adopt the correct attitude. Here is an incident from the period of the four pious Caliphs which will illustrate this point.

When 'Ali ibn Abi Talib reigned as fourth Caliph, a married couple complaining of marital discord came to him to request a settlement. In the light of the above-mentioned Qur'anic guidance 'Ali ordered that a board of arbiters, one from the husband's family and one from the wife's family, be set up, which should make proper enquiries into the circumstances and then give its verdict. This verdict was to be accepted without argument by both sides.

As recorded in the book, Jami' al-Bayan, by at-Tabari, the woman said that she gave her consent, on the book of God, whether the verdict was for or against her. But the man protested that he would not accept the verdict if it was for separation. 'Ali said, "What you say is improper. By God, you cannot move from here until you have shown your willingness to accept the verdict of the arbiters in the same spirit as the woman has shown."

This makes it clear that a true believer should wholeheartedly accept the arbiters and their verdict in accordance with the Qur'anic injunctions. Once their verdict is given, there should be no further dispute.

TWO WAYS OF DIVORCING

However, it has to be conceded that life does not always function smoothly, like a machine. Despite all safeguards, it sometimes does happen that a couple reaches a stage of such desperation that they become intent on separation. Here the *shari'ah* gives them guidance in that it prescribes a specific method for separation. The Qur'an expresses it thus: "Divorce may be pronounced twice, then a woman must be retained in honor or allowed to go with kindness."[15]

This verse has been interpreted to mean that a man who has twice given notice of divorce over a period of two months should remember God before giving notice a third time. Then he should either keep his spouse with him in a spirit of goodwill, or he should release her without doing her any injustice.

This method of divorce prescribed by the Qur'an, i.e. taking three months to finalize it, makes it impossible for a man seeking divorce suddenly to cast his wife aside. Once he has said to his wife (who should not at this time be menstruating), "I divorce you," both are expected to think the situation over for a whole month. If the man has a change of opinion during this period, he can withdraw his words. If not, he will again say, "I divorce you," (again his wife should be in a state of "purity") and they must again review the situation for a further month. Even at this stage, the husband has the right to revoke the proceedings if he has had a change of heart. If, however, in the third month, he says, "I divorce you," the divorce becomes final and the man ceases to have any right to revoke it. Now he is obliged to part with his wife in a spirit of good will, and give her full rights.

This prescribed method of divorce has ensured that it is a well-considered, planned arrangement and not just a rash step taken in a fit of emotion. When we remember that in most cases, divorce is the result of a fit of anger, we realize that the prescribed method places a tremendous curb on divorce. It takes into account the fact that anger never lasts — tempers necessarily cool down after some time — and that those who feel like divorcing their wives in a fit of anger will certainly repent their emotional outburst and will wish to withdraw from the position it has put them in. It also takes into account the fact that divorce is a not a simple matter: it amounts to the breaking up of the home and destroying the children's future. It is only when tempers have cooled down that the dire consequences of divorce are realized, and the necessity to revoke the decision becomes clear.

When a man marries a woman, he has to say only once that he accepts her as his spouse. But for divorce, the Qur'an enjoins a three month period for it to be finalized. That is, for marriage, one utterance is enough, but for a divorce to be finalized, three utterances are required, between which a long gap has been prescribed by the *shari'ah*. The purpose of this gap is to give the husband sufficient time to revise his decision, and to consult the well-wishers around him. It also allows time for relatives to intervene in the hopes of persuading both husband and wife to avoid a divorce. Without this gap, none of these things could be achieved. That is why divorce proceedings have to be spread out over a long period of time.

All these preventive measures clearly allow frayed tempers to cool, so that the divorce proceedings need not reach a stage which is irreversible. Divorce, after all, has no saving graces, particularly in respect of its consequences. It simply amounts to ridding oneself of one set of problems only to become embroiled in another set of problems.

Despite all such preventive measures, it does sometimes happen that a man acts in ignorance, or is rendered incapable of thinking coolly by a fit of anger. Then on a single occasion, in a burst of temper, he utters the word "divorce" three times in a row, "*talaq, talaq, talaq!*" Such incidents, which took place in the Prophet's lifetime, still take place even today. Now the question arises as to how the would-be divorcer should be treated. Should his three utterances of *talaq* be treated as only one, and should he then be asked to extend his decision over a three-month period? Or should his three utterances of *talaq* on a single occasion be equated with the three utterances of *talaq* made separately over a three-month period? There is a *hadith* recorded by Imam Abu Dawud and several other traditionists which can give us guidance in this matter: Rukana ibn Abu Yazid said "*talaq*" to his wife three times on a single occasion. Then he was extremely sad at the step he had taken. The Prophet asked him exactly how he had divorced her. He replied that he had said "*talaq*" to her three times in a row. The Prophet then observed, "All three count as only one. If you want, you may revoke it."[16]

A man may say *"talaq"* to his wife three times in a row, in contravention of the *shari'ah's* prescribed method, thereby committing a sin, but if he was known to be in an emotionally overwrought state at the time his act may be considered a mere absurdity arising from human weakness. His three utterances of the word *talaq* may be taken as an expression of the intensity of his emotions and thus the equivalent of only one such utterance. He is likely to be told that, having transgressed a *shari'ah* law, he must seek God's forgiveness, must regard his three utterances as only one, and must take a full three months to arrive at his final decision.

In the first phase of Islam, however, a different view of divorce was taken by the second Caliph, 'Umar ibn al-Khattab. An incident which illustrates his viewpoint was thus described by Imam Muslim.

In the Prophet's lifetime, then under the Caliphate of Abu Bakr and also during the early period of the Caliphate of 'Umar, three utterances of *talaq* on one occasion used to be taken together as only one utterance. Then it occurred to 'Umar ibn al-Khattab that in spite of the fact that a system had been laid down which permitted the husband to withdraw his first, or even second *talaq*, men still wanted to rush into divorce. He felt that if they were bent on being hasty, why should not a rule be imposed on them binding them to a final divorce on the utterance of *talaq* three times in a row. And he proceeded to impose such a rule.

This act on the part of the second Caliph, apparently against the principles of the Qur'an and *sunnah*, did not in any way change the law of the *shari'ah*. To think that this led to any revision of Islamic law would be to misunderstand the situation: the Caliph's order merely constituted an exception to the rule, and was, moreover, of a temporary nature. This aptly demonstrates how the Islamic *shari'ah* may make concessions in accordance with circumstances.

Each law of the *shari'ah* may be eternal, but a Muslim ruler has the power to make exceptions in the case of certain individuals in special sets of circumstances. However, such a ruling will not take on the aspect of an eternal law. It will be purely temporary in nature and duration.

Various traditions in this connection show that the second Caliph's treatment of certain persons was not in consonance with the *shari'ah*. The rulings he gave on these occasions were in the nature of executive orders which were consistent with his position as a ruler. If he acted in this manner, it was to punish those who were being hasty in finalizing the divorce procedure.

It is a matter of Islamic historical record that when any such person was brought before 'Umar for having uttered the word *talaq* three times on one occasion, he held this to be rebellious conduct and would order him to be flogged on the back.[17]

Perhaps the most important aspect of this matter is that when 'Umar gave his exceptional verdict on divorce being final after the third utterance on a single occasion of the word *talaq*, his position was not that of a powerless *'alim* (scholar) but of a ruler invested with the full power to punish — as a preventive measure — anyone who went against Qur'anic injunctions. This was to discourage haste in divorce. By accepting a man's three *talaqs* on the one occasion as final and irrevocable, he caused him to forfeit his right to revoke his initial decision, thus leaving him with no option but to proceed with the divorce.

On the other hand, the Caliph had it in his power to fully compensate any woman affected by this ruling. For instance, he was in a position to guarantee her an honorable life in society and if, due to being divorced, she was in need of financial assistance, he could provide her with continuing maintenance from the government exchequer, *baitul mal*, etc.

Today, anyone who cites 'Umar's ruling as a precedent in order to justify the finality of a divorce based on three utterances of the word *talaq* on a single occasion should remember that his verdict will remain unenforceable for the simple reason that he does not have the powers that 'Umar, as Caliph, possessed. 'Umar's verdict was that of a powerful ruler of the time and not just that of a common man. It is necessary at this point to clear certain misunderstandings which have arisen about the extent of agreement which existed on 'Umar's ruling. Of all the Prophet's Companions who were present at Medina at that time, perhaps the only one to disagree was 'Ali. As a result of this, certain *'ulama* have come to the conclusion that the Prophet's followers (*Sahabah*) had reached a consensus (*'ijma*) on this matter.[18] But the consensus reached was not on the general issue of divorce, but on the right of Muslim rulers to make temporary and exceptional rulings, as had been done by 'Umar. It is obvious that the Companions of the Prophet could never have agreed to annul a Qur'anic injunction or to modify for all time to come a prescribed system of divorce. All that was agreed upon was that exceptional circumstances warranted exceptional rulings on the part of the Caliph. He was entitled to punish in any manner he thought fitting, anyone who digressed from the *shari'ah*. This right possessed by the ruler of the time is clearly established in the *shari'ah*. Many other instances, not necessarily relating to personal disputes, can be cited of his exercise of this right.

CONCLUSION

From the above discussion it becomes clear that the *shari'ah's* prescribed method of divorce entails the pronouncing of the word *talaq* at intervals of one month over a three-month's period, the third pronouncement making the divorce final. However, just as there are always cases of abuse of the law, there are always cases of divorce carried out by the improper method of uttering the word *talaq* three times on the one occasion.

When the law is misused in this way, there are two ways of dealing with the offenders. Either he can be made to consider his three utterances of *talaq* as only one, in which case he can still benefit from the right to revoke his initial decision, or he may, as a punishment, be forced to suffer the consequences of his irresponsible behaviour, i.e. immediate separation from his wife and resulting destruction of his home and family life. Such a punishment meted out to one man can be a strong deterrent to others. Once it is understood how grave are the consequences of a hasty divorce, few will be inclined to follow the same path.

The executive order of 'Umar ibn al-Khattab was not meant to become a permanent law of the *shari'ah* to be generally enforced at all times. It was meant only to discourage deviation from the *shari'ah* and to engender respect for the proper way of divorce. Although an exception to the general rule, 'Umar's verdict could at some future date be adopted, if the circumstances so warranted it, and it could be enforced just as it was in the past, provided that whoever made such a ruling was vested with the same political power as 'Umar ibn al-Khattab. The right to pass an executive order belongs only to an administrator. The common man has no such right, whatever the circumstances, because, he does not have the requisite power to deal with the social consequences of such a ruling.

AFTER DIVORCE

The question that arises immediately after divorce is of ways and means to meet one's necessary expenses. One's answer is to resort to the Islamic law of inheritance. If women were to be given their due share according to Islamic law, there would be no question of a woman becoming destitute. But, sad to say, the majority of Muslim women fail to get their due share of inheritance from their deceased fathers and husbands as stipulated by Islamic law. If they could do so, this would be more than enough to meet such emergencies.

However, Islam has not just left women's financial problems to the vagaries of inheritance, because parents are not invariably in possession of property which can be divided among their children. Further arrangements have been made under the maintenance law, but this has no connection with the law of divorce. The answer to this question must be sought therefore in the Islamic law of maintenance. Here we shall briefly describe some of its aspects:

1. In case the divorced woman is childless or the chidren are not earning, according to Islamic law, the responsibility for her maintenance falls on her father. That is, her situation will be the same as it was before marriage.

To quote from *Fath al-Qadir*[19]:

> The Father is responsible for bearing the expenses of his daughter till her marriage, in the event of her having no money. The father has no right to force her to earn, even if she is able to. When the girl is divorced and the period of confinement is over, her father shall again have to bear her expenses.[20]

2. If the divorced woman has a son who is an earning member of the family, the responsibility for her maintenance falls entirely upon him.

All that rightfully belongs to a wife, will be the duty of the son to provide, that is, food, drink, clothes, house and even servants, if possible.[21]

3. In the case of the father being deceased, and where even her children are unable to earn, her nearest relatives such as brothers or uncles are responsible for her upkeep. In the absence of even this third form, the Islamic *shari'ah* holds the State Treasury (*baitul mal*) responsible for bearing her expenses. She will be entitled to receive the money for her necessities.

Because of the number of provisions made under Islamic law for women it has never been the case in Islamic history that Muslim divorced women have been cast adrift, helpless, with no one to look after them.

Indian columnist, Khushwant Singh has remarked that we do not hear of Muslim women committing suicide or being tortured like Hindu women, which is a proof that Islam has already given them adequate liberty and has made enough provision for them to be supported in times of emergencies.

A new dimension has been added to the issue since the women of this day and age can leave their homes to work, and are therefore not as entirely dependent on men as they used to be in the past: there is no need then to make laws which provide for them at the expense of their menfolk. When they are earning like men, what is the point in making such a law? Only in exceptional cases, surely, do they need to be looked after, and ways and means of doing so can generally be worked out quite satisfactorily on a personal level.

Notes

1. *Encyclopaedia Britannica* (1984), vol. 7, pp. 163-164.
2. Ibid.
3. Ibid.
4. Bertrand Russell, *Autobiography*, (London, 1978), pp. 563-564.
5. *The Hindustan Times*, (New Delhi), October 12, 1985.
6. Abu Dawud, *Sunan, Kitab at-Talaq*, 2/255.
7. Qur'an, 2:236.
8. Qur'an, 33:49.
9. Qur'an, 4:130.
10. Ibn Majah, *Sunan, Kitab an-Nikah*, 1/636.

11. Qur'an, 4:21.
12. Ibn Majah, *Sunan, Kitab an-Nikah.*
13. Abu Dawud, *Sunan, Kitab at-Talaq,* 2/255.
14. Muslim, *Sahih, Kitab ar-Rada',* 2/1091.
15. Qur'an, 2:229.
16. *Fath al-Bari,* 9/275.
17. *Fath al-Bari,* 9/275.
18. *Rawai' al-Bayan,* 1/334.
19. A standard book on Islamic Law.
20. Al-Shaokani, *Fath al-Qadir,* 3/344.
21. Ibn 'Abidin, *Radd al-Muhtar 'ala ad-Durr al-Mukhtar,* 2/733.

CHAPTER 9

Dowry

THE CUSTOM OF DOWRY IS NOT ISLAMIC

The custom of giving dowry — a practice which has never been sanctioned by Islam — is greatly on the increase among the Muslims of India and Pakistan. As this custom is not prevalent among the Muslims of other countries, it seems quite clear that it has been borrowed by Indian and Pakistani Muslims from the Hindus of the sub-continent. The latter, in accordance with their ancient law, did not give their daughters any share in the family property, but on the occasion of their marriage — as a measure of compensation — they gave them dowries, part of which took the form of household goods.

In imitating this Hindu custom in India, Muslims are denying their daughters their rightful share in the family property to which they are entitled under Islamic law. The practice of "compensating" for this by giving them wedding presents and labelling these *jahaz* or "dowry" (*jahez* in Urdu) is, in reality, a deliberate evasion of the Islamic law of inheritance.

There is a body of opinion among certain Muslims which has it that *jahaz* is the *sunnah* (way) of the Prophet, because he himself gave his daughter, Fatimah, a "dowry" on the occasion of her marriage to 'Ali ibn Abi Talib.

FATIMAH'S DOWRY

As a justification for giving dowry, in the modern sense of the word, this proposition is clearly unacceptable, for, according to early records, the "dowry" which the Prophet gave to Fatimah consisted of only the barest of household necessities.

According to 'Ali ibn Abi Talib, the Prophet Muhammad prepared for Fatimah a sheet, a leather bag for carrying water, and a pillow filled by *idkhar* (grass).[1]

'Abdullah ibn 'Amr, enumerates them as a *khamil* (a single sheet of cloth), a leather bag for carrying water and an *idkhar* filled pillow made of leather.[2]

Asma, the daughter of 'Umyas, relates that when Fatimah left for 'Ali's house, it was quite unfurnished except for a flooring of sand, a pillow of date palm bark, a pot of water and a drinking vessel. Even the sheet which Fatimah was given had to be divided in two so that one half could be spread for sleeping on and the other half could be worn.[3]

If, nowadays, a girl's dowry had to be defined purely in terms of household necessities and limited to the same few items which the Prophet gave to Fatimah, it seems unlikely that anyone would consider it becoming to give a dowry at all.

Then the question arises as to why the Prophet felt obliged to give anything to Fatimah at all, when it had never been the custom to give presents to the bride. This feeling of obligation can be traced to the quality of the relationship which had grown up between 'Ali and himself. When 'Ali was just a boy, the Prophet requested his father, Abu Talib, to confide him to his care. From his very childhood, then, 'Ali had been under the guardianship of the Prophet. Because of this long, close association, they had become more like father and son, rather than just cousins. Considering that the Prophet had borne all 'Ali's expenses right from the time he came to him, it was but natural that on the occasion of his marriage, the Prophet, as his guardian, should give him some necessary items with which to set up his home.

DOMESTIC NECESSITIES

It is clear that the verb *jahhaza*, as used in the traditions, never had the meaning which it has acquired in modern times. In Arabic, it simply meant the "furnishing of provisions."[4]

Nowadays, it is commonly held that at the time of her marriage, a girl should be given an ample dowry to enable her to set up her new home with ease. But this is a wholly non-Islamic concept and has no bearing whatsoever on the ideal of marriage in Islam. Had it been a traditional Islamic practice, we should certainly have seen the precedents set for it in the Prophet's own lifetime. As it happened, the Prophet gave household items only to Fatimah, largely on account of his close relationship with 'Ali, and gave nothing at all to his other three daughters on the occasion of their marriages. Had dowry-giving been an established *sunnah* of the Prophet, he would surely have given it to his other daughters as well.

THE REAL GIFT

One regrettable aspect of dowry-giving in recent times is that it is becoming more and more a matter of ostentation. Nothing could be more un-Islamic in motivation than this. Even the practice of performing a marriage quietly, without any flamboyant display of wealth, but subsequently giving a lavish dowry to enable the bride to set up her home is contrary to Islamic practice. It was certainly not the *sunnah* of the Prophet. Fatimah was his favorite daughter, but he neither gave her a lavish dowry nor did he send things to her home after the wedding. Even when Fatimah made a request to him for something of a material nature, he only gave her the benefit of his counsel.

Different versions of Fatimah's request have been recorded in many of the books on Hadith. It seems that she had to do all the housework herself, which she found physically very taxing. During the early period of her marriage, the Prophet had received a number of captives who were to be used as slaves. 'Ali told Fatimah about this and suggested that she should go and ask her father to give her one of them. When Fatimah came to the Prophet, he asked what had brought her there. But, feeling too shy to ask anything of him, she merely said, "I have come to say *salam* to you," and she went back home without having explained her difficulties to him. The Prophet later came to her house and asked why she had really come. Then Fatimah said, "O Prophet of God, both of my hands have boils on them. I have to keep grinding and kneading the flour, so I wanted a servant." The Prophet replied, "Whatever God has decreed, that you will receive. And I will tell you something better than that. That is, when you go to bed, glorify God 33 times and proclaim His glory 33 times and praise him 34 times. This makes full one hundred. Such action on your part is better than that of having a servant."[5]

In spite of these events having been faithfully recorded, there are still many people who seek to justify the giving of huge dowries by citing the example of the Prophet's gifts to Fatimah. But, would any one of this number advise a daughter with blistered hands to forget about having a servant and praise God instead? Would any one of them, on hearing her bewail her lot because of difficulties with in-laws, advise her simply to turn to God? By any standard of consistency, that is exactly what they ought to do.

If any misguided scoffer were to allege that Islam was an imperfect religion in that it failed to lay down guidelines for every eventuality in our lives, all Muslims would be up in arms against him. But, in practice, Muslims themselves make the same assertion, if tacitly, whenever they accept the ways of other religions as being more practicable than those of Islam.

Certainly, in the case of dowry, Muslims have unashamedly adopted a Hindu custom. Similarly, other rites performed during Muslim marriages have been derived from the customs of other nations. If Muslims suppose that just taking a pride in Islam is the sole prerequisite for their being honored in the court of God, they will eventually have to do penance for having entertained such a grave misconception. They would do well to reflect upon how the Jews took enormous pride in the *shari'ah* of the Mosa, without this, however, preventing them from being cursed by the Almighty.

MAHR — THE DOWER

Islam has successfully maintained an even balance in society between men and women by giving its unequivocal endorsement to a practical division of labor, whereby women are placed in charge of the internal arrangement of the household, while men are responsible for its financing. The home is thus organized on the pattern of a microcosmic estate, with the man in a position of authority. The Qur'an is specific on this issue:

Men are the protectors and maintainers of women because God has made some of them to excell others and because they support them from their means. All the righteous women are the truly devout ones, who guard the intimacy which God has (ordained to be) guarded.[6]

For largely biological reasons, women are well adapted to domestic pursuits while men, for similar reasons, are better suited to work outside the home. These physical and mental differences between men and women are, in practice, what underlay Islam's division of familial responsibilities into internal and external spheres, with the woman dealing exclusively with the home and family and the man providing the funds.

MAHR MU'AJJAL

At the time of the marriage, the groom hands over to the bride a sum of money called *mahr* (dower) which is a token of his willing acceptance of the responsibility of bearing all necessary expenses of his wife. This is the original meaning of *mahr*, although this custom has come to have different connotations in modern times.

There are two ways of presenting *mahr* to the bride. One is to hand it over at the time of the marriage, in which case it is known as *mahr mu'ajjal*, or promptly given dower. (The word *mu'ajjal* is derived from *'ajilah*, meaning "without delay.") During the time of the Prophet and his Companions, *mahr mu'ajjal* was the accepted practice and the amount fixed was generally quite minimal. The giving of *mahr* by 'Ali to Fatimah, the Prophet's daughter, is an illustration of how this custom was respected. (It has been recorded in detail in the books of Hadith.) After the marriage had been arranged, the Prophet asked 'Ali if he had anything he could give as dower in order to make Fatimah his lawfully wedded wife. 'Ali replied, "By God, I have nothing, O Messenger of God." The Prophet then asked, "Where is the coat of armor I once gave you?" 'Ali replied that it was still in his possession (although he later admitted "by the Master of his soul" that it was in a dilapidated condition and, as such, was not even worth four *dirhams*). The Prophet then instructed him — "since I have married you to Fatimah" — to send the coat of armor to Fatimah, thereby making his union lawful. This then was the sum total of Fatimah's dower.[7]

Rabi'ah Aslami, who tells of how he used to serve the Prophet, was asked one day by the latter why he did not get married. Rabi'ah replied that it was because he had nothing to give to his wife-to-be. The Prophet mulled the whole matter over, then asked him to go to a certain Ansar tribe and say that the Prophet had sent him to get married to a particular woman. Rabi'ah did as the Prophet advised, conveying his message to the tribesmen, and was duly married to the woman in question. But he greatly regretted having nothing to give her by way of dower. He came back to the Prophet and told him of his feelings. The Prophet then arranged for the dower by requesting the Chief of the Aslam tribe, Burayda Aslami, to "collect for him (Rabi'ah Aslami) gold equal in weight to one date stone." Rabi'ah relates how the people of his tribe did just that, whereupon he took the collected gold from them, and went to the Prophet. The latter told him to take it to the girl's family, and tell them that this was her dower. Rabi'ah did so. They accepted it with pleasure, saying, "It is much, it is good."[8]

MAHR MU'AJJAL

Another way of giving dower, according to the *shari'ah,* is to hand it over, not on the occasion of the marriage, but after a certain period of time, the duration of which is fixed by the man. This has to be settled at the time of the marriage if *mahr* is not to be handed over immediately. This form of dower is called *mahr mu'ajjal,* "a period of time." This has often been wilfully misinterpreted as implying an indefinite postponement of the giving of dower. But this is quite erroneous, for a definite date has always to be fixed for the discharging of this responsibility.

Mahr mu'ajjal, however, can take the form of some service performed by the husband, one notable example of which was the grazing of cattle by the Prophet Moses. When Moses left Egypt for Madyan, he married Safoora, the daughter of the Prophet Shu'ayb. His *mahr mu'ajjal* was settled and paid off by binding himself to grazing the cattle of his elderly father-in-law for a period of eight to ten years. Only after performing this service for a full ten years did he leave Madyan for Egypt.[9]

THE OPINIONS OF JURISTS

The system of dower favored by the *shari'ah* entails immediate handing over of *mahr*. This was the practice followed by all of the Prophet's Companions. Deferred dower is an alternative, but is not ranked equal in merit of a prompt discharging of this responsibility. It is simply a form of concession made to those who are unable to meet the requirements of *mahr* at the time of marriage.

Further details on this subject may be found in the books of *Fiqh*. In his book, *Al-Fiqh 'ala'l Madahib al-Arba'ah*, 'Abdur Rahman al-Jaziri devotes 85 pages to the subject of dower. The issue of the two systems of dower, *mu'ajjal* and *mu'ajjal*, is discussed in four pages. Although jurists have their differences on this matter, these are of a minor nature.

The different sects of *sunnis* do not differ in *usul*, or the fundamentals of religious belief, but only in minor rules of practice and in certain legal interpretations. Since, in some respects, separate doctrines are broached, four schools of jurisprudence have been established, known as Hanafi, Shafi'i, Hanbali and Maliki.

All of these schools agree that delay in handing over the dower, whether in full, or in part, is lawful, provided that the period fixed for payment is not indefinite. The Shafi'is also stipulate that the "period of payment should have been fixed in time."[10]

NO HEAVY BURDEN

The dower, which may be in cash or in kind, has to be fixed taking into account the bridegroom's position in life. That is, it should never be more than he is easily able to afford, whether it be a lump sum in cash or some article of value. The jurists have different views to offer on what the minimum amount should be, but all are agreed that it should be substantial enough for something to be bought against it. Any amount which is sufficient for a purchase is acceptable as dower.[11]

There are no traditions which encourage an increase in the dower, whereas there are many traditions which enjoin the fixing of smaller dowries. In all such cases, Islam lays down guidelines rather than issuing strict commandments. That is why Islam has not totally forbidden any increase in the dowry, and it is left to tradition to carry on the principle of fixing smaller sums. There is a well known saying of the Prophet Muhammad, according to 'Abdullah ibn 'Abbas, that "the best woman is one whose dower is the easiest to pay."[12]

Another saying refers to such a bride as "the most blessed woman."[13] "The state of blessedness," according to a third saying, resides in "her being easy to deal with and taking less dowry."[14]

'Aishah was once asked how much dower the Prophet gave his wives. She replied that it was 12 *auqiyah* and 1 *nash* (one *nash* being equal to half an *auqiyah*, that is, about 500 *dirhams*). This was the only dower of the Prophet Muhammad for his wives.[15] "But," she added, 'Umm Habiba's dower consisted of 4000 *dirhams*, this sum having been fixed by the Christian King of Abyssinia, Najashi, who had performed this marriage by proxy."[16]

NON-PREFERABLE WAY

The second Caliph, 'Umar ibn al-Khattab, once while addressing a gathering asked them to refrain from fixing heavy dowers in marriage. On hearing this, a woman stood up and, addressing the Caliph on the pulpit said, as God Himself has said, "If you have given much wealth to your women do not take anything from it." On hearing what the woman had to say, 'Umar withdrew his words, saying, "The woman is right, 'Umar is wrong."[17]

It is clear then that although the fixing of higher amounts to be given as dower is not strictly forbidden from the legal point of view, this practice is generally considered to be socially undesirable. That is why the dowers of the Prophet and his Companions were kept very low. According to the records we have, there is no single instance of any one of them having fixed substantial dowers either for himself or for his daughters.

THE COMPANIONS AND THEIR MARRIAGES

In the first era of Islam, marriage was a simple affair, without pomp or ceremony. Any expenditure incurred in its performance being quite minimal, it did not become a burden on either family. The wedding celebrations of the Companions were, in keeping with this principle, quite free of any ostentation. There is a saying of the Prophet that "the most blessed marriage is one in which the marriage partners place the least burden on each other."[18] Certainly, the most trouble-free marriage is one in which the existing resources are sufficient to meet all normal requirements.

There was once a case of a certain individual having become engaged without having anything to give as dower. When this came to the attention of the Prophet, he asked him over and over again if he really had nothing to give. When the man replied in the negative, the Prophet, far from telling him that he should borrow money and then get married, asked him if he had not learned certain parts of the Qur'an by heart. On receiving an affirmative answer from him, the Prophet said, "I therefore marry you to that woman. The dower you give will be that part of the Qur'an which you have committed to memory."[19] In other words, he should have to teach that part of the Qur'an to his wife.

The simplicity which marked the occasion of marriage in the days of the Prophet is well illustrated by 'Abdur Rahman ibn 'Auf, one of the foremost of the Prophet's Companions, who was married in Medina with as little ceremony as possible, not even thinking it necessary to invite the Prophet or any of the Companions. Imam Ahmad tells of how the Prophet came to know that 'Abdur Rahman was married: 'Abdur Rahman ibn 'Auf came to the Prophet with the scent of saffron upon him, and when the Prophet asked him about this, he said, "I have married." The Prophet then enquired as to how much dower he had given his bride. "Gold equal in weight to one date stone," he replied.[20]

A WRONG CUSTOM

In modern times the Islamic spirit has almost vanished from the responsibilites connected with the arranging and performing of a marriage. Muslims nowadays prefer to follow local custom rather than the guidelines of Islam. One manifestation of such a misguided practice is the fixing of heavy dowers — much in vogue in the brides' families, as this is regarded as safeguarding the girls' interests. In this regard the *Dictionary of Islam* says:

> The custom of fixing heavy dowers, generally beyond the husband's means, especially in India, seems to be based upon the intention of checking the husband from ill-treating his wife, and, above all, from his marrying another woman, as also from wrongfully or causelessly divorcing the former. For in the case of divorce the woman can demand the full payment of the dower.[21]

The fixing of a substantial dower for the above purposes rests on the suppositon that the dower has to be fixed at the time of marriage, but not handed over on that occasion. This gives it a "deterrent" value, which it could not otherwise have, i.e. if it was immediately paid.

This supposition is quite un-Islamic. As mentioned above, there are only two lawful forms of dower in Islam, one being *mahr mu'ajjal*, which is handed over at the time of the marriage, and the other being *mahr mu'ajjal*, which is to be given later, but at a definite point in time. That is, the man must fix a date for its payment, and must abide by it. The third custom, according to which a dower is to be given, without any time being appointed for the fulfillment of this due, is not in accordance with the Islamic *shari'ah*. Whatever is done on this basis is certainly unlawful.

SURE SOLUTION

What parents try to achieve — unsuccessfully — through the fixing of heavy dowers, is stability in their daughters' marriages. But such stability relates more to the girl's appreciation of the realities of life than to the manipulation of the dower, or to any other material consideration. It is unfortunate that a great deal of wishful thinking is indulged in in our present society, whereas what is needed is a keener awareness of the root cause of familial and societal problems. The commonest manifestations of these are quarrels with in-laws, and sometimes even the breaking up of the home. The main reason for the increasing frequency of such tribulation in married life is the absence of any real appreciation on the part of the bride of what her new role in the family is supposed to be.

The bride comes from her parent's home where she has had the unstinted affection of her father, mother, sisters and brothers. This relationship, and the place in the family which it gives her, are usually taken for granted, and seldom regarded as factors in life which have to be striven for. She is seldom conscious that these very valuable elements in family living are not just hers for the taking when she enters her new home as a married woman. They have to be worked for, and she has to show herself deserving of them; only then can she claim the kind of love and regard which she had had as a matter of right from early childhood in her parents' home. This initial lack of awareness on her part is very often the cause of major rifts later on in her married life.

A girl is the flesh and blood of her parents. She is loved by them whether she is good or bad, whether she is active or idle, whether she helps her parents or not, and she can safely expect them to continue to love her, regardless of the circumstances of her life, and regardless of how her own character develops. But she has no such blood relationship with her in-laws. Love from them will never be unconditional, but will exist, cease to exist, increase or decrease, in direct relation to the impression which her character and abilities make upon them in the general round of daily living.

For the bride, entering the marriage bond is like undergoing a series of tests, the outcome of which will determine whether her married life will be stable and happy, or exactly the reverse. If a girl feels like a fish out of water in her new home, it simply means that she has to make greater efforts to understand and adapt herself to her new environment. Wise parents will warn their daughters in advance that they must learn to mold themselves to new sets of circumstances.

A girl who enters marriage with a correct appreciation of what is required of her will make the transition with the greatest of ease. She will soon, by virtue of her character and accomplishments, earn the same honorable position in her parents-in-law's home as she had in her parents' home solely on account of their love for her. For such a girl, entering marriage will be as easy as changing her habits of dress with the change of the season.

In the case of a girl who enters marriage, uninstructed by her parents as to the realities of life in her parents-in-law's home, friction is likely to arise because she does not consider her new home her real abode in life. She does not think of it as being her own home. As a result her parents-in-law will be repelled rather than attracted by her and they, too, will not think of her as their own. In such a situation it is the girl herself who has to pay the price. Her life will be fretted away, with little sense of fulfillment; she will be fortunate indeed if her afflictions are only psychological. It is a matter of great regret that girls in this position seldom realize that their woes have no basis in fact, but stem largely from their unpreparedness for the married state. Such a situation is invariably aggravated when the girl's parents, spurred on by her complaints, attempt to intervene. Their hostile attitude in the long run only causes their daughter to suffer more. Whenever there is a clash between the weak and the strong, it is always the former who suffer and, of course, within the bonds of marrige, it is always the girl who is in the weaker position. Parents do not realize the damage they do to their own daugther's life in waging an unending war against her in-laws. But, as the old saying goes, "Every father is a fool where his children are concerned."

Where parents are blinded by their affection for their daughter, it is up to the girl herself to think objectively. Suppose, as a customer in a shop, she attempted to appropriate items for which she had not paid. Obviously these goods would be withheld from her by the shopkeeper. You have to give before you get. Similarly, in her parents-in-law's home, if she demands their attention, care and affection without having given any of these things to them, she cannot expect them to behave towards her with absolute perfection. You must pay the price of the goods you wish to possess.

The parents-in-law's home is a kind of training and testing ground in which the girl must be willing to learn, to adapt and to prove her mettle. She must leave behind her the fairy tale existence of her parent's home and enter the realms of reality. The bride who does not grasp these imperatives will most likely be a failure both as a wife and as a daughter-in-law. It is the girl who is prepared to look the hard facts of life in the face who will make her marriage a resounding success.

Notes

1. An-Nasa'i, *Sunan, Kitab an-Nikah*, 5/135.
2. Al-Haythami, *Majma' az-Zawa'id wa Manba' al-Fawa'id, Kitab al-Manaqib*, 9/210.
3. Ibid., 9/209.
4. See, Qur'an, 12:70.
5. Al-Haythami, *Majma' az-Zawa'id wa Manba' al-Fawa'id, Kitab al-Adkhar*, 10/122.
6. Qur'an, 4:34.
7. Ibn Kathir, *As-Sirah an-Nabawiyah*, 2/544.
8. Ahmad ibn Hanbal, *Masnad, Kitab al-'Ilm*, 4/58.
9. See, Qur'an, 28:27-29.
10. Abdur Rahman al-Jaziri, *Al-Fiqh 'ala'l Madahib al-Arba'ah*, 4/153-156.
11. Ibid., 4/107.
12. Al-Haythami, *Majma' az-Zawa'id wa Manba' al-Fawa'id, Kitab an-Nikah*, 4/281.
13. Al-Baihaqi, *Sunan al-Kubra, Katib as-Sudaq*, 7/235.
14. *Kanz al-'Ummal, Kitab an-Nikah*, 16/322.
15. Ad-Darimi, *Sunan, Kitab an-Nikah*, 2/141.
16. Abu Dawud, *Sunan, Kitab an-Nikah*, 2/235.
17. Ibn Hajar al-'Athqalani, *Fath al-Bari*, 9/167.
18. Al-Haythami, *Majma' az-Zawa'id wa Manba' al-Fawa'id, Kitab an-Nikah*, 4/255.
19. Abu Dawud, *Sunan, Kitab an-Nikah*, 2/336.
20. Ibid, 2/336.
21. Thomas Patric Hughes, *Dictionary of Islam*, p. 91.

CHAPTER 10

Hijab in Islam

HIJAB IN THE LIGHT OF THE QUR'AN AND HADITH

This chapter is based on an authoritative Arabic book titled *Hijab al-Mar'ah al-Muslimah fil Kitab was-Sunnah*, by Muhammad Nasiruddin al-Albani, a famous scholar and traditionist. It was translated by this writer and initially published in condensed form in the quarterly, *Islam and the Modern Age*.[1]

The third edition of the original work with some additions is before me. The question of *hijab* (veil), or *purdah* in Urdu, the author tells us, has been discussed in light of the Qur'an and Hadith.

From the author's point of view, a woman's face is not included in the parts of the body that need to be compulsorily covered. He suggests, however, that it is better to cover it. He agrees with those who, in spite of holding the view that the face is not to be covered as a rule, nevertheless advocate the covering of the face in order to discourage mischief, in view of the general moral degradation in present-day society. Here is one of the traditions referred to by him to support his argument.

'Aishah says that Muslim women used to attend the morning prayer led by the Prophet wrapped in a sheet of cloth. Afterwards, when they returned home, it was so dark that they could not be recognized.

This narrative makes it clear that their faces were not covered. Had their faces been covered, the question of their being recognized would not arise. The phrase "because of the darkness they could not be recognized" makes sense only if the faces, by which individuals are recognized, were uncovered.

Muhammad Nasiruddin al-Albani takes a similar stand as regards the covering of a woman's hands, quoting a famous tradition narrated by Ibn 'Abbas. It says that once the Messenger of God addressed the women to urge them to give alms (*sadaqah*). Afterwards Bilal ibn Rabah, a Companion of the Prophet, spread a sheet, on which the women began throwing their rings.

After quoting this tradition the author quotes Ibn Hazm:

> Ibn 'Abbas saw the hands of women in the presence of the Prophet. This proves that the face as well as the hands are not included in the parts of the body to be covered. Indeed all other parts except these have to be veiled.[2]

He further writes:

> My heart bleeds to see the way many women of today adorn themselves, crossing all limits of decency. But the remedy does not lie in declaring forbidden what Allah has permitted.

He goes on to say that it is clear from the Qur'an, the Hadith and the practice of the Companions and *tabi'un* (companions of the Prophet's Companions) that, whenever a woman steps out of her home, it is incumbent upon her to cover herself completely so as not to show any part of her body except the face and the hands.[3] According to Muhammad Nasiruddin al-Albani's findings the following rules of *hijab* are applicable:

1. The whole body, except for the exempted parts should be covered.
2. But any veil which in itself becomes an attraction is to be avoided.
3. Garments should not be semi-transparent.
4. Dress should not be tight fitting.
5. Garments should not be perfumed.
6. The form of dress should not in any way resemble that of men.
7. It should not resemble that of non-believers.
8. Garments should not reflect worldly honor.[4]

The first rule of *hijab* has been derived from the following passages of the Qur'an:

> Say to the believing women to turn their eyes away (from temptation) and to preserve their chastity; to cover their adornments except such as are normally displayed; to draw their veils over their bosoms and not to reveal their finery except to their husbands, their fathers, their husbands' fathers, their sons, their step-sons, their brothers, their

brothers' sons, their sisters' sons, their women-servants, their slave girls, male attendants lacking in natural vigor, and children who have no knowledge of sex. And let them not stamp their feet when walking so as to reveal their hidden trinkets. Believers, turn to Allah together in repentance, that you may prosper.[5]

The second verse in this connection is as follows:

Prophet, enjoin your wives, your daughters and the wives of true believers to draw their veils close round them. That is more proper, so that they may be recognized (as virtuous women) and not molested. Allah is Forgiving and Merciful.[6]

The author interprets the wording of 33:59, "to cover their adornments except such as are normally displayed," to mean that the hands and face are exempt from covering. He draws his argument in support of this from the Hadith.

After studying many *ahadith* in connection with the verse from *surah* 33 of the Qur'an, he writes: "It is clear from the instances drawn from the Qur'an and the Hadith that, although it accords with the *shari'ah* and it is preferable for a woman to cover her face, it is not compulsory for her to do so. It would be better if women followed this practice, but there is no harm if they do not."[7]

The second rule of *hijab*, according to Muhammad Nasiruddin al-Albani's research, is that *hijab* in itself should not be a source of attraction. It should not become a display of finery referred to in the Qur'an as *tabarruj*:

Stay in your homes and do not display your finery as women used to do in the days of Jahiliyah (period before Islam). Attend to your prayers, give alms to the poor, and obey God and His Messenger. God only wishes to remove uncleanliness from you (members of the family), and to purify you.[8]

According to the author, the intention of this verse is that a woman should not display her beauty and attraction in such a way as to produce carnal desires in the hearts of men. Since the purpose of the gown (*jilbab*) is to hide such attractions, it is, therefore, unimaginable that the gown itself should become a source of attraction.[9]

He states, moreover, that in Islam the displaying of feminine attractions is a habit so important to avoid that it has been bracketed in the scriptures along with such unlawful things as polytheism, adultery and theft. He has collected a number of *ahadith* to support his argument.

The third rule of the *hijab*, according to the writer, is that the garment should not be thin because a thin cloth can never provide cover. And a diaphanous garment only accentuates the attraction of a woman and becomes a potential source of mischief.[10] The author quotes many sayings of the Prophet Muhammad, one of which is as follows:

> Towards the end (in the last phase) there will be women among my followers who will appear naked, or as good as naked, even when wearing clothes.

The fourth condition set by the writer is that the garment should be loose-fitting. He again supports his argument by quoting various sayings of the Prophet. Finally he has given an instance where Fatimah (the Prophet's daughter) expressed her disapproval of a dead woman being wrapped in such a shroud as might display her body as being a woman's. He writes: "See for yourself how the dearest daughter of the Prophet considered the use of such a cloth detestable as would not properly drape feminine parts of a dead woman's body. Certainly such a garment for a living woman would be far worse."[11]

The fifth condition of *hijab* is that the garment should not be perfumed (while going out). There are many traditions forbidding women to wear perfume while going out. After quoting four traditions, he writes: "Ibn Daqiq al-'Id writes that in this *hadith* a woman is forbidden to go to the mosque wearing perfume, because it stimulates carnal desires in men. So when it is forbidden for women wearing perfume to go to the mosque, their use of perfume when they go out shopping, or for any other purpose, is all the more sinful. Al-Haythami writes that going out wearing adornments and perfume is a major sin, even if it is done with the husband's permission."[12]

The sixth conditon of *hijab* is that a woman's garments should not resemble those of men. Here is one of the traditions he has quoted to this effect:

> The Prophet has condemned men who imitate women and women who imitate men.[13]

From this tradition the writer comes to the conclusion that a garment which in most parts resembles those of men is not permissible for women, even if it covers her adequately.[14]

The seventh rule of *hijab* is that it should not resemble that worn by non-believers. Muhammad Nasiruddin al-Albani says that any similarity to non-believers must be avoided, in matters of worship, festivals and dress.[15] The Qur'an states this briefly, but the *sunnah* provides the detail. One of the verses of the Qur'an on which he bases this argument states that it is "so that they may not be like those who were given the scriptures before this..."[16] He quotes Ibn Taymiyya and Ibn Kathir who construe this verse as meaning that imitation of non-believers is not allowed in Islam.

Then he quotes the tradition in which the Prophet forbade adopting the ways of non-believers in prayers, funeral prayers, sacrifice, food, dress, etiquette, etc.[17]

The eighth rule of *hijab* is that a woman's garments should not reflect worldly honor. Here is a *hadith* to this effect:

> One who wears the mantle of fame in this world will be made to wear the robe of dishonor in the hereafter.[18]

His concluding remarks are: "The garment should cover the entire body of a woman except the face and hands, and should not become an attraction in itself. Neither should it be thin, nor tight. It should not accentuate the body. It should not be perfumed or resemble those worn by men or non-believing women. It should not suggest fame."[19]

THE TRANSLATOR'S VIEWS

The Qur'an says: "Say to the believing women to turn their eyes away (from temptation) and to preserve their chastity; to cover their adornments except such as are normally displayed."[20]

The wording of the verse, "except such as are normally displayed," gives rise to the question of what it is that has been exempted here from being covered. The theologians and the commentators have two views on the subject. These two views are based on the fact that beauty is of two kinds — one natural (by birth) and the other artificial (that is acquired by the use of make-up, etc.). One group says that the word 'beauty' here refers to both kinds of beauty, whereas the other group believes that it is artificial beauty which is referred to in this verse.

Ibn Mas'ud, Hasan, Ibn Sirin, and Abul Jawza' have interpreted this verse as referring to the kind of beauty which depends on clothes, ornaments, etc. They are of the opinion that when a woman goes out, she should not display these deliberately. However, if any part of such adornment is unintentionally exposed, for instance, if a gust of wind displaces the covering sheet momentarily, this is deemed excusable.

The other point of view finds support from 'Abdullah ibn 'Abbas, 'Abdullah ibn 'Umar, 'Ata', 'Ikrama, Sa'ib ibn Jubayr, Abu ash-Sha'tha', Dahhak, Ibrahim Nakh'i, etc. They infer from the phrase 'such as are normally displayed' the exemption of face and hands.

This interpretation is based on the tradition recorded by Abu Dawud in his *Sunan*: 'Aishah says that once Asma bint Abu Bakr came wearing a thin garment. The Prophet turned his face away from her and said: "Asma, it is not proper for a woman after having reached puberty to expose any part of her body except these." Then he pointed to his hands and face.[21]

That is why there are two theological schools of thought. The Hanafis and Malikis believe that the face and hands are not to be covered, while the followers of Imam Shafi'i and Hanbali maintain that a woman has to be fully veiled. In this view, natural as well as acquired beauty have to be completely veiled. It is unlawful for a woman to unveil any part of her body when she goes out. To them, what is exempted is that which gets exposed unintentionally. They will be excused for that. Thus the face and the hands are the parts that are forbidden to be exposed unnecessarily.[22]

Maulana Shabbir Ahmad 'Usmani gives the following commentary pertaining to this verse of the Qur'an:

To this writer the interpretation of *zīnah* (beauty) as adornment would be more appropriate and comprehensive in this context. The word adornment encompasses all kinds of beauty, whether natural or acquired; whether inborn beauty or that of beautiful garments or make-up. In short, a woman is forbidden to display adornment of any kind before anyone not permitted by the *shari'ah*. If a woman cannot keep these parts veiled as ordained for reasons beyond her control, or for any compelling reason, she cannot be held responsible for that (provided it is not likely to generate any mischief.)

It is evident from the Hadith and *athar* (the sayings and deeds of the Prophet's Companions) that the face and hands are exempt because it is not possible to keep them covered while performing various chores of daily life and even religious rites. If they are ordered to be strictly covered, it will create great difficulties for women in carrying out their jobs. The theologians have considered the feet also to be exempted parts. It must be clearly understood, however, that unveiling is permitted strictly on the basis of necessity. Men are forbidden to set their eyes on them. Perhaps this is why before exempting women from covering their face and hands (verse 31), men are commanded to lower their gaze and guard their modesty in verse 30. Thus the permission to unveil a part of the body does not give licence to others to set their eyes on them.[23]

EXPERIMENTAL VERIFICATION

Of all the family problems in advanced countries, divorce tops the list. The fact that the majority of marriages in these countries end up in divorce has ruined family life completely, for children do not enjoy the love and care of parents who are still alive, whereas it was formerly only death which separated children from their parents. Children there grow up like uncared-for weeds, adding to the list of criminals. It is generally accepted that the majority of juvenile delinquents are the product of broken homes.

Divorce was not so common in former times. Then how has it reached such proportions now? The sole reason for this is traceable to the promiscuity of what in religious terminology is called unrestricted society. This life style devoid of moral constraints has made it possible for men and women to live together like the fish in the sea. With such a life style, permissiveness is unavoidable. One's loyalties keep changing. In a segregated society, where interaction between men and women is almost non-existent, a man associates only with his spouse, which keeps him from forming new loyalties, while in a free society he comes upon new faces every day, one better than the other. He then feels like abandoning the old face in preference to the new and more attractive one. What is happening in the West is that the couple live together for some time after marriage and when they come across a better face, they go in for divorce to start a new life. This fact has been plainly stated by the *Encyclopaedia Britannica*. Commenting on the increasing rate of divorce in western society, it says:

> Actors, authors and other groups that have many contacts with the opposite sex tend to have a high divorce frequency.[24]

This western report links the high rate of divorce to regular contacts. This is significant in that it proves that the degree of freedom of the sexes in society has a marked bearing on the instability of married life. Where segregation of the sexes in society creates stability in married life too much freedom creates the kind of instability in married life which ends in divorce.

Putting a stop to freedom in society could be an experimental verification of the restricted society being a proper society Only the placing of restrictions in society can provide a deterrent to divorce. While the lack of restrictions in society weakens the fabric of family life and creates many social evils, constraints, on the other hand, strengthen family bonds, which greatly benefits the human race in different ways.

Notes

1. *Islam and the Modern Age,* Urdu Edition (New Delhi), January, 1973.
2. Muhammad Nasiruddin al-Albani, *Hijab al-Mar'ah al-Muslimah fil Kitab was-Sunnah* (1914), p. 31.
3. Ibid., p. 7
4. Ibid., p. 13
5. Qur'an, 24:31.
6. Qur'an, 33:59.
7. Muhammad Nasiruddin al-Albani, *op. cit.,* p. 31.
8. Qur'an, 33:33.
9. Muhammad Nasiruddin al-Albani, *op. cit.,* p. 31.
10. Ibid., p. 56.
11. Ibid., p. 63.
12. Ibid., p. 65.
13. Ibid., p. 67.
14. Ibid., p. 77.
15. Ibid., p. 78.
16. Qur'an, 57:16.

17. Muhammad Nasiruddin al-Albani, *Hijab al-Mar'ah al-Muslimah fil Kitab was-Sunnah* (1914), p. 80.

18. Ibid., p. 80.

19. Ibid., p. 110.

20. Qur'an, 24:31.

21. Abu Dawud, *Sunan, Kitab al-Libas,* 4/62.

22. Muhammad 'Ali as-Subuni, *Rawai' al-Bayan,* (Beirut, 1980), 2/155.

23. *At-Tafsir al-'Uthmani,* with notes by Shaikh Mahmud ul-Hasan (Bijnor, 1950), p. 458.

24. *Encyclopaedia Britannica* (1984), vol. 7, p.163.

CHAPTER 11

Success in Marriage

When 'Abdullah ibn Ja'far's daughter was about to be married, he gave her this piece of advice: 'O my daughter, avoid being haughty or making a prestige issue of anything, for both are keys to the lock of divorce. Avoid anger and discontent too, for they engender malice.'

This is the best counsel a father could give his daughter at the time of her marriage. After the wedding, she goes to live in another's home. Now, instead of living with her own kith and kin, she is under the roof of people with whom she had no blood relationship. Where, in her parents home, displays of anger or arrogance, or other shortcomings, were overlooked by her parents and siblings, it is a very different story in her in-law's home, where even the smallest of errors may cause her to fall from grace.

The in-laws do not have the same soft corner for her that comes naturally to her parents. In the new house, every action sets off a reaction. There, overweening pride cannot just be ignored, and no one is willing to forget the slightest misdemeanor.

The only way that a new bride can make things easier for herself is to adjust to her new environment. She should avoid doing or saying anything which could possibly invite an unpleasant reaction. It also helps if she is tolerant of things which are not to her liking and, if someone's behavior is contrary to what she expected, makes allowances for this and refrains from brooding over it. This is the only way for a girl to make a success of her life in her new home. No other course is possible.

It is an unwise father who teaches his daughter to be assertive in her in-law's house in the mistaken belief that this will give her the upper hand. A wise man would tell his daughter to adopt a conciliatory stance. The success or failure of married life depends entirely upon the bride's willingness or unwillingness to adapt.

TWO EXAMPLES

Two opposite cases come to mind. One is of a daughter who, being the apple of her parent's eye, never did even the most trifling of household chores. She just idled away her time. After her marriage, she made no attempt to change her ways. But this was not acceptable in her in-laws' house. There were sharp differences over her behavior and when bickering became a daily affair, her carefree life came to an end.

She now found herself with a whole new set of problems. Even so, she did not care to practice introspection. She always blamed her in-laws. One day, after fighting with them, she came back to her parents with a sorry tale. But she only told them her own side of the story, with no mention of how she herself had behaved: she talked only of how she had been treated. She did not tell them that whatever treatment she had received was the result of her never taking any interest in the household affairs. She had, in fact, never looked upon her in-laws' house as her own home. To her, home was her parents' house, even after she was married. Unaware of this, her parents became very critical of the way their daughter had been treated.

Like most other parents, they were quite credulous about everything she told them, and, supposing their own child to be in the right, put the entire blame on the in-laws. This led to their becoming entangled in a long feud. The ensuing mental agony took its toll. The girl fell sick, and after a prolonged illness, succumbed to tuberculosis. Thus ended her unhappy life.

The other is the case of a wise woman. Initially, she found herself in an unhappy situation in her in-laws' home because of her unattractive appearance. At first, this was discussed behind her back, but soon she had to suffer the humiliation of open insults from the women of the household. This was very hard on her, but she refrained from telling her parents about it, having decided that she would completely ignore unsavory comments. Instead, she privately resolved to be helpful to the others, and voluntarily took over all of the household work. She cared for the needs of every member of the family and made sure that no one had any reason to complain against her.

This was the beginning of a long and trying period. It took not months, but years for things to change. But finally, a stage came when she was the most popular member of the family, having earned everyone's affection and respect. No better than a maid when she had arrived, she had now become the virtual mistress of the house.

The secret of a successful marriage is the ability to forge bonds of loyalty. Such bonds come into being quite naturally with one's own parents, brothers and sisters. They are so strong that they can never be broken. There can be no doubt about this. But similar bonds do not exist in the in-law's house. They have to be established. The only solution for the new bride entering her parents-in-law's home is to transfer her loyalty to all of the people to whom she is now related by marriage. When she says 'my home' it should mean her new abode. The focus of her attention should now be her in-laws, from whom she should seek support, rather than from her parents. She must become a part of the family and have everyone's well-being at heart. Experience teaches us that this is the way to make a success of married life.

GUARANTEED SOLUTION

It is undeniable that happiness in marriage is closely linked with awareness. Awareness can make a marriage. Its absence can mar it.

If it were given any serious thought, it would become evident that trouble with the in-laws is a problem created by default. It is also more imaginary than real. Unfortunately ours is not an aware society. And we are paying the price for that in different ways. One of them is the increasing discord between brides and their in-laws.

Certain historical factors have caused the members of our community to live in a world of make-believe. They are ignorant of the realities of life, and, because of this lack of awareness, they are suffering for it in every walk of life. Marital problems are part of this inheritance.

The parental home is a haven where a girl receives natural affection. The in-laws' home is a place where, by her own efforts, she has to create a niche for herself. A daughter, being the flesh and blood of her parents, will be loved by them, regardless of whether she is good or bad, whether she is a source of worry or happiness, whether she works diligently or just idles away her time.

Things could not be more different in the in-laws' home. There she has no blood relations and must, therefore, prove herself worthy of affection by the way she conducts herself. There, affection has to be a two-way affair, unlike in her parental home, where affection was unconditionally assured.

For a girl, marriage is like undergoing a long series of tests. At first she feels like a fish out of water. But, if the parents have been wise and forewarned her of possible pitfalls, she will be mentally prepared to cope with new challenges. This will make it easier for her to adapt to the new situation. It is only if the girl is both intelligent and willing to adapt that she can learn how to do this by herself.

A girl with intelligence and/or wise parents will have few problems in marriage. For her, entering wedlock is no more complicated than changing her habits of dressing with the change of season. She establishes a position of respect for herself through her own exemplary conduct.

Problems are bound to arise when the girl is lacking in intellect and the parents are also ignorant. The position is further aggravated when the girl does not consider the new home to be her own and is, consequently, not regarded as a member of the family into which she has married. What she suffers, as a result, is self-inflicted. What is actually at fault is her own poor understanding of what is required of her as a daughter-in-law, but she very conveniently blames all her misery on her in-laws.

As the old adage has it, "Every parent is foolish when it comes to his own children." When girls go to the extreme of complaining about imaginary wrongs, parents tend to take their stories quite literally. And that is how feuds are started. The outcome is always unpleasant for the one who starts it, and the girl, being of the weaker sex, is always the loser.

Why is it that a girl's complaints about her in-laws do not always appear to be based on fact? It is because they present only one side of the case. The very fact that only one side of the story has been told means that it is lacking in veracity. Does a customer have any right to complain that a shopkeeper has not delivered the goods, when he himself has not paid for them? If a girl looks at her problems without bias, she will realize that balancing up the two sides of the question is really the crux of the matter. If she does not deliver what the in-laws expect, she cannot expect to get what she wants either.

The truth is that the in-laws' house is a place where one learns the secret of living. It is only when the girl is no longer under the protective cover of her parents that the facts unravel. Then the reality of the in-laws' home makes the parental home seem like an illusory world. Any girl who fails to learn this secret is bound to have an unsatisfactory married life, while the girl who comes to terms with reality can look forward to an untrammelled life of wedded bliss.

THE JOINT FAMILY

These days girls consider living in a joint family a problem. They would much rather live elsewhere with their husbands. Educated girls in particular try to convince their husbands that they, as a couple, should live separately after marriage. On the face of it, this appears to be a good idea. But often the initial charm wears off, and they feel that their situation is worse than if they had opted for the joint family system. I have seen many girls who managed to wean their husbands away from their parents. But then after living alone for some time, life became so burdensome for them that it seemed little better than a treadmill. In a joint family, a woman makes only psychological sacrifices, whereas in a nuclear family it is her whole existence which is sacrificed. The latter is much more difficult than the former.

Making an assessment of the woman's role in western society, Arnold Toynbee wrote: "Middle-class woman acquired education and a chance at a career at the very time she lost her domestic servants and the unpaid household help of relatives living in the old, large family; she had to become either a household drudge or carry the intolerably heavy load of two simultaneous fulltime jobs."[1]

It is because girls are upset by certain unpleasant aspects of joint family living that they opt for living alone with their husbands. Such decisions are emotional. If only they worked half as hard in the joint family situation as they did when living alone with their husbands, their lives could be considerably more comfortable and convenient.

Life is never free from troubles. It is only by handling it intelligently that we can lessen them. Living with others certainly has its problems, but they are far fewer than one experiences when living separately. Wisdom lies in opting for the easier course.

MENTAL WORRIES

What can become a major domestic problem is the presence of stepchildren. The very existence of children from a previous wife can cause such estrangement of the husband and his new wife, that it can lead to the ruination of the family.

It is natural for a woman to love her own child, and as soon as she becomes a mother, her whole attention is focussed on the newborn baby. This is the beginning of the problem. The children of the previous wife start to feel they no longer have any place in their own home. The undercurrent of tension mounts, leading to a situation which is disastrous for all concerned.

A child who has his own mother to stand by him and show him affection feels safe and secure. But the orphaned child, the stepchild, is never sure of his ground. Unless his stepmother gives him constant reassurance in the form of interest and affection, he is bound to feel neglected and humiliated. It is the feeling of humiliation which becomes the most problematic in a joint family. But there is a simple solution to this imbroglio. The stepmother must realize that some restraint must be shown in her display of love for her own off-spring — something which will do them no harm, because they are already secure in the knowledge that this is their own, real mother — and she must also learn to be more effusive in displaying affection for her stepchildren. And then, whatever the circumstances, keeping her emotions under control and showing unfailing courtesy at all times helps to prevent any possible misunderstanding.

We have a real life example in the second marriage of Maulana Syed Sulayman Nadwi[2] to Salima Khatun (1905-1986). When he married her in 1923, he already had a son by his first wife, called Abu Suhayl. Whenever Salima Khatun wrote a letter to someone, instead of signing off with her own name, she would write "mother of Abu Suhayl" in the traditional style. Later she had four children of her own, but there was no change in her attitude. She continued to be "mother of Abu Suhayl." Her own son, Dr. Salman Nadwi,[3] is a famous personality, but she never referred to herself as "mother of Salman." She was a deeply religious lady. She outlived her husband by 34 years, but her old ways did not change.

This trait was reflected in all aspects of her dealings. Quite naturally she must have been very fond of her own children, but she did not make it obvious. The result was that Abu Suhayl got along well with his step brothers and sisters as if they were his real brothers and sisters. There was never any tension in the family.

Ninety percent of domestic problems are psychological in nature and ought to be dealt with as such. Whenever a mother-in-law has a complaint, she should ask herself if she would have complained if her daughter had done the same thing. Similarly, a daughter-in-law should do some soul-searching, putting her mother in place of the mother-in-law.

If they seriously think about it, both the mother-in-law and daughter-in-law will find that their differences do not have any solid basis in fact. Most of their complaints are imaginary and as such, should never find expression in word or deed. They deserve to be confined where they originate, i.e. in the mind.

Notes

1. *Time*, March 20, 1972.
2. A noted scholar. After the death of 'Allama Shibli Nu'mani, he completed the remaining five volumes of *Sirah an-Nabi*. He died in 1953.
3. He is now the professor of Islamic Studies at the University of Durban in South Africa, and has written several books.

CHAPTER 12

Conclusion

If it were put to a writer that he could the better serve humanity by stepping out of his study and jumping into the boxing ring, he would surely retort that there is more to solving the problems of the world than just punching people on the nose. He would, indeed, point out that the intellectual can best operate in his own chosen sphere, and that it is not physical brashness which counts in this life, but the sharpening of awareness.

Imagine a reversal of the social structure which entailed a surgeon working in a butcher's shop, a teacher sitting on the roadside selling vegetables, or a microbiologist digging ditches. In each case, the change of workplace and role would render useless and irrelevant the innate and acquired skills, the knowledge and the moral excellence of these highly qualified, highly experienced professionals. Their competence and effectiveness would, moreover, be eroded by the sense of frustration and disorientation engendered by surroundings which clearly degraded them.

In luring women out of their natural sphere — the home and the bosom of the family — "emancipation" has pitchforked women into the same humiliating situation as our imaginary professionals. Once out of their homes, they find themselves forced, in uncongenial surroundings, to play unfamiliar roles for which neither training nor biology has fitted them. They are even worse off than our surgeon, teacher and microbiologist, for they have not only to contend with the professional hostility of their male counterparts, but must constantly be on their guard against being exploited and debased. In the meanwhile, their valuable domestic skills, innate maternal instincts and fine moral acuity become submerged and nullified in the treadmill of their daily working existence.

True progress for women cannot be achieved by encouraging them to make their entry into every field of life. A better approach would be to increase their knowledge, skills, alertness and awareness in the sphere to which they already belong. The more a woman is endowed with these qualities, the more effective will be the part she plays in all the activities of daily living. The woman who is intellectually aroused can perform the greatest of services, whereas, if she is left ignorant and untutored, she will never — even if she is brought to the forefront of things — be able to play a role of any significance.

There have been many women in history who never emerged from their homes, but who exerted a great influence upon the outside world. A notable example is Nur Jahan, a widow taken to wife by the Mughal Emperor, Jehangir, in 1611. Although according to time-honored custom, Nur Jahan lived almost exclusively in the palace, all historians are agreed that she exerted a strong influence, through Jehangir, far and beyond the palace walls. This is not to say that she never committed blunders. She did, the greatest of which was her conspiracy to have her own son-in-law, Shaharyar (married to the daughter of her deceased husband), succeed Jehangir, who, on the contrary, wished Prince Khurram (Shah Jahan), the ablest of his three sons, to be his successor. This was a plot which led to great strife and bloodshed, but, leaving this aside, the example of Nur Jahan certainly shows to what extent a capable woman can influence the affairs of the outside world. We reproduce here what historians have to say of her:

> Nur Jahan enjoyed great influence and authority and became a power behind the throne. Nur Jahan exercized a strong influence on her husband and looked after him with unparalleled care and devotion. Under her influence Jehangir restrained himself from excessive drinking. She relieved him of much of the drudgery of administrative routine and anxiety. She enhanced the splendor of the Mughal court and ably seconded the efforts of her husband in patronizing learning and art and disbursing charity.[1]

HISTORIC FEAT

The allegation that woman cannot perform great services when confined to the home is, therefore, clearly refuted by Islamic history. Housework is also undoubtedly great work, but the work which concerns the outside world and which is generally accepted as great work, can also certainly be performed by women, without passing beyond the threshold of their own homes.

An outstanding instance of the power wielded by Muslim women is their conversion of the Tartars (Mongol), who laid waste the world of Islam in the thirteenth century Hijra. Having been the direct enemies of Islam, the Tartars accepted its tenets and proclaimed themselves its guardians. 'Ghazan Khan (reigned 1295-1304) was able to embrace Islam amid general acceptance by his army, and his successors were all Muslims. Within less than 40 years, after Hulagu's terrible invasion, his descendants had become patrons of Muslim culture.[2]

How this miraculous conversion took place is explained by Professor T.W. Arnold:

> It is interesting to note that the propagation of Islam has not been the work of men only, but that Muslim women have also taken their part in this pious task. Several of the Mongol princes owed their conversion to the influence of a Muslim wife, and the same was probably the case with many of the pagan Turks when they had carried their raids into Muhammadan countries.[3]

After the Tatars had slaughtered the male Muslims on a massive scale, they took the women captive and brought them into their homes as mistresses and wives. From within the Tartar homes, these Muslim women were to play a crucial role, for, filled as they were with the zeal and fervor of Islam, they burned with the desire to serve its cause, and set about converting their capturers with a large measure of success. Those Tartars who were not immediately converted by their womenfolk at least softened to such a degree in their attitude towards Islam that when they came into contact with Muslims elsewhere in the world, they were very easily converted. This was thanks to the preliminary seeds having been sown within their very own homes.

The first Tartar ruler who converted to Islam was Barka Khan, who ruled from 1256 to 1267. It appears that his mother was a Muslim, and had trained him in the ways of Islam from early childhood. His formal conversion came just after his coronation, when he had a conclusive discussion on Islam with a Muslim merchant. Ghazan Khan's brother, Aljai, whose wife was a Muslim, succeeded him in 1304. It is said that it was his wife's persuasion which brought about his conversion. Indeed, most of the Tartar chiefs and military men converted in the same way. Indeed, their Muslim wives and mothers so impressed upon their minds the greatness of Islam, that the whole course of Islamic history was thereby changed.

The influence of Muslim women is in no way diminished for its being in the more mundane settings of the modern world, for although, physically, they remain within the domestic sphere, mentally they go with their husbands wherever life's exigencies may take them. In so doing, they share both their hearts and their minds. The relationship of every wife to her husband is of great depth: it is she who is his chief adviser and sharer in his joys and sorrows. Thus she is associated at every moment with all his thinking, all his activities. Where the household tasks are concerned, her involvement is direct: so far as external tasks are concerned, she exercises over them a kind of benevolent remote control.

A woman's work relates, albeit indirectly, to all of life's activites. While the importance of a woman's role in life is at all events comparable to that of a man, it should be borne in mind that this role will always be the more effectively performed by those women who are keener in their awareness.

It is a little understood fact that the role a woman plays does not depend upon her physical environment, but rather on the degree to which her intellect has been cultivated. The importance accorded to the male sphere of action as opposed to the female sphere, rather than to the type and quality of the actions performed therein, has been given undue emphasis, thus attaching to a woman's domain an unwarranted stigma of inferiority. It is to combat this acquired sense of inferiority that so many women feel the necessity to emerge from their homes and to take up the cudgels in the world of commerce and industry, science and technology, law and medicine. It is regrettable that they do not stop to consider that, though they are the weaker sex, as a matter of biology they are the strength of the stronger sex. Therein lies the secret of woman's power.

Notes

1. *Encyclopaedia Britannica* (1984), Vol. 9, p. 383.
2. *Encyclopaedia Britannica* (1984), Vol. 9, p. 993.
3. T.W. Arnold, *The Preachings of Islam* (1976), p. 415.

Index

Living Islam

By Ruqaiyyah Waris Maqsood

This book examines the social aspects of Islam, clearly outlining the aims and duties of every Muslim in respect of vital issues in Islamic life and conduct. The subjects dealt with include human rights, the sanctity of life, women's rights, the duties of the Muslim in the workplace, the family, sexual relationships, alcohol, drugs, crime and punishment, 'green' issues, and the true meaning of jihad. Reference is made in each chapter to the relevant passages of the Qur'an and Hadith.

The aim of the book is to show how Muslims strive to bring God-consciousness (taqwa) into every area of their daily lives, from the important and profound to mundane and simple tasks; and how, in this devotion and urge to serve, striving for the pleasure of their Lord, they find fulfilment and happiness.

ISBN 81-85063-27-3 Page 310, Price Rs. 325

Muslim Prayer Encyclopaedia

By Ruqaiyyah Waris Maqsood

An indispensable guide to the content and practice of Muslim prayer, based on a comprehensive study of all the authentic Hadith of the Prophet Muhammad as presented in the collections of Bukhari, Abu Dawud and Muslim.

ISBN 81-85063-29-X Page 328, Price Rs. 395

The Essential Arabic

A Learner's Practical Guide

By Rafi'el-Imad Faynan

This practical guide to modern Arabic is presented in a very simple and easy-to-grasp style. Unique in its approach, it explains the language by analyzing sample sentences in the kind of crystal clear manner which leaves a lasting impression on the reader's mind. The step-by-step approach of this easy-to-use guide will be found useful not only for beginners, but also for more advanced students. It can also be a handy tool for teachers of the language. One is finally left wondering how the hitherto dreaded learning of Arabic could have been made so delightfully simple...

ISBN 81-85063-26-5 Pages 184, Price Rs. 200

MUHAMMAD
A PROPHET FOR ALL HUMANITY
MAULANA WAHIDUDDIN KHAN

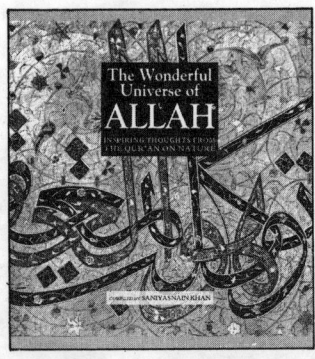
The Wonderful
Universe of
ALLAH
INSPIRING THOUGHTS FROM
THE QUR'AN ON NATURE
SANIYASNAIN KHAN

WOMAN
BETWEEN
ISLAM
AND
WESTERN
SOCIETY
•••
Maulana Wahiduddin Khan

QURANIC WISDOM FOR MODERN LIVING
PRESENTING
THE QUR'AN
A BRIEF INTRODUCTION TO ALL THE
114 CHAPTERS OF THE QUR'AN

RELIGION
and
SCIENCE
Maulana Wahiduddin Khan

The
Beautiful
Promises of
Allah

WORDS
OF THE
PROPHET
MUHAMMAD
SELECTIONS FROM
THE HADITH
COMPILED BY
MAULANA WAHIDUDDIN KHAN

THE LIFE OF THE PROPHET
MUHAMMAD
MUHAMMAD MARMADUKE PICKTHALL

HIJAB
IN ISLAM
Maulana Wahiduddin Khan

The Beautiful
Commands of
ALLAH

WOMAN
IN ISLAMIC SHARI'AH
Maulana Wahiduddin Khan

INDIAN
MUSLIMS
The Need For A
Positive Outlook
Maulana Wahiduddin Khan

The
Sayings
of
Muhammad
compiled by
Sir Abdullah Suhrawardy
with a Foreword by
Mahatma Gandhi

ISLAM -
Creator of the
Modern Age
MAULANA WAHIDUDDIN KHAN

QURANIC WISDOM FOR MODERN LIVING
A TREASURY OF
THE QUR'AN
BOOK 1: THE OPENING
COMPILED BY
MAULANA WAHIDUDDIN KHAN

MUHAMMAD
A MERCY TO ALL THE NATIONS

AL-HAJJ QASSIM ALI JAIRAZBHOY
WITH A FOREWORD BY HIS HIGHNESS THE AGA KHAN

Heart of the Koran

Lex Hixon

The Soul of the Qur'an

INSPIRING PRAYERS TO KINDLE HEART AND MIND

SANIYASNAIN KHAN

Steps to Leadership

from the Qur'an and Words of the Prophet Muhammad

compiled by
Abdur Ghani Ahmad Barin

The Muslim Marriage Guide

Ruqaiyyah Waris Maqsood

Living Islam
TREADING THE PATH OF THE IDEAL

RUQAIYYAH WARIS MAQSOOD

BASIC DICTIONARY OF ISLAM

RUQAIYYAH WARIS MAQSOOD

THE MUSLIM PRAYER ENCYCLOPAEDIA

A COMPLETE GUIDE TO PRAYERS AS TAUGHT BY THE PROPHET MUHAMMAD

Ruqaiyyah Waris Maqsood

HISTORY
of the Prophet
MUHAMMAD

PHILIP K. HITTI

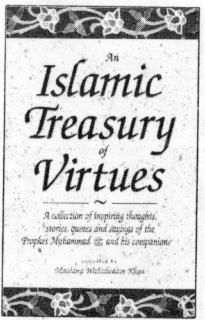

An Islamic Treasury of Virtues
~
A collection of inspiring thoughts, stories, quotes and sayings of the Prophet Muhammad ﷺ and his companions

compiled by
Maulana Wahiduddin Khan

Islam AND MODERN CHALLENGES

Maulana Wahiduddin Khan

ISLAM AND THE MODERN MAN

Maulana Wahiduddin Khan

The Essential Arabic
A Learner's Practical Guide
ما يَلزَم من العَرَبيّة

Rafi'el-Imad Faynan

THE HOLY QUR'AN
TRANSLATION AND COMMENTARY BY
ABDULLAH YUSUF ALI

The Qur'an
The Noble Reading

TRANSLATION AND COMMENTARY BY
T.B. IRVING
(AL-HAJJ TA'LIM ALI)

The Qur'an
TRANSLATION
القرآن الحكيم

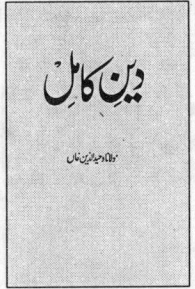
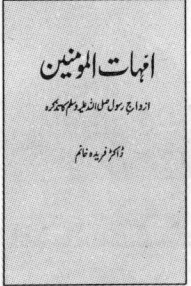

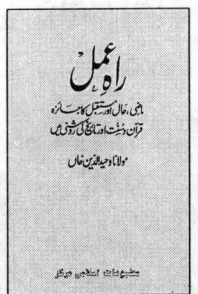